THE VODKA DIARIES

RICHARD SAYETTE

A PEACE CORPS WRITERS BOOK

THE VODKA DIARIES: A PEACE CORPS VOLUNTEER'S ADVENTURES IN RUSSIA

A Peace Corps Writers Book—an imprint of Peace Corps Worldwide
Copyright © 2018 by Richard Sayette
All rights reserved.

Printed in the United States of America
By Peace Corps Writers of Oakland, California

For information, contact peacecorpsworldwide@gmail.com.
Peace Corps Writers and the Peace Corps Writers colophon
are trademarks of PeaceCorpsWorldwide.org.

ISBN-978-1-935925-92-7
Library of Congress Control Number: 2018940354

First Peace Corps Writers Edition, June 2018

Special Thanks to:
Marian Haley Beil and the Peace Corps Writers
Roger Gaire and Claire Allen for Editing/Proofreading
Sheenah Freitas of papercranebooks.com for the Cover Design and Formatting Expertise

Dedicated to my drinking buddies; past, present and future.
Nostrovia!

ACKNOWLEDGEMENTS

I would like to acknowledge my fellow Peace Corps Russian Far East II volunteers, the Russian and American Peace Corps staff, my wonderful host family and all of my Russian friends in Vladivostok and Artyom. During the writing of this work, I decided to alter the names of some of my colleagues as I had not discussed this project with them and wanted to protect their reputations. The portrayal of events stem from my perspective and memories; given that it has been twenty-four years since my return from Russia, I apologize for any discrepancies. Of particular note, the friendship and time spent with my host family, Vitaly, Tanya Kulgina and her family, Ken and Winnie Hill and the entire city of Artyom were vital to my success and enjoyment as a Peace Corps Volunteer.

I would also like to thank my wife Heather and daughter Siena who continuously inspire me to reach for the sky and tolerate my frequent storytelling with smiles.

RUSSIA IS A RIDDLE WRAPPED IN A MYSTERY INSIDE AN ENIGMA.

—WINSTON CHURCHILL

A WELCOMING NOTE FROM PEACE CORPS HQ—SUMMER 1993

"The idea of sending Peace Corps Volunteers to Russia and the former Soviet Union is one that has intrigued and excited Americans since the agency's inception in the early 1960s. At the same time, however, it seemed the most unlikely of ideas, given the antagonistic relationship between the United States and the USSR, as well as Peace Corps' traditional emphasis on the "third world" nations of Asia, Africa and Latin America. With the dissolution of the Soviet Union and its sphere of influence in Eastern and Central Europe, however, the Peace Corps is now moving quickly to meet a challenge unprecedented in its thirty-year history. Since 1990, Peace Corps has sent English teachers, business advisors and environmental advisors to Hungary, Poland, Czechoslovakia, Romania, Bulgaria, Albania, Latvia, Lithuania and Estonia. The great challenge ahead of the Peace Corps is now to move quickly to aid the republics of the former Soviet Union. The first Peace Corps volunteers in Russia began their service as business advisors in early 1993. The beginning of a Peace Corps program in Russia marks the beginning of the end of half a century of mistrust and hostility. This is a new world for the Peace Corps and for Americans in general, and Peace Corps volunteers in Russia will face enormous challenges. Suspicion harbored for years will have to be overcome and an exchange of ideas will have to work its way through and between two completely different systems of thought and philosophies of life. Ambiguity and chaos will be the norm for life in Russia during its difficult transition to integration with the West, and as Volunteers in Russia, there is no question that working and living in a country that is simultaneously deconstructing and reconstructing itself will be confusing and often frustrating. The Peace Corps has always prided itself on an ability to provide flexible and adaptable Volunteers, and the program in Russia will be a true test of this ability . . ."

THE VODKA DIARIES

AUGUST 3, 1994

Consciousness comes slowly, painfully. I lean forward, straining to come to a sitting position on the couch, my tongue stuck to the roof of my mouth, blood pounding against my temples with each minimal bit of exertion. I reach for my glasses and a shooting pain racks what hours earlier had been my brain, a disquieting gurgle rocks my stomach. I slither to the edge of the couch, the cold floor sending a shock up my spine. Balancing like the Tower of Pisa, I make my way down the hallway, blindly heading to what I hope is the bathroom. Life is laughing in my face as the sunshine bounces off the linoleum floor, blinding me with a snide, punishing cackle. I urinate while leaning against the wall, rubbing my head with my free hand. I close my eyes to the sound of urine hitting water, letting me know that I am on target. I step across to the shower, the powerful spray digging into my face as my legs fight to keep me upright.

What a way to start my Peace Corps experience! I'd arrived in Seattle a day earlier than necessary to spend time with my old friend David Harris, somehow thinking it wise to go "all out" on the night before my Peace Corps initiation. One bourbon turned into several as we recounted tales of our high school, college, and traveling hijinks. A final 3 a.m. glass of Scotch and a cigar and I vaguely remember climbing into a taxi, looking at my watch and wondering how I would be able to get up and function in three hours.

The Peace Corps' instructions had been to meet at the Westin Hotel in downtown Seattle to join my fellow Peace Corps volunteers for three days of introduction to "The toughest job you'll ever love!" I got dressed, called a taxi, and managed to get my duffel bag into the trunk without puking. The next hour was a blur as we drove across town, apparently hitting every pothole, before pulling into the Westin driveway. I made it to my room without having to look anyone in the face, living in fear that I would later be remembered by one of my fellow volunteers as the disheveled, red-eyed slouch they had seen in the lobby. I had two hours for a power nap and the opportunity for the Advil to kick in prior to the first meeting. I dove onto the king-sized bed, fully dressed, clenching the pillow tightly against my face. In what seemed like seconds, the wake-up call shattered my slumber.

With a slightly upbeat gait, I took the elevator down to the meeting room where I donned my best smile in preparation for giving a confident first impression. Paper arrows taped to the corridors pointed me toward the "Peace Corps Orientation" from which the sound of nervous laughter grew louder as I closed the distance. I took a deep breath, exhaled, and then stuck my head through the doorway. A circle of men and women stood, hands jammed into pockets. In an effort to come across as just another rosy-cheeked American idealist setting out to change the world, I smiled awkwardly and introduced myself, offering an outstretched hand. In front of each chair was a file with a big red, white, and blue Peace Corps logo on the cover. Sitting down, I opened the file looking for clues as to what my two-year commitment would entail. The collective energy electrified the air.

"Hello and welcome to Seattle!" A woman barely pushing thirty shouted out in staccato bursts addressing a group thirsty for information. "I would like to congratulate all of you for taking the first step in changing your lives forever." Her smile was directed at each of us as she looked around the room. "You have volunteered to contribute to a world in which peace and understanding will thrive and the old ways of confrontation and conflict will cease to take the forefront in US/Russian policy. . . ." The words wafted past me, as I scanned the circle, sizing up my fellow trainees. Seven women and nine men ranging in age from mid-twenties to mid-seventies. I regained my focus on the speaker, as the tenor of her voice shifted from exuberant to apologetic, just in time to catch her explaining that our visas had not yet been forwarded, so we would begin our training in Seattle instead of Russia, depriving us of two weeks in Russia. I would have preferred an extra two weeks in my hometown to say goodbye and attend the wedding of my friend Willie, but as we were repeatedly advised, patience and flexibility are two of the key attributes you need to survive in the Peace Corps. Despite this change in scheduling, it felt good to have finally begun my odyssey after having already been delayed for fifteen months. Once all the official administrative announcements had been made, the formal introductions began. One by one, we stood and gave our names, hometowns, and the reason we had signed up for this great adventure. Most went something like this: "My name is John. I am from Wyoming. I joined the Peace Corps because I wanted to experience another culture," followed by a brief work and educational history. Our Peace Corps program focused on small-business development, so each of us were required to have an MBA or ten years of work experience.

Chuck, at a grandfatherly 79, was the oldest in our group. His wife of 45 years was suffering from Alzheimer's disease and she no longer recognized him. He felt that he had little to offer by staying by her side and decided to dedicate his remaining years to sharing his knowledge and experiences with others. Sitting next to Chuck was Louise, who although considerably younger than Chuck, was still the second oldest. Louise had four grown children, all of whom had families of their own. She decided that she wasn't yet ready to surrender her time to pampering the grandkids, so she volunteered for a 27-month adventure. Lannette fit my expectation of the typical Peace Corps volunteer to a tee. Dressed in a hippie-style skirt, with a salt-and-pepper ponytail and wrists jingling under the weight of a dozen clanking bracelets, she told us that her dream of joining the Peace Corps in the late 1960s had been put on hold due to getting married and having a child. Now that her son was in college and her husband no longer in the picture, she was ready to seize the opportunity that she thought had escaped her.

As the introductions moved around the circle, testaments of a yearning for adventure and a chance to make a difference poured forth. On one level, each of us had volunteered to serve our country and dedicate two years to the hope of improving America's image abroad, forgoing a salary. While not in the same category as the sacrifices of our military, our commitment of our time and energy to a concept would take us far from home to live in conditions far less comfortable than what we were accustomed to in our own country. Unlike US State Department or NGO staff, we weren't getting paid, didn't stay in nice hotels, or get opportunities to be wined and dined. We would live at the level of our Russian counterparts, eat what they ate, and become part of the local communities.

When my turn to speak arrived, I steadied my nerves and spoke of my MBA degree in International Business, my three years training and work as a classical French chef, and finally of my two years backpacking around Europe and Asia. I thought the chef comment would impress the women in the group: who doesn't love a chef? My travel experiences had given me a greater sense of empathy and interest in other cultures, which contrasted greatly to the perceptions of those who rely on the media for sensationalized video of other countries that seems to focus only on the pain and suffering. My time alone on the road had strengthened my problem-solving skills, forcing me to rely solely on my own thoughts and abilities—hopefully this would put in a better position to adjust to life in Russia as a volunteer.

When I sat back down, the next to speak was John Collins. At twenty-five he was one of the younger volunteers. He had a strong Southern accent and a boxer's frame—the pugilist, not the dog—although it wasn't easy to distinguish with his bushy beard and beer belly. He had been living in St. Thomas in the Virgin Islands when he received his acceptance letter from the Peace Corps and he'd eagerly quit his job as the computer specialist at Radio Shack to head off on a new adventure. His laugh was contagious and I recognized a kindred spirit. Gary stood up next. He was the "anti-Peace Corps" Peace Corps volunteer, with a preppy appearance and quick wit that leavened his conservative leanings. Realizing that his initial comments had generated a few sneers, he pulled out his passport to show a photo of himself with shoulder-length hair standing in front of a surfboard. The final person to speak was Karl, a self-proclaimed army brat and playboy, who explained that he was seeking an adventure and wanted a "lifestyle change." He seemed more polished than the rest of us, speaking with an ease that reminded me of a politician.

As a group, we had sold our possessions, ended relationships, said goodbye to our families and friends, and were now prepared to start a new life on the other side of the world. Our Peace Corps advisor cautioned us that to survive the stress and hardships that we were sure to encounter during our 27 months, we would need to depend on each other for emotional support, guidance, and friendship. The next two years would require hard work, perseverance, patience, and above all, flexibility. It was scary: we had reached the point of no return. Getting on that flight to Russia meant having little to no contact with our prior lives, our families and friends, our support networks. A package or letter sent from the US would take up to 3 months to reach us and phone service would be available to only a lucky few. We wouldn't be staying in high-end hotels with comfortable bedding, we wouldn't have access to Western foods or groceries nor, most strikingly, unlimited hot water to bathe. Instead of cringing at these images, we felt a strengthening of our collective reserve and our commitment to succeed.

AUGUST 7, 1994

Because of the visa delay we moved from our upscale lodging at the Westin Hotel to the freshmen dorms at the University of Washington. This must have been fate's way of gradually preparing us for our ultimate destination.

Two volunteers were assigned per room and meal tickets for the school cafeteria were handed out. Somehow both Karl—the army brat—and I ended up with our own rooms, with neither of us feeling guilty enough to inform the Peace Corps staff of their error. Accentuating the feeling that we were being treated like teenagers, we were given a generous stipend of $10 per day to supplement the cafeteria meals provided by the university. Watching the unloading of our baggage from the bus gave onlookers quite a chuckle, as seventy bags—ranging from giant designer suitcases to duffel bags, all bursting at the seams—filled the sidewalk. We dragged our luggage up two flights of stairs, down a long dark hallway reminiscent of "The Shining" and into our rooms. We were allotted ten minutes to settle in before the start of our first Russian-language lesson.

The lessons were taught by two Russian instructors who had been flown in from Vladivostok so that we wouldn't fall behind on our timeline. The standard process is for Peace Corps trainees to spend the first three months living with a host country family and spending eight hours a day, six days a week learning the local language and getting instruction on local culture and business practices. Natasha, the younger of the two instructors, reminded me of a beautiful Russian spy from a James Bond movie; she wore a silky, snug-fitting summer dress that highlighted her figure. Natalia, motherly in both personality and features, gave a warm and reassuring smile. Our first ninety-minute lesson consisted of repeating Russian words and phrases, focusing on the difficult pronunciations that begin with a series of consonants before the introduction of a vowel. An example would be *Hello*, which begins with the letters "zdrv." We had been asked to learn the Russian alphabet prior to arriving, so although most of us couldn't speak a word of Russian other than the word *vodka*, we would be able to forgo that part of our education. Starting tomorrow, we will jump to three ninety-minute language lessons a day.

Two additional Russian-language instructors are scheduled to arrive tomorrow, which will improve the student-to-instructor ratio. The lessons are tiring, as we are forbidden from speaking English and continually repeat strange sounds foreign to the English tongue. This is then followed by hours of verb conjugation and tedious attempts to memorize vocabulary words. Fortunately, having grown up in New Jersey, I had an uncanny ability to talk with my hands to get my point across. With four students paired to each teacher, it is impossible to daydream without getting scolded. Natasha and Natalia are tough on us, as if trying to compensate for their own sense of foreignness—both were traveling outside of Russia for the first time.

Despite or perhaps because of the strenuous schedule, I have gotten to know several of my fellow trainees quite well. We spend all our waking hours together, whether in class, the cafeteria, or in the study hall after dinner. After three days of this busy schedule I needed a break from "group think" and, with minimal effort, was able to talk Chris Willis, a soft-spoken Midwesterner, into joining me for a beer at one of the local brewpubs. We hadn't spent much time together, so sitting in a bar for a beer or two was a great way to build those ties that we were supposed to be developing for future support. Well, one pitcher quickly turned into two and then three and before I knew it the bar was closing and it was after one a.m. We stumbled back to the dorm, dreading the six a.m. breakfast that would kick off another full day of lessons.

AUGUST 10, 1994

Struggling though three lessons each day is wearing me down. Tempers are getting short and the initial niceties tossed back and forth have been replaced with sarcasm and snide looks. Cliques of various sorts have formed, which has put schisms into our unified front. The age and cultural differences are a major contributing factor, although hearing comments such as "Those drunks came in at two in the morning and woke us up" indicate that the loss of the "feel-good" sentiment formed in the first week may partially be due to my own behavior. Group play dates are worked into our schedules to regain the camaraderie and induce a bit of stress relief. Two days ago it was volleyball followed by sojourns to the local brewpub, which had already become my home away from home. The bartenders treat us as mascots and are quick to offer free pitchers knowing that we are surviving on limited funds. John Collins, the laid-back Southerner and my primary partner in crime, has convinced me to treat every night as if it will be our last night in America. This has led to a reduction in both my savings and sleep. A $10 daily stipend doesn't go far in Seattle, even with discounted pitchers of beer. Sundays are free days with no formal lessons and August is a beautiful time of year here; we have been spending as much time as possible outdoors. Since our arrival, we have been greeted each morning with sunny, clear skies and temperatures averaging in the high 70s.

Before arriving, each of us had our own life complete with a sense of privacy and of being in control of how we spent our time. Now our new routines consist primarily of classwork, study, and sleep, giving us limited independence. The trips to the brewpub prove to be a great release and fortunately this has not negatively impacted my language lessons. Strong language skills will be vital to our survival, considering that very few Russians in our designated area will speak English.

AUGUST 13, 1994

Our departure is scheduled for August 18, two weeks after our initial meeting at the Westin Hotel. This being our final weekend in America, we were given Saturday afternoon in addition to Sunday to complete any last-minute shopping. Ready for one final weekend, John and I pooled our resources for a bottle of Captain Morgan rum and a 2-liter bottle of Coke to get the party started. Like bees to flowers, Gary, Karl and Holly joined us within minutes in the Commons area, under a sun that was high and bright amid pure blue sky. Holly, in her twenties and from Ohio, had a sweet smile and a hint of trouble in her eyes that intrigued me. A slight breeze ruffled the branches overhead, but not enough to interfere with the flight of our Frisbee. We spent the day laughing, running, and enjoying the fresh air with little thought to shopping.

AUGUST 14, 1994

Growing up in the 1970s I had experienced nuclear attack drills at school and can recall hiding under the desk as a first grader, not knowing whether to laugh or pee my pants when the alarm warned of an incoming missile attack. The awareness of a Great Enemy bent on our destruction left indelible memories on all of us and made the ideological and cultural differences between Russia and America much harder to forget. Nonetheless, it wasn't until I took our language teachers Natasha and Natalia to the local supermarket that I saw just how foreign we are to each other. The variety of options for every item was mind-boggling for them. I remained a respectful few feet behind, witnessing their exploration of our American world. They whispered as we passed aisles full of coffee and tea, toothpaste and breakfast cereals. Movies and soap operas from the US often reached the Russian market, but it was assumed that their displays of abundance were part of the West's propaganda. The Russian government had fueled so much fear and mistrust of American capitalism that any indication contrary to this viewpoint came across as propaganda. On the walk back to the dorms, Natasha, in a moment of deep reflection, explained to me that now she can understand why we Americans are always smiling.

AUGUST 15, 1994

The Peace Corps staff in DC announced today that our visas have arrived and that we will be flying out as planned on the 18. I have had little time to think about what life will be like in Russia as I have been so fixated on learning the language and getting to know my fellow trainees. I guess I spent a bit of time imbibing at the brewpub as well, but that doesn't fit the narrative. Anyway, with time getting short, a sense of panic has kicked in and I dedicate every free moment to studying, hoping to make up for the past two weeks of partying. I ask myself whether I will be able to communicate with the Russians and then, realizing my weakness, dive back into my books. When I broach this subject with my fellow trainees, I find that I am not alone in my worries. In addition to our lack of language competency, we worry that we won't have the necessary survival items and then dart off to buy battery-heated socks, rolls of duct tape, and other sundry items.

AUGUST 18, 1994

The past two weeks have thoroughly tested our patience and raised questions about the Peace Corps administration's competence. How badly can they screw things up? We are on an emotional roller coaster. Last night I called my family to say goodbye again and promised to write once I arrived in Russia. This morning, news of another delay was declared. For the second time in as many weeks I called my family to let them know that our departure has been postponed. Our bags were packed. We were excited, despite the anxiety coursing through our veins, and couldn't wait to head to the airport. We were told that seven of our eighteen visas had arrived in Seattle and that the unlucky eleven of us that were still missing visas, including me, would remain in Seattle until our visas were processed by the Russian embassy in DC. The lucky seven will depart tonight for Vladivostok aboard an Alaska Airlines flight. This forced separation of our group created a strange sense of loss that seemed almost comical considering that only two weeks earlier, none of us had even met. I was frustrated that the Peace Corps staff in DC failed to advise us that we were short eleven instead of waiting until everyone was packed and ready to go. Our patience is being tested and we haven't even gotten to Russia yet!

To help us deal with the frustration, a conference call was set up with Ken Hill, the Peace Corps' Russian Far East country director, who was in Vladivostok. He apologized for our delay and told us how much he was looking forward to meeting us. His concern and sincerity seemed genuine and the call boosted our spirits as much as possible considering that we were back to waiting in the University of Washington dormitories. Also on the call was the assistant country director for our program, who was stuck in Washington, D.C. having his own visa problems. Since being accepted into the Peace Corps and given an assignment fifteen months ago, the poor organization and lack of clarity has me wondering whether anyone is in charge. Every deadline has been missed and I wonder how we will be supported once we are on our own in the field. It was hard enough explaining to my family that I was moving to Russia to work as a volunteer after spending the past two years earning an MBA without having to explain the continual delays. I could hear the concern in my parents' voices and felt like I had to apologize for the Peace Corps, which pissed me off even more.

AUGUST 24, 1994

Today is my grandmother's eighty-second birthday. I called to wish her a happy birthday and she began to cry, which made me realize for the first time just how far away I would be from home and family. When I first informed my family of my decision to join the Peace Corps and move to Russia, my grandmother had chided me, "What do they have in Russia that you can't get in New York City?" Overall, family and friends have been supportive, although I am sure there have been plenty of conversations behind my back pertaining to my sanity. I had applied during my last semester of graduate school at the University of South Carolina. While everyone else was talking about how much they were going to earn at their banking or finance jobs, I talked about my future move to Russia and how I was going to change the world, drink vodka, and meet attractive Russian women. I don't regret my decision: I figure that I will have the next forty years to work. This opportunity may never again be available.

Brian, our assistant country director, called this afternoon to tell us that the remaining eleven visas had been sent via Federal Express and should arrive in Seattle tomorrow. He and his wife Gail had been scheduled to join us tonight, but unfortunately their visas are still missing so they will continue to wait in DC. The eleven of us are antsy in our purgatory: no longer connected to our former lives and not yet afoot in our new ones. The mounting delays have been a disappointment and it is hard not to lash out at Brian, as he is our first line of contact with the Peace Corps administration.

AUGUST 25, 1994

The priest was dressed in multiple layers of black that seemed far too warm for this time of year, but he never wiped at his brow or seemed the least bit uncomfortable. He spoke slowly, as if wanting to make sure we understood every heavily accented word, while he guided us through Seattle's oldest Russian Orthodox Church. He gave a brief account of Russia's religious history and the historical relationship between the Orthodox Church and the Soviet government. I was intrigued by the solemnity of his movements and the way he crept around the issues regarding the recent political and economic collapse of Communism and Russia itself. He embodied a sense of spirituality and mystique that was tied into the composition of the church itself.

Following our tour, the priest walked us down quiet suburban streets until we came upon the Russian Consulate. After an awkward few minutes in the lobby, the consul general appeared and seemed almost angry that the United States was providing humanitarian assistance to his country. I had wondered whether the Russians would resent our presence and whether this had been the reason for the delay of our visas. The consul general's attitude, although not outright antagonistic, was far from welcoming and it increased my anxiety concerning how we would be treated once in Russia.

When we returned to the dorms that night, a note was pasted to each of our doors saying that our visas had finally arrived! In a further effort to improve morale, Brian had set up a conference call with the seven members of our group that had already arrived in Russia. We huddled around the speakerphone, eager to hear every minute detail, as they regaled us with their adventures. For twenty minutes, we stood around the phone with stupid grins on our faces listening to tales of cockroaches the size of small dogs, inedible food, and the difficulty our friends had understanding the language. Instead of feeling shock or disgust, we were radiant. The call ended with a plea for us to bring mosquito nets, glove liners, and as many pairs of socks and underwear as possible due to the difficulty of doing laundry.

SEPTEMBER 4, 1994

Today is my fifth day in Russia. I am writing while crouching on a tiny twin bed under the limited light that has crept in through the window through a layer of grime and a filter of floating dust. Our flight from Seattle seemed much longer than the actual thirty-five hours of travel time, not least in part due to Alaska Airlines' policy of not providing free booze on international flights. Adding to this was the suspicious nature of the Russian authorities, who refused to allow us to get off the plane to stretch our legs at either of the two refueling stops. Our first welcoming view of Russian soil was dampened by our concern that we would end up in a huge fireball on a Siberian tarmac when the Russian ground crew fueled our plane with lit cigarettes dangling from their lips. Apparently there is no OSHA in Russia!

We were a mess from the long flight, lack of sleep, and general exhaustion when we finally landed in Vladivostok's international airport. It was 9 p.m. local time (7 a.m. Seattle time). I was expecting the third degree going through customs and immigration, which turned out to be a breeze: we were whisked through to the front of a long line of Russians returning from abroad. We walked out into the Russian night, the air scented with the smell of roadside barbeques, car exhaust, and sweat. A curtain of humidity pressed into my skin, making me keenly aware that quite a bit of time had passed since my last shower. In zombie-like fashion, dragging our suitcases and backpacks, we blindly followed our training director to a school bus for the ride to the dormitory where we would be spending our first few nights.

The bus had all the glamor of the school busses I rode in when a child in New Jersey, complete with gum and graffiti plastering the seat backs. Exhausted, we stared out the windows, taking in the scenery as we bumped along the highway. The sky, dark but for a hint of pale moon, seemed an ominous welcome. It was surreal. Our eyes strained to catch anything of interest in the passing landscape. Houses set in woodsy enclaves, the rusty hulks of deserted vehicles, and the occasional pedestrian made for unremarkable impressions. The scenery changed abruptly as we entered the city limits. Eight and ten-story cement skyscrapers lined the highway. People scurried in and out of the shadows, moving from doorway to doorway. Small groups of teenagers clustered around street corners, discernible only by the glowing tips of their cigarettes. The traffic became heavy, slowing our passage to a crawl—slow enough that we could see the faces at the bus stops and on the passengers riding in cars alongside us, all exhibiting an almost frightening lack of expression.

The smell of burning refuse and grilling meat from roadside barbeques filtered in through the windows as we passed an outdoor market. It reminded me of my travels through Southeast Asia, and it was far from what I had expected here. Finally the bus struggled up a long winding driveway and stopped in front of a four-story brick dormitory. We slung our bags over our shoulders and trudged up a set of stairs. The smell of stale cigarettes marked the entrance and grew stronger as we walked down the hallway toward the office. Karl and I were roommates, which was fine since I enjoyed his company and sense of humor. He had a mischievous twinkle in his eyes and had earned my envy by—supposedly—sleeping with one of the Russian instructors. Our dorm contained two small cots, a tiny refrigerator, and a desk that had seen better days. A plastic chandelier with more bulbs missing than glowing hung from the ceiling with a backdrop of red shiny wallpaper that fought to stay attached to the walls. The windows were cracked and caked with dust, which wasn't too bad since the view was of the garbage dumpster.

We were fortunate in that we had the only room with a private bathroom and shower. Our toilet was even equipped with a toilet seat, a rarity in the dormitory. Our exuberance was quickly dampened when we tried the shower spigot. There were two temperatures: cold and really fucking cold. Had I had not been covered in two days' worth of sweat and grime I might have made do with a splash of water on my face and a double dose of deodorant, but I was way past that point. The lady at the front desk advised us that the city was waiting until late October to turn on the hot water in an effort to conserve energy. There was a severe energy crisis plaguing eastern Russia, despite the large quantities of coal coming out of local mines, because the government preferred to sell the coal to China, Japan, and South Korea for the foreign currency. Hyperinflation had relegated the ruble to a fraction of its value over the past year and the average Russian had seen his life savings reduced by 80 percent in the past two years.

I awoke the first morning to the unfamiliar cadence of Russian voices. I reached for my glasses, saw Karl starting to move, and decided that for the good of my bladder I had better get to the bathroom first. Once showered and dressed, I walked out to the lobby, which was slowly filling with the rest of my jet-lagged colleagues. Excitement and nervous laughter filled the air. When everyone was accounted for, our guide herded us into a cafeteria where waitresses served us a breakfast of gray hot dogs, cold spaghetti speckled with congealed butter, and bowls of reddish salmon caviar. Mugs of instant coffee were brought to the table along with powdered milk and rocky, unrefined sugar. I was the only one with an appreciation for caviar; I slathered slices of bread with butter before layering on the caviar. It was hard to figure how the others preferred the hot dogs and spaghetti, but I wasn't about to argue.

After breakfast, we were led down a dimly lit hallway into the heart of the university, where the strong presence of ammonia and disinfectant stung our eyes. We finally came upon a classroom and got the first glimpse of our fellow American trainees. Hugging, back-slapping and emotional head-nodding occurred as if it had been years and not days since they left us in Seattle. Our schedule for the next two and a half months would be composed of an intensive training program at the university, with classes running from 8:15 a.m. to 5:00 p.m. six days a week. Classes would be divided between language training, and cultural and technical development so that we would have a better understanding of both personal and business culture. Our three weeks in Seattle had provided a limited language foundation, but we had far to go. Local businessmen, both Russians and expats, were scheduled to lecture us about the commercial difficulties in the Russian Far East as well as on basic Russian business etiquette. I hung on every word, imagining myself as a young Gordon Gekko, wheeling and dealing with Russian businessmen in my American suit and shiny shoes. My colleagues showed a similar eagerness, and the training staff felt compelled to caution us repeatedly on managing our expectations. "You will only get frustrated if you come in with the attitude that you are going to save the world. Try to listen first, because you will need to really understand the business climate before offering your American expertise," they advised.

The first day of class brought out a renewed enthusiasm, which was something that had gradually dwindled after our first week in Seattle despite how we were told that "If you fail the language test at the end of your training you will be sent home!" With so few English speakers here, our safety and survival depends on our ability to pick up the language. The warnings inspired me and I couldn't wait to establish a routine to test my new limits. After our first day spent in a classroom conjugating verbs and repeating vocabulary words, I succumbed to my inner demon and snuck away with John for a quick beer. We were supposed to spend an hour relaxing before dinner, but instead we joined a group of Russian students leaving the university and climbed aboard a tram with the hope of ending up in the downtown area, where John had seen a bar on a prior visit to the city. I had assumed that John's ten days of experience in-country would have better equipped his navigational abilities, but the look of confusion as he tried to figure out the tram map indicated otherwise. Everyone seemed to be staring at us as if a flashing fluorescent sign shouted "Americans."

While still in the United States, my opinion of Russia had consisted of scenes of blistery arctic winds and heavily bundled comrades right out of a Dostoevsky novel. Now with sweaty hands gripping a bus pole in ninety-degree temperatures, I would have paid dearly for a gush of the arctic breeze, particularly as the combined perfume of sweat, sausage breath, and exhaust had me praying that our stop would be next. The tram zigzagged wildly, bumping around on the roughly paved streets while we strained to see any familiar signs through the dirt-encrusted windows. I looked over at John and without having to say a word, we both moved toward the door. Suddenly the tram came to an abrupt stop and the mass of sweaty people swayed forward. Everyone except for the two of us began shouting, until two men forced their way to the door. They climbed up the outside of the tram and onto the roof, where they reconnected the poles that attached the tram to the electric wires overhead. The lights flicked back on and the men returned to the inside of the tram to a chorus of cheers. Fortunately, the next stop was the final stop and we pushed our way through a horde of people eager for a breath of fresh air and a glimpse of the blue sky.

The scene we embarked upon reminded me of a depression-era movie. Raggedly dressed babushkas squatted on wooden crates, their hair wrapped in bandanas, as they scooped sunflower seeds out of burlap bags into cones made of newspaper. Their gnarled hands grasped the proffered coins from a few of the commuters while they continued screaming out to others in an effort to gain another sale. Kiosks lined the outer area of the station, most little more than wooden shacks stuffed to the breaking point with Russian cigarettes, chocolate bars, and counter-to-ceiling displays of vodka bottles. It had been six hours since my lunch of borscht and cucumber salad, so my heart jumped when I saw a Snickers bar. I took out a 500-ruble note and handed it to the clerk, pointing at the shelf and mumbling "Snickers." She stared at me with a look of incomprehension. "Sneekers," I repeated, motioning toward the candy bar again. She understood and took the bill, handing me back my change and the Snickers bar. I beamed, proud at having conducted my first transaction in Russia.

We continued along a cobblestone street where the crowds thinned, allowing us to walk side by side under the imposing shadows of Stalinesque concrete buildings. The only color present came from the fluttering Russian flags that adorned every building. The pedestrians kept their eyes to the pavement, focused solely on getting home. We came upon the central square, which bordered the port, and were greeted with the outline of tanker ships and cranes, a drabness that contrasted sharply with the bright blue sky. The plaza was quite large and pulsated with the shrieks of vendors pushing trays of watches, flower bouquets, and postcards at the passersby.

I bought a packet of post cards from an overly zealous vendor with enough cleavage bursting from her dress to make up for the overpriced cards. We sat on an empty bench, contemplating our new lives while soaking up the new surroundings. A child pedaled past us on a bicycle and he turned to stare at us, causing him to lose his balance and head into the street where he collided into the side of a passing car. It sounds dramatic to say that it seemed to occur in slow motion, but I watched his little body sail through the air before hitting the pavement. The car screeched to a halt. The driver stepped out and stared. People began shouting and the driver shouted back and then he jumped into his car and sped off. The boy lay on the ground, a pool of blood spreading from his still body. A single shoe leaned against the crumpled bicycle, the back wheel slowly spinning.

We wordlessly stood up and hustled away toward the port, where the last rays of sun glistened off the bay. The width of the beach fluctuated from a measly twenty meters to more than a hundred as it wound toward the limestone cliffs. Again, my only point of comparison was from movies and I was reminded of the 1960 Fellini film "La Dolce Vita" as heavyset women, stuffed like sausages into their bathing suits, paraded around with potbellied men in what could only generously be referred to as Speedos. Nobody braved the frigid water. The children played across the litter-strewn beach, their screams mixing with those of the seagulls. Teenage couples sat on benches, fingers interlocked, in the throes of young love. The girls were waving cigarettes in movie-star fashion while the boys tried to appear nonchalant, flexing their biceps and looking tough. We kept walking and after a few blocks came to a small café. We knew it was a café because the sign outside said "Café." Otherwise, you couldn't have identified the type of establishment, due to the blackened windows. We stepped inside, past a welcoming swarm of flies. We hesitated, but since this was the only restaurant we had seen, we continued. We were the only patrons. A waitress gave us a cursory look before turning back to filing her nails. For some reason I felt it would be rude to walk out, so we waited. After several minutes without further acknowledgement, we made coughing sounds hoping for some form of acknowledgement. "Should we leave?" we asked each other. We had been warned about poor customer service, but this was ridiculous. We walked out, slightly unnerved.

Upon arriving in Russia, each of us had been given $14 worth of rubles by the Peace Corps for pocket money, a sum small enough, they casually remarked, to prevent us from getting into any trouble. So they thought. Having built my confidence with the Snicker's purchase, I was ready to try my luck with a beer. Back at the central plaza we found a beer kiosk, selling both Russian and foreign varieties. After a moment's hesitation, I forked over half my ruble allotment and loaded ten Australian Foster's Lager cans into John's backpack. Proud of our achievement, we took our stash to a nearby bench and I cracked open my first beer in Russia. There is no refrigeration at the kiosks so the beer was an ambient 80 degrees. But the sense of accomplishment was incredible. The second beer went down a little faster and by the third, our goofy grins returned, further setting us apart from the stoic Russian alcoholics on nearby benches.

The Peace Corps staff had lectured us to take every precaution when traveling on public transportation, specifically advising us not to draw any attention to ourselves since the busses and trams were full of criminals looking for an easy target. Our success in getting downtown, buying beer, and finding the correct tram led to a false sense of security and we chatted away in English on the way home, oblivious to the interest we had aroused. Two Russian sailors pushed through the crowd toward us and we tensed, fearing a confrontation. Fortunately, they made toothy grins, put us at ease, and we shook hands as they introduced themselves. Every eye on the tram was now focused on the four of us. I shrugged off the crushing handshake squeeze while fumbling with my few words in Russian. We began an incredibly ridiculous conversation that included lots of pointing and pantomiming with repeated efforts by the Russians to get us to come to their house to drink vodka. We feigned ignorance of their intentions and managed to get back to the university without offending them.

I stumbled into the dorm cafeteria and took a seat at the end of the table, doing my best to hide my buzz from the others, since I didn't want to advertise our misbehavior. After seeing what was for dinner, I wished that I had eaten something from one of the street vendors. Mounds of gray mashed potatoes, curdled in a pile of slimy chunks of similarly coagulated grease, filled my plate. I used the spoon to poke and prod the mass, hoping for divine interference. A handful of scrawny green beans stuck out from under the potatoes giving mind to a clump of weeds growing through cracked pavement. Bricks of brown bread, with the taste and texture to match, were placed on the table. This was a far cry from the soft, sweet-smelling bread we had been given at breakfast. My plastic knife snapped when I tried to cut through the crust. This gastronomic travesty brought tears to my eyes. I make no apologies for being a foodie and although not a picky eater, I couldn't imagine suffering on this diet through the next twenty-seven months. Three years apprenticing as a classical French chef, four years working in top restaurants, and now my dietary choices consisted of this substitution for edible food.

After dinner, I returned to the dorm room and began to read from a packet of background information provided by the Peace Corps with respect to the Russian Far East. I owed it to myself to learn as much as possible about the geography and demographics. We were in a part of Russia called *Primorye or Primorsky Krai*, which borders North Korea and China to the south and the Sea of Japan to the east. The population of the region is two million people, with 800,000 living in its largest city, Vladivostok. The Russian naval and nuclear submarine bases, formerly of the USSR, are entrenched along the coastline, creating a security consciousness that is much greater than in other parts of Russia. Indigenous animals such as deer, bears, and even Siberian tigers are here, which caused quite a bit of consternation on our first day when the local paper featured report of a young couple attacked the prior night by a tiger while they waited for the train. The couple had been mauled and the boyfriend killed and partially eaten. This brought on my first nightmare in twenty years as I dreamed of being pinned under a car by a crazed tiger swiping at me with outstretched claws. I vowed never to take a train in Russia.

SEPTEMBER 5, 1994

During our Saturday morning class, two current Peace Corps volunteers visited with us. They were part of the original Russian Far East Peace Corps group of fifty-two, who had arrived during the winter of 1992. A year later they were down to twenty-four volunteers and now after eighteen months, they were down to nine. They had experienced significant difficulties and had been "mentally and physically unprepared" for the hardships that come from being a pioneer group. The chore of finding food, lovingly referred to as "hunting and gathering," immediately turned into a full-time activity since there was little available in the outdoor markets and no super-markets or grocery stores. The Peace Corps, learning from that first entry into Eastern Russia, started our training program a few months earlier in the year to coincide with the peak of the harvest. This allowed us to learn how to prepare for winter like the Russians by stocking up on dried and canned goods, establishing relationships with the local communities, and most importantly, learning which of the kiosks had foreign connections allowing for an occasional box of mac & cheese or Oreo cookies.

We are living under a constant cloud of suspicion from the Russians.

They ask us with incredulous glares why we would give up the "good life" in America to live without hot water, a steady supply of electricity, and all the other amenities we have back home. It is a fair question and is difficult to answer without sounding condescending. Russian propaganda had painted everything American with a decadent and immoral brush and now it hurts their pride to acknowledge that the Evil American Empire is providing humanitarian assistance. Most Russians in this area have had little, if any, interaction with foreigners, which only adds to the suspicion.

We continued with our brutal language lesson schedule as well as being introduced to the basics of doing business in Russia. The Peace Corps has brought in local business owners, bankers, and tax lawyers to expand our network and increase our understanding of just how different Russian business is from that in the States. One afternoon we met two of the volunteers who operate business centers in Vladivostok. The term *business center* in Russia is new, as is the concept of business itself, so that instead of focusing immediately on helping clients put ideas into action, here it is necessary to explain some of the basic constructs first, such as marketing and financing, since they didn't grow up with lemonade stands and paper routes. The mission of the Peace Corps business centers is to help Russian entrepreneurs write business plans and prepare grant requests in the hope of securing start-up capital from nongovernmental organizations (NGOs) or to locate a foreign business partner. Obtaining funding from foreign agencies was vital, since the only local alternative was to borrow from the Russian mafia. The hyperinflation drained Russian ruble bank accounts, and only a few well-connected people had accounts in foreign currencies.

We hadn't received any information specifically related to the mafia, but their presence was hinted at during every discussion. During our second day of class, a loud explosion thundered through the university. We heard doors slamming in the hallways and then the sound of people running. We ran out of the classroom, following our teachers despite not knowing why we were running or where we were heading. We ended up in the university courtyard, where we could see smoke billowing from the twisted metal of what had been a car. This turned out to be the result of a car bomb that had targeted a rival businessman. On one level, it was exciting to witness such violence, but also quite a wake-up for us to take extra precautions when out in public.

Organized crime is so prevalent and such a part of everyday life that it is impossible to separate legal from illegal activity. In Russia, if you refer to an individual as being connected to the mafia, it connotes political clout and the ability and will to use violence to achieve the desired result. Without a trustworthy and even playing field within the legal system and because of the reluctance of law enforcement to get involved in cases involving the mafia, the common man has no leverage in the court system. This in turn means greater reliance on an alternate means of resolution, i.e., the mafia. Living in this Wild West environment is dangerous since both Russian and foreign businesses operate with a constant sense of fear. This attitude permeates society, especially seen in the aggressive tone of the young men in the streets, which can be intimidating, especially with my poor understanding of the language. The lower-level mafia violence is primarily directed toward local shop owners. Supposedly special care is taken to avoid targeting foreigners for fear that would bring an end to foreign investment, but every foreigner that spoke to us had a story to counter that opinion.

SEPTEMBER 6, 1994

We can't get enough new information about our new home in the Russian Far East. We spend our nights poring over regional maps and discussing the pros and cons of possible job sites. The idea of being assigned to a small village fills me with dread. To improve my chances of a plum assignment, I have been sweet-talking the selection committee and I bribe them with chocolate when nobody is looking. I'm a city guy and, having never ridden a horse or worked a day in the field, I would be totally out of place in a small farming village. Some of the assignments will be in the two largest cities in the Russian Far East: here in Vladivostok and in Khabarovsk, which lies twelve hours north by train along the Amur River. Others will work with village collectives and town administrations. In addition to receiving our job assignments today, we will also meet and move in with our host families. No longer will we have the nightly support sessions with our fellow volunteers to quiet our nerves and apprehensions. We will each be on our own with a Russian family, speaking only Russian and on our best behavior as we try to adapt to the Russian culture and norms. These families have agreed to adopt us for two months to teach us the survival skills that we will need to live on our own. The families have been instructed to help us understand Russian culture and traditions as well as to work with us on our rudimentary language skills. It's said there is no better way to learn a language then to live it, but it's a daunting task. Some Russian families sign up for the money, which at eight dollars per day is a considerable sum, while others sign up for the opportunity for their family to interact with an American. It is a standard Peace Corps regulation that trainees spend twelve weeks with a host family, but since our visas were delayed, we will have a shorter period. It is hard to explain what I am feeling as I prepare to meet my host family. I wonder whether they will be warm and welcoming or whether I will be an outsider in their home. Will they respect my privacy? Will they be kind? Most importantly, will they feed me something other than gray hot dogs and coagulated spaghetti?

When I'm nervous, it becomes immediately obvious: perspiration gathers along my brow and above my lip. As I wait, I continually wipe my palms against my pants. I am reminded of puppies at the pound trying their best to look cute within their cages while prospective adoptive families pass by. The host families are likely just as nervous, wondering whether their American will require high maintenance or be easygoing and ready to absorb all they have to offer. Irina, one of our language instructors, tapped me on the shoulder and then grabbed my hand. "Your turn," she said as she nodded in the direction of the door. She led me outside and into a classroom where a hearty-looking couple in their late fifties sat fidgeting. Hand in hand, they smiled awkwardly, as Irina motioned for me to sit beside them. I cracked a cautionary smile as I bent toward the chair, but as I was leaning down, they had moved to stand. I stumbled back to my feet and the three of us stood awkwardly smiling at each other, unsure of the protocol. Fearful of making a social gaffe, I used the two-handed Bill Clinton handshake with the husband. Feeling his calloused grip, I instinctively squeezed tighter to compensate for my weak, soft hands.

"*Ochen Priatno*," I said, showing off the best of my Russian-language skills. The husband introduced himself as Uri and then pointed at his wife, who he introduced as Jenya, which I interpreted as *Jenna*, the Russian word for wife. I felt awkward addressing her as "wife" and as the moment of silence grew, I just blurted out "Mama." They burst into a smile and within seconds we were all laughing.

The only English they had mastered was *Hello*, so we spent the first two minutes smiling stupidly at each other while Irina tried her best to sell me like a used car dealer, pointing out my positive attributes and bragging that I was one of the teachers' favorite students. She followed up by telling me in English how lucky I was to have them as a host family. I wanted to impress them. I wanted them to feel lucky that they got me, but with only three and a half weeks of language lessons, I was pushed to the limit of my conversational abilities and found myself repeating memorized phrases about my family and favorite hobbies. They responded in a flurry of Russian that went right over my head. I had no idea what to say after that, so I returned to smiling stupidly.

"Mama" is a healthy woman with a bright smile and an aura that makes you immediately want to hug her. Her husband, also a bit portly, had a twinkle in his eyes and seemed equally friendly. For ten minutes Irina translated our questions and answers before excusing herself to help with the next pairing. She had been a security blanket during the introduction, but with her gone, I was left on my own. I asked them questions to get them talking and to make them feel more comfortable, especially since it didn't really matter at this point if I understood their replies; I nodded in false understanding. When they asked me questions, I responded by guessing at what they wanted to know, hoping that nothing came out as outrageous or inappropriate.

My host parents had been cautioned about the strange eating habits of some of the volunteers, with the emphasis being on the seven or eight who now claimed to be vegetarians after witnessing the food options at the cafeteria. Vegetarianism is a difficult concept for Russians to grasp. It baffles them when one of the Americans turns away a meal containing beef, chicken, or pork, since meat was often in scarce supply, prohibitively expensive, and seen as a delicacy or special-event ingredient. My passion for food and eating came across quickly when they asked me what I liked to eat, as I recited the names of the Russian dishes I had memorized. They smiled as I spewed out the words for both common and traditional dishes and I smiled back in mutual admiration: they were obviously good eaters. After twenty minutes of conversation that included pantomiming and picture-drawing, I figured out that they had an 18-year-old son named Timofey who was studying medicine, and that their apartment was within walking distance of the university. When I asked them why they had volunteered to be a host family, they replied that they thought it important for their son to spend time with an American. It was the answer I had hoped to hear. After that, the conversation got fuzzy; the more I nodded, the faster they spoke. Every third sentence I would ask them to repeat something or to speak more slowly. Eventually they were talking comically slow and again we burst out in laughter.

Mama joined me to retrieve my baggage from the dorm, while my host father brought the car around to the back door. Mama's snickers and head-shaking showed her displeasure at our accommodations, giving me confidence that their home would be more enticing. Papa was waiting for us in a two-door Toyota sedan and got out to help me load my bags into the trunk. I'd decided that since I was calling her Mama, I might as well call him Papa. He seemed to like this as well and together we stuffed my duffel bag and other possessions into the trunk before I climbed into the back seat. Seeing the extent of my worldly possessions, or at least the possessions that I would be living off of for the next two years, crammed into the trunk was a humbling experience.

Papa drove off, weaving between other cars and massive potholes while trying to shout over Mama, who was simultaneously pointing out objects from the opposite window and yelling at him to slow down. The last mile was straight up the side of a mountain that offered breathtaking views of the city and surrounding bays, but made my legs quiver in anticipation of having to walk up and down every day to get to the university.

By Russian standards, my family is middle class. They have a two-bedroom apartment on the seventh floor of an eight-story concrete building, entirely indistinguishable from the adjacent concrete apartment buildings. Laundry gently sways on lines across countless balconies, blocking the view of the shimmering bay as well as taking up much of the balcony. Once we pulled up in front of their apartment building, we had to lug the bags up seven flights, since the elevator was out of service. With the advent of Perestroika, the Russian government gave up responsibility for the buildings and allowed the current occupiers to take ownership. This meant that suddenly the shared space, including elevators, hallways, and stairways, had to be kept up by contributions from the tenants. No one wanted to pay for a new lightbulb for the stairwell when it was expected that it would be stolen the next day. With high inflation, most middle-class Russians didn't have the funds to contribute to the repairs or upkeep. Thus, the elevator had not been serviced or maintained for two years, leading to its current state.

The barely lit stairwells gave me an eerie feeling that I was not just far from home geographically, but chronologically as well. As we lugged my 90 pounds of jeans, T-shirts, and other necessities up the seven flights of stairs, I kept asking them to stop so that I could catch my breath. During these pauses, I suspected that they saw me as a weak American; neither of them had a problem with the effort required. I saw my grandparents' faces in theirs and wondered what my life might have been had my ancestors not fled Russia at the turn of the century. I would have grown up in a similar environment. It sounds contrived to say that I could see the hope, love, pain, and joy in their eyes, but I felt a bond was uncanny given that we had known each other less than an hour. I was emotional, feeling nervous and excited as I watched them unlock the door to both their home and lives. I am living a novel. A Russian novel where I am not Rich Sayette from Morristown, New Jersey, but an explorer entering the world of Pushkin, Gogol, and Dostoevsky. A world in which every door leads to a new experience.

The outer steel door of their apartment was bolted into cement walls and had a thick metal lock. The inner door had a smaller, yet still formidable lock that required two separate keys. Timofey, their son, must have heard us, since he stood in the hallway with a curious expression. He was quite thin in contrast to his parents and seemed timid in his mannerisms. I shook his hand and he returned my grip awkwardly, before reaching out to take one of my bags. Mama and Papa took a seat on a bench in the hallway and began to remove their shoes, patting a place between them for me to do the same. Timofey headed off, struggling under the weight of my duffel bag. He returned a few seconds later indicating that I should follow him, which I did in my stocking feet.

The hallway led past a living room and a bathroom that he pointed to while uttering words that I failed to catch. There were three doors at the end of the hallway, one of which led to a bedroom furnished with a foldout couch, dresser, and a large desk that covered most of the floor space. Two bright yellow parakeets bravely chirped from the safety of their cage, giving me either a glorious welcome or a warning to watch myself. I don't like birds, and from the clamor I sensed that the feeling was mutual. The walls were papered from floor to ceiling with depictions of scenes from St. Petersburg. There were fountains caught in mid-flow under an awning of autumn trees, massive cathedrals, and winter scenes showing dachas with smoking chimneys. Timofey spoke in a quiet, slow manner, as if he interpreted my lack of Russian-language abilities as a lack of intelligence. I didn't understand what he said, but from his manner it didn't seem to be

"Rich, so glad you are staying with us and getting to have my room while I sleep in the living room on the sofa". He seemed eager to return to the comfort of the living room, where his parents were setting out a welcoming feast. Mama scurried back and forth from the kitchen, her arms heaped with casserole dishes emanating wonderful aromas that had me salivating after surviving for several days on cafeteria food and Snickers bars. Timofey again said something I couldn't understand and then pointed to the couch, indicating that I should take a seat.

Intricate paintings and family photographs covered most of the wall space. The living room, warm and sunny from the wall-to-wall windows, had a very inviting aura that helped ease the tension. A large armoire in the middle of the room was packed with wine and Champagne glasses, while opposite a television stood out in contrast to the antique décor of the rest of the room. I sat awkwardly on the couch with my knees brushing against the coffee table watching as the three of them made trips to the kitchen to bring out additional platters. My stomach grumbled under the assault of wonderful smells. Papa took a seat next to Timofey and we began the same basic conversation that we shared at the university, as if to get Timofey up to speed. I repeated the memorized phrases telling Timofey about my two brothers, my two stepsisters, and describing where New Jersey was in respect to New York, California, and the two Disney resorts. The awkward silences were becoming more the norm and it was a relief when Mama brought out the last of the dishes and took a seat next to me. She gave a final instruction to Papa and then patted my leg with her hand and motioned for me to dig in, repeating the phrase *Coushit, coushit* meaning "eat, eat." Two words never sounded so good.

Before I even had a chance to pick up my fork, Papa set down a bottle of cognac on the table, and three snifters dangled precariously between his fingers. He placed one glass in front of Mama before doing the same for himself and me. Timofey didn't get one, which I assumed was due to his age. Papa made a toast in which I recognized little more than the sound of my own name before he reached across the table to clink glasses with me. The cognac burned on its way down, but I stoically stifled any facial grimace. Papa immediately refilled our glasses while Mama began heaping spoonfuls of salads, rice, chicken, and mushrooms onto my plate. The importance of toasting in Russian culture had been stressed during our training, with our instructors going so far as to force us to memorize a few basic toasts to acknowledge the hospitality of our host families. Per Russian custom, the host always gives the first toast in which he thanks the guests for coming. The second toast is offered immediately afterwards by the guests to thank the hosts, and the third toast in succession is led by the men, who stand in honor of the women before slamming down the third glass in as many minutes. I stood up and made my rehearsed toast to my new family and again we clinked glasses. It was barely noon, a bit early in the day to be drinking cognac, much less three shots. Fortunately, there was no lack of food to absorb it. I dug into a beet salad that was so fresh that each bite resonated like an orchestra as it hit my tongue. Fish marinated in a delicate vinaigrette, smoked kielbasa, and a dozen other wondrous platters came to me as Mama watched my plate like a hawk for any open space upon which she could slam down another spoonful. She eagerly scanned my face after each forkful to judge my reaction. I recognized this from my own behavior back home and wanted to convey my appreciation. After a particularly delicious bite, I leaned over and gave her a hug. Everything was delicious and beautifully presented, leaving me with a goofy smile. The pleasure I felt at having been matched with a family that appreciated food was equaled by the relief on their faces in knowing that their American was a good eater.

Within thirty minutes it felt as if I had eaten enough to last me for the entire twenty-seven months I was scheduled to spend in Russia. The only time that I put down my fork was to reach for the snifter that Papa was continuously refilling with cognac. Mysteriously, the more I drank, the easier it was to communicate. I found myself in the midst of conversations describing my life in much greater detail than I had thought possible only hours earlier. I don't know whether they understood a thing I said, but they nodded their heads in a similar fashion as I had when pretending to understand them. After the last of the dishes had been cleared of food and the empty plates brought into the kitchen, Mama brought out a pot of tea and a package of European crackers. It felt like the right time to present them with the gifts that I had brought from home. The gifts included a book of New York City photographs, souvenir T-shirts, and NY Mets and Jets baseball caps. Using the book as a guide, I pointed out where I had lived and where my family had grown up in Brooklyn, Queens, and the Bronx. After spending enough time looking at the book to be polite, they brought out a book of photographs of Russian cities, including St. Petersburg, where their daughter Irina and her two children lived. I followed along with forced enthusiasm as the massive amount of food began to settle in my gut. I fought the desire to close my eyes, fearing that falling asleep in the middle of them showing me photos of their family would be a serious faux pas. Once through the photo album, Timofey brought out a world map. We huddled over it and they were amazed to see just how far New Jersey was from Vladivostok: an exercise I had gone through dozens of times since finding out about my Peace Corps assignment. Vladivostok is twelve time zones away from New Jersey, making it exactly half way around the earth from my family.

After the meal, Papa offered to take me on a walk, which seemed like a good idea, although not nearly as enticing as the prospect of taking a nap. On the way down the stairs, Papa explained that his name was Uri Nikolayevich. Nikolayevich translated to son of Nicolai. I asked whether he preferred Papa to Uri and he smiled and said that Papa would be fine. We were more at ease with each other, probably because we were now quite inebriated. Once outside, it was easy to get a good view of the city since the apartment stood near the top of a hillside that overlooked the bay. I figured we would stick to the road alongside the buildings, and was therefore surprised when Papa turned and faced the steep incline leading to the top. He couldn't possibly think that I was going up there? The top of the hill looked to be half a mile up, the steep incline covered with thick brush. Boulders and trees stood out almost perpendicular to the mountain as my eyes traced the goat-paths that zigzagged to the top. Papa took the first steps forward. I took a deep breath and followed. In seconds we were both gasping and I smiled inside, guessing that he too must have been feeling the pain coming up the stairs on the way up to the apartment. Dark patches of sweat appeared on our shirts and the combination of cognac and garlic filled the air after each exhalation. Somehow we reached the peak, but neither of us could utter a word as we stood hunched over, hands firmly planted on our knees as we gasped for breath.

After taking a few minutes to regain his composure, Papa began to point out the sights. He pointed left toward the Golden Horn Bay, which is home to Vladivostok's main harbor, the Regional University, and the Russian naval base. The Golden Horn Bay had gotten its name when the first European freighter arrived in the 1860s and the captain saw the horn-shaped expanse of water reflecting the fading sunset, which gave the water a golden hue. As it was still early in the day, the bay was dark blue and utterly beautiful under a cloudless sky. The traffic and activity below seemed calmer than it had at street level. For twenty minutes we stood in silence admiring the view and feeling proud of the accomplishment of having made it to the top. Papa suggested that we should reward ourselves with some more cognac, or at least he said something to me that contained the word "cognac," which is the same in Russian as it is in English or even French for that matter. Again, not wanting to be rude on my first day, I nodded with a smile!

I was grateful that the descent required only a fraction of the effort that the climb up had. When we reached the street, Papa walked past the entrance to our building. I didn't question and followed along until we reached a small shop on the ground floor of one of the neighboring apartment buildings. Russians refer to these shops as kiosks, which confused me since the outdoor booths were also called kiosks. From my limited time here, I recognized the convenience of having kiosks everywhere I looked, despite most having identical products. We stopped in and Papa grabbed a bottle of Champagne and a loaf of bread. This brief delay allowed me enough time to muster my strength to climb the seven flights back up to their apartment. The bread, wrapped in wax paper and warm to the touch, gave off a wonderful aroma and the desire to tear into it propelled me forward. Papa explained that the "lift," as the elevator is called in Russian, had been broken for three months and was unlikely to be repaired anytime soon, so I had better get used to taking the stairs.

After climbing the seven stories and making it back into the apartment, I kicked off my shoes and collapsed on the couch next to Timofey, who was intently watching a Russian game show on television. He made every effort to explain what was happening, but my lack of Russian, much less Russian slang, made it difficult and he eventually gave up. All I wanted was to take a quick nap before Papa busted out the cognac again, but not wanting to seem rude, I feigned interest in the program. I could barely keep my eyes open and was trying to figure a way to catch a few minutes of sleep when I noticed Mama resetting the table. I watched in disbelief as she began bringing out a new series of plates loaded with fish, chicken, and assorted vegetables. Barely two hours has passed since the end of the earlier feast, which I had assumed was our dinner. I had eaten accordingly. Now, seeing another feast unfolding, all fears of not having enough to eat faded and gave rise to the new fear that I would outgrow my clothes before even making it to the end of my two-month home stay.

Papa opened the Champagne and we began the second meal of the afternoon! I felt compelled to eat everything put before me, although the size of my bites gradually decreased in size as I visualized Mr. Creosote, the grotesque character in Monty Python's "The Meaning of Life" who explodes after eating one last thin wafer mint after a huge meal. Mama seemed so pleased that I was enjoying the meal that I didn't have the heart to say "no more." Finally, when I couldn't handle another bite, I translated the words for "I don't have any room," which got my point across.

SEPTEMBER 6, 1994

Papa was behind the wheel. Mama was in the front seat gripping the dashboard with whitened knuckles, while Timofey and I were crammed into the back seat fighting for space with an overstuffed picnic basket. Mama had packed cakes, sandwiches, and assorted homemade treats for my first family trip to the coast and Papa was scaring the shit out of us as he drove with reckless abandon, weaving in and out of traffic. Russians are quick to point out that Vladivostok is considered the "San Francisco" of Russia, and I was eager to get outside of the city to see some of this beauty, but after a few minutes with Papa Andretti, I wasn't so sure. I squeezed my eyes shut and braced for a collision every other minute while trying not to laugh at Mama slapping him whenever she was brave enough to let go of her grip on the dashboard. Papa appeared calm, a big smile on his face as he ducked Mama's assaults. Three years ago there were only a few hundred cars in Vladivostok, so traffic rules were lenient—only the wealthy had cars and they in turn were responsible for making the laws. Over the past year the mafia, in cahoots with the Russian navy, brought in thousands of used Japanese cars and trucks on the naval vessels so that now the streets flowed with a myriad of inexperienced and unlicensed drivers. This kept the pedestrians on their toes since the roads were so peppered with potholes: cars often detoured across sidewalks and into opposing lanes of traffic to avoid having to slow down for the potholes. At one point of our journey we were driving fifty miles an hour and cars were zooming past us in the opposite direction on both sides.

We finally arrived at the coast and it was indeed beautiful. A sea-scented breeze blew along the rocky cliffs. Seabirds soared high above, circling before diving down to the surface for their own lunch. It was too windy to eat outside, so we sat in the car and ate chicken and potatoes, washed down with warm vodka and tea. It was fun and I enjoyed being accepted as part of the family. Mama kept a close eye on Papa's drinking, which in turn kept me relatively sober. Although drinking takes away some of my apprehension in speaking Russian, it also detracts significantly from my ability to focus the following morning during my language lessons. It seems absurd, but by keeping up with Papa when we drink, I have earned his respect and we have gotten close. Russians take great pride in their ability to drink and consider it rude to reject a proffered glass. I also didn't want to appear as a "soft" foreigner. To Timofey, who doesn't drink, we often look ridiculous pantomiming and shouting to each other in a combination of Russian, English, and gibberish.

SEPTEMBER 9, 1994

Each night I get back from the university feeling more tired than the day before. We spend six hours each day reciting Russian vocabulary and grammar. We take daily exams to test our survival skills, including giving and receiving directions, ordering food, and shopping. Despite the pressure, I am amazed at how much I have learned in such a brief period. To ease the pressure, occasionally some of us will stop at the bus stop on our way home from class to drink warm Russian beer and watch the Russians watching us. This gives us a chance to vent without the concern of offending an eavesdropping instructor or one of the Peace Corps staff. Once back with our host families, we are again surrounded by the Russian language and are forced to concentrate on every word.

On most days my first desire upon returning to the apartment is to hide away in my room to collect my thoughts and let my mind wander. The problem with this is cultural in nature: our Russian host families take our desire for privacy as an insult to their hospitality. I didn't want to offend them.

The Peace Corps staff has split us into groups of four for an exercise that will test our survival skills by sending us out on field trips to the small villages outside of Vladivostok. They want to test our ability to use public transportation and they want to force us to ask directions and to speak with ordinary Russians. My travel buddies are Holly, John, and the grandfatherly

Chuck. I have a crush on Holly and find myself pushing to be in her study groups. I often catch myself staring at her from across the room. Back home I wouldn't have thought twice about asking her out, but our group is small and she is one of the few people that I consider a friend. I don't want to put this at risk. At times the attraction seems mutual as she smiles at me when our eyes catch and I wink back as if we have our own little inside joke. John continues to be the partner in crime he's been since we met in Seattle. We share the same warped sense of humor and penchant for beer, which helps us pass time and fight off the occasional feelings of home-sickness. In contrast, Chuck, the 79-year-old former insurance agent, has begun to wear me down. He has fallen behind in our language classes, and as if to compensate, has become quite outspoken on every topic. Together we make a strange travel group as I take turns with John and Holly guiding Chuck to ensure that he remains in the group.

Our assignment was to take a bus from Vladivostok's main bus station to the city of Artyom, an hour north, and then return later in the afternoon by train. Our teachers' nervousness was contagious and we immediately forgot the phrases that we had spent the past two weeks memorizing. This led to our teacher's breaking protocol and helping us purchase our tickets before leading us onto the correct bus. Once on the bus, we settled into our seats and stared out the window, lost in thought. I began to contemplate, not without trepidation, what my life would be like in two months when I would be on my own and expected to travel and live like a local. Toyota Land Cruisers, the vehicle of choice for the Russian mafia, zoomed past our bus kicking up clouds of dust as we putt-putted along the roadways. Due to the poor road conditions there was a continual shift in speed as the driver slowed for potholes and for stray cars speeding toward us in our own lane. A haze of cigarette smoke filled the bus, which when mixed with the gas fumes that seeped into the cabin through the cracked flooring, made for a wonderfully noxious perfume. My stomach became queasy and I hoped that I wouldn't toss my breakfast over the seat in front of me. I looked over at Holly and saw a greenish tint to her cheeks as well. Our eyes met and we shared a moment of "what the fuck have we gotten ourselves into" before returning to our own thoughts.

After an hour of stop-and-go traffic, the bus stopped in front of a typical Communist-era bus depot and everyone disembarked, including the driver, which made it quite apparent that we had reached our destination and should also disembark. We didn't know if we were in the right place, as there had been no announcement, and there were no signs stating the name of the station. We started laughing and then shyly quieted down, as the stares of the passersby created an eerie feeling that we had violated some sacred norm against laughing in public.

Apartment buildings stretched off in both directions, neither indicating which way led to the city center, the finding of which was the goal of our exercise. Not being able to reach a consensus about which way to go and too humble to ask for directions, we followed a group across the street to another bus stop and then clambered onto the first bus that stopped. Chuck muttered continually that he thought we were lost while the other three of us glared anxiously out the window looking for a sign that we had guessed correctly. The road eventually narrowed to a single lane and within minutes, the buildings gave way to farmland. Realizing that we had gone in the wrong direction, we got off at the first stop and crossed the street so that we could take a bus back in the opposite direction. We were frustrated and I bit my tongue so as not to scream at Chuck, who seemed on the verge of complete panic, chanting "I told you we were going the wrong way."

After ten agonizing minutes at this lone country bus stop, we heard the diesel engine of another bus and fortunately it stopped in front of us. I leaned in and asked the driver, in my best Russian, if he was going to the city center. He nodded and motioned for us to climb aboard, probably quite puzzled as to why four foreigners would apparently be lost in the middle of nowhere. The bus took us past the Artyom bus station and continued for another half-mile before reaching a large plaza where a large sign stated "Artyom Center." Thirty busses were lined up side by side and my confidence grew. We got off and looked around, walking in a small circle.

"Where to now?" Holly asked. Not even Chuck ventured a guess this time. Our goal was to find the city administration building where there was a Peace Corps business center staffed by Linda, a volunteer from the first group. Again too shy to ask directions, we walked toward the unknown, passing a school, several stores, and dozens of identical concrete apartment buildings. We took it all in, eager to be the first to spot a building that would resemble a government administration building. I asked a woman for directions and after struggling to understand, she smiled and pointed straight ahead. Fresh air and the thought of success brought out our smiles and soon, the swagger returned to our steps. Our attempts to fit in apparently were less successful, as everyone stared unabashedly as we passed.

A woman with a big smile, salt-and-pepper hair, and a Western business suit walked toward us. It was Linda. After several minutes of small talk, she invited us to join her for lunch in her apartment, since the only restaurant in town was closed for remodeling. We were anxious to see how volunteers actually lived once away from the host families, so this was a much better option than dining out anyway. Her apartment was sparsely furnished, with a small living room, kitchen, and bathroom. The kitchen struggled to accommodate the five of us, as Linda served spaghetti followed by tea and cookies. The initial camaraderie faded and our conversation lagged. Linda seemed as uncomfortable hosting us as we were in invading her space. She directed most of her conversation toward Holly, leaving Chuck, John, and me to talk among ourselves. When the last of the cookies had been eaten, she offered to take us to the train station so that we could get back to Vladivostok. We had hoped to get a tour of the city, but none of us complained about cutting short our trip. Once onboard the train, I quickly took a seat next to Holly, leaving John to sit next to Chuck.

It was during times like this, when I was close to Holly, that I struggled to determine whether the attraction was mutual. At times she was withdrawn, but minutes later she would grab my arm and whisper something in my ear to make me laugh. We were all feeling vulnerable being far from home without the security of being surrounded by our lifelong friends and family. There was a strong desire to grab ahold of something and to feel connected. I wanted Holly to fill this void for me. I wanted the emotional connection, but at the same time feared the possible rejection and awkwardness that would be sure to follow. If we had only been drinking, the liquid courage would have pushed me over the line of caution.

The train's lack of accoutrements and décor matched that of the bus, but now we had the added benefit of stifling heat and a veil of acrid body odor to accompany the familiar cigarette smoke. The clickety-clanking from the bumpy track echoed in the heavy silence. Passengers stared ahead, no one smiling or showing any emotion. We too remained quiet. Thoughts of where I would end up living, what my life would be like living on my own, and whether I would eventually sleep with Holly filled my head. The ride passed quickly and soon we were getting off at the Pervaya Retchka [First River] train stop, only a short tram ride to my host family's apartment. We nodded goodbye to each other and headed off on our own. I was exhausted when I reached the apartment, but felt obligated to tell Mama about my travels while sipping tea at the kitchen table. She warned me to be careful after hearing how we got on the wrong bus, while laughing at our ineptitude. She and Papa have become very protective, as if my difficulty in understanding the language and my being an American are signs of limited toughness and intelligence.

After dinner Mama helped me wash my clothes. That may sound strange, but their washing machine was the size of a football helmet and the clothes had to be wrung out by hand and then hung to dry. After watching me struggle for twenty minutes when I tried to do it myself, Mama volunteered to finish the rest so that I could get a good night's sleep. I felt guilty accepting her help, but not guilty enough to refuse the offer.

SEPTEMBER 24, 1994

Entering the third week with my host family, I feel much more at ease than I would have thought possible. I come home from class and kick off my shoes before taking a seat at the kitchen table to chat about the day's events with Mama. My language skills have increased exponentially, seemingly without my notice. Six days a week we sit through our lessons and then come home to practice our new vocabulary. Sundays we relax and spend time with our host families. All of us yearned for these Sunday excursions and the opportunity to get out of the city.

This Sunday I readily accepted Papa's offer to go to the family's dacha, an hour north of the city. Their dacha is a small cottage surrounded by fenced-in gardens. The fence prevents the quick snatch of a tomato or squash by an otherwise honest neighbor or passerby. Smaller dachas owned by less affluent families consist solely of plots of land where a variety of summer vegetables are grown, while wealthier families have dachas that more closely resemble an American country home. Regardless of one's place in Russia's social hierarchy, dachas play a vital role in survival because it can be difficult to find food during the winter. Vegetables and fruit are pickled, canned, or dried to last during the lean months. My family has a closet filled with jars of pickled cucumbers, tomatoes, and other vegetables, buckets of potatoes and carrots covered in soil, as well as a still that Papa built to make wine. On the one occasion when I got to try a sip, it took all of my perseverance to swallow.

Once we arrived at the dacha, there was little small talk. I have never spent any time on a farm and my only experience gardening consisted of picking blueberries as a child, so I was a bit nervous about holding my own in front of Papa. Wearing jeans, a flannel shirt, and work boots, I figured I could at least look like I knew what I was doing and tried my best to mimic Papa and Timofey. I knelt in the soil, my virgin hands pulling carrots and potatoes from the earth. I occasionally wiped the perspiration from my brow with dirt-smudged hands. Over the afternoon I braved thorns gathering berries and swatted flies and bees to collect cucumbers, squash, and peppers. The garden was the size of a basketball court and every inch was planted with some type of fruit or vegetable. As the sun began to set, we piled several heaping baskets and burlap bags stuffed with produce into the back seat of the car. Despite the blisters, I felt very accomplished, and of course hungry.

I was ready to climb into the back seat, figuring we were done for the day, when Papa called me back. With a big smile, he stood next to the *banya*, which is a rustic version of a sauna. I wasn't sure exactly what he had in mind, so I shrugged and followed him inside. Papa placed a bundle of logs and sticks down on a metal grate. He lit a match and then deftly got a fire going. Soon smoke was pouring from the *banya*'s chimney and Papa's smile was even bigger. He stripped off his clothes and motioned for me to do the same. Once undressed, I was instructed to lie face-down on the higher of the two benches. He poured water over the coals and the room filled with steam. He poured more water and the sizzling got so loud that I could barely hear his voice. He poured water over a birch branch still covered with leaves and then waved it over the coals so that it absorbed the heat. I closed my eyes, not sure what to expect. I had heard about other volunteer's experiences in which they were beat with branches, so with butt cheeks clenched, I prepared for my own beating. I focused on the sunlight filtering in through cracks as he slapped at my neck and shoulders with the branch, the steaming leaves making a snapping sound every time they hit my skin. He worked his way down my back before reloading the branch with more steam. Now I realized why Timofey had turned down the offer to join us. The smacks got more forceful as he advised me that he was beating the heat into my skin. Leaves were flying off in all directions. This continued for several minutes until he was convinced that I had gained a true appreciation for the *banya* process. I thought we were finished, and I stood up to dress, but he pointed instead toward the corner of the *banya*. I moved over and he pulled a latch, sending a bucket of ice-cold water crashing over my body. "*Xorosho?*" he asked with a big smile inquiring as to whether I was enjoying the experience. I nodded affirmatively while trying to decide whether he was a sadist or just plain nuts. Papa motioned me back to where he now took his turn on the bench. After the surprise drenching, I had no qualms beating him with the same gusto with which he had beaten me.

I continue to have difficulty connecting with Timofey. Sometimes he follows me around the apartment asking me questions about my life in America, while at other times he completely ignores me, hiding away in the back bedroom as soon as I return from the university. Since he doesn't drink alcohol, I suspect that he feels excluded from our nightly discussions around the kitchen table sharing a late bottle of cognac or Champagne. I had hoped to have a brotherly relationship with him, but the distance I feel gives me little reason to believe that we will get close.

SEPTEMBER 27, 1994

I woke up sweating and shivering, apparently a bad reaction to the latest round of immunization shots that the Peace Corps provides. It really sucks to be sick in someone else's home, as they feel compelled to care for you and you have no choice but to let them, regardless of your desire to be left alone. I tried to sleep it off, but Mama brought me tea and hot soup every hour until it got to the point where I pretended to feel better just to get a few consecutive hours of sleep. She was concerned that the Peace Corps would blame her for my illness, so was pulling out every home remedy known to mankind. I have lost seventeen pounds since my arrival, primarily due to walking to and from the university each day. The first few days I had to stop at least twice to catch my breath on the way home, but now my legs and lungs have adjusted and I barely break a sweat. I noticed that I had moved my belt in two notches, which was surprising considering how much I was eating at the apartment. This too gives Mama concern, as she doesn't want the Peace Corps to think that she isn't feeding me enough.

After three weeks, I finally felt it time to make my foray into Mama's kitchen, asking if she would mind if I watched her prepare dinner. This not only flattered her, but also gave us a greater foundation from which to build a relationship. I explained that I loved to cook and had trained as a chef in America. With a huge smile, she grabbed my hand, led me into the kitchen, and tied an apron around my waist. Within minutes we were elbow to elbow rolling out dough. She invited me to food shop with her and since there are no supermarkets she showed me where to pick up everything from fresh produce at a farmer's market to Asian spices at one of the Korean markets. I taught her how to make pizza and she instructed me on the finer points of *pelmenyi*, the Russian version of ravioli. Mama got such a kick out of cooking together that she began to brag to the other host mothers. This led to Tiffany complaining in class one morning that her host mother had insisted that Tiffany teach her how to make pizza.

As we neared the completion of our first month in Russia, the Peace Corps decided that it was time to send us on an overnight field trip to prepare us for our eventual assignments. We were told to pack a bag for two days: we would travel by bus to the city of Spassk, 250 miles to the north, where we would have the pleasure of touring a sausage factory and dairy farm. Spassk, in addition to its strong agricultural industry, is also the city in which Dostoevsky was imprisoned, giving him the basis for his novel "One Day in the Life of Ivan Denisovich." Any opportunity to avoid a few days of language lessons was welcomed as much as the ability to get away from the noise and pollution of Vladivostok. We were working hard and under a great deal of stress to learn Russian, so a few days off seemed the perfect way to refocus our energy. The hotel in Spassk was a state-run facility that had all the charm of a bus depot, but no one complained since it brought back the comradery we had felt in Seattle. The hotel smelled of disinfectant and the dim fluorescent bulbs in the hallways gave way to equally nondescript rooms.

After a quick pep talk by our instructors, we were given the afternoon to explore the city. Several of us went straight to the nearest alcohol kiosk to purchase vodka and Champagne for our evening entertainment. A bottle of Stolichnaya vodka cost the equivalent of a dollar and a bottle of good Russian Champagne cost less than two dollars. We were still a little nervous when it came to speaking Russian to strangers, so the fact that we had been able to conduct these minor transactions successfully was a source of great pride. As silly as it sounds, we were intimidated by the thought that a salesperson would have trouble understanding us. Sometimes they'd ask us to repeat ourselves just to hear our accents, since there were so few foreigners in that part of Russia.

After a quick dinner in the hotel cafeteria, John and I invited a group to our hotel room with the sole purpose of getting drunk and letting off a little steam. In a show of unity, each of us opened our own bottle of vodka at the same time and toasted to a successful trip before bringing the bottles to our lips. There is a Russian tradition in which the top of the bottle of alcohol is thrown away, symbolizing that those in attendance will finish the bottle in honor of their friendship. If you wimp out, offense is taken: you've proven that you don't value their friendship. This night, the five of us sitting in a dank Russian hotel room followed suit, making a show of tossing the caps into the trash before taking big chugs from our bottles. It was a relief to spend time with each other, joking and commiserating over our host family mishaps and misadventures. This brought forth memories of our days in Seattle when we'd collectively expressed our fears and apprehensions about life in Russia.

Our behavior may seem sophomoric, but we have been taxed trying to become proficient in the language while living under a microscope in a stranger's home. We came to the country speaking little more than basic greetings and now we were reaching the level at which we were almost conversational, feeling like we had a chance of surviving on our own.

Gary was the first to finish his bottle and triumphantly held it upside down over his head. Within seconds we were all sitting around the table holding empty bottles over our heads, laughing like idiots. Once the alcohol was gone the room began to feel small and we decided to venture out to see the town. Our bus driver had told us about a disco within walking distance of our hotel, and this became the goal of our exploration. We stumbled along the sidewalks in our American clothes, talking exuberantly in English as if we were in New York or Chicago and not a small town in the Russian Far East. The sound of the music filtered through the empty streets and we walked toward it like lemmings heading for the cliff.

As the beat grew louder, our excitement increased along with our sense of adventure.

We turned a corner and were met with flashing strobe lights pulsing to the beat of techno music in the cool night air. The disco was set inside a fenced-in parking lot with a canvas barrier that prevented those outside the fence from seeing in. Before I could get acclimated to the scene, I smelled kielbasa and my nose steered me in the direction of a street stall grill where several men waved fans over the coals. My colleagues made for the ticket booth while I made a beeline toward the food.

Conversations ceased in midsentence as my colleagues strode up to the ticket booth. Beside the beer kiosk, groups of young women gawked, cigarettes in hand, with their miniskirts and blouses skin-tight against slinky hips and perky breasts. They blew smoke to the stars in false acts of sophistication from brightly colored lips. The young men, pretending to ignore them, exhaled smoke with their chests thrust forward and biceps innocently flexed. Seeing any group of foreigners in their town was unusual, much less a group of loud, smiling Americans with wallets full of rubles. Karl, John, and Gary immediately disappeared from my view, while I stayed behind to finish the last bites of my kielbasa sandwich. I noticed a few people watching me, so I refrained from licking my fingers and wiped my hands on a napkin before making my way toward the ticket booth. I thought of my host brother Timofey and assumed that these young adults, probably only a few years younger than me, didn't have enough money to buy a ticket, so I did a quick count and asked the clerk for seventeen tickets so that everyone could come inside. The ticket agent asked me several times how many tickets I wanted before counting them out and taking my money, which was the equivalent of three dollars. The Russians stared at me bewildered as I handed out the tickets.

Once inside I quickly caught sight of Gary, who was standing on the edge of the dance floor with a beer in each hand. He handed me one as we surveyed the crowd. We seemed to be the main topic of conversation, with all eyes upon our every move. After a few minutes, the novelty wore thin and the partiers returned to doing their own thing. Several of the young women strutted past us, casting sidelong glances to gauge our interest. We introduced ourselves to a few of the braver women, stating the obvious: that we were Americans visiting on business. We received guarded replies and eventually found ourselves back with Karl and John, who stood out like a pair of sore thumbs. We took long draws from our beers while ogling the gyrating women grooving to the beat.

"Why are we standing here instead of shaking our own asses on the dance floor?" asked Karl, ever the instigator, before strolling into the undulating crowd. With a communal shrug, the three of us followed and soon each of us was dancing with a Russian woman. My partner looked like every other woman, with a short skirt hiked up to mid-butt cheek, high heels, and a top that apparently belonged to a younger sibling. She grabbed my hand and eventually maneuvered us to the center of the dance floor, where we circled, groped, and rubbed against each other. We were moving with the music, faster and faster, and my mind became a blur. It felt like I was in the midst of an acid trip with my mind lost in a fog of booze, sound, and lights. Her hands grasped my ass, pulling me to her, which made me smile until I realized that her goal was to steal my wallet.

I slid her hand toward my hip and within seconds her hand returned to my wallet. I palmed my wallet and placed it into my front pocket, pretending to be oblivious to her intentions as she leaned forward, kissing me hard while grinding against me. I felt her hand searching the back of my pants for the wallet. Finding the back pockets empty, she checked my front pockets and I felt—more than saw—her smile as if she had miraculously outsmarted the drunk foreigner. I was having fun knowing that I was strong enough to prevent her from taking my wallet and curious as to how far she would go. Between songs she led me to the fence, where she again began kissing me while trying to slide her hand inside my front pocket. I moved her hand away a few times and then watched as she turned her attention away from me to a group standing to our right. I realized that the game had gone far enough when three men moved in our direction. Sensing my awareness, she tried in one last desperate attempt to grab my wallet but before she could get it out of my pocket, I twisted her wrist and slipped her arm behind her back. The group was now only a few feet away, close enough for me to see the hostility in their eyes. I was outnumbered and my friends were drunk and distracted. I pushed the woman in their direction and walked toward the entrance, where two policemen stood guard.

One of the guards recognized something was amiss and he approached. Knowing that I had to get in the first word, I reached out and grabbed his flashlight, shining the light on the woman, who now stood behind one of the men. I repeated the word *vor*, meaning thief, and then mimicked the act of someone picking my pocket. The guard took both the woman and the man she'd been hiding behind aside and made them empty their pockets. After a quick exchange of words that were outside of my vocabulary, he escorted them outside the gate. My buzz diminished as the realization of what an idiot I had been hit home. What was I thinking? By flashing money, even though it was a pittance by our standards, I came across as flaunting my wealth instead of as being generous. I found Gary, John, and Karl at the beer kiosk and convinced them to walk back to the hotel with me in exchange for paying for their beer.

We returned to find Kurt, Chris, and Charlie draped over drab lobby chairs, each drinking vodka out of individual bottles. We collapsed alongside them and took sips as they were offered, while John regaled them with our disco exploits. In the middle of telling us a story, Charlie jumped to his feet, tottered uneasily, mumbled something unintelligible, and then staggered up the stairs toward his room. Twenty minutes passed before we finished the bottles, and as Charlie hadn't returned, we set out to find him. He lay face-up, fully clothed on his hotel bed. With little else to keep us occupied, John grabbed a green magic marker and, amid continuous laughter, the five of us took turns writing on his forehead, cheeks, and chin. I wrote "Rich was here" across his forehead. John and Gary played a game of Tic Tac Toe, and Chris and Karl added their own graffiti. I don't remember returning to my room or even falling asleep, but I must have been concerned about Charlie retaliating because I awoke securely ensconced in our room with a chair forced under the doorknob.

I was thoroughly hung over and dreading the thought of spending the next ten hours on an old school bus with thirteen of my fellow hung over Peace Corps trainees. I beat John to the shower to wash away as much of my headache as possible, or at least to ease the pain enough to allow me to swallow a few Advils. Afterwards, I dressed, packed my bags, and somehow made it downstairs to the breakfast table. I looked around and saw that most of my colleagues' faces were cloaked in the same painful grimace. Even to summon the energy to nod hello seemed too demanding. It was at this time that I remembered Charlie and asked if anyone had seen him. Suddenly we all began to laugh hysterically. Chris, who was Charlie's room-mate, told us that although he hadn't actually seen Charlie, he did note that Charlie had spent an unusually long time in the bathroom. When Charlie finally made his way down to the cafeteria, his face was scrubbed clean and pink with either extreme embarrassment or anger. His scowl made it apparent that it was the latter and that he wasn't very impressed with our handiwork. We tried to keep straight faces, but it was too much, and soon laughter again erupted.

We loaded our bags onto the bus in zombie-like trances. Our hang-overs made the rough roads and stench of exhaust unbearable. When we arrived at our first stop, a dairy factory outside the town of Ussurisk, things only got worse. We were given a tour that included walking between rows of cows standing in their own filth. The manager extolled the virtues of his herd while the smell of sour milk and feces sent waves of nausea through my body. The sun was at full strength with the temperature in the high 90s. The walls felt like they were closing in on me and I prayed that I wouldn't hurl, although this could only improve the smell. Every time I raised my head in an effort to pay attention, I would see Gary or John in similar discomfort. The tour ended with the manager bringing out samples of a chunky yogurt drink called kefir. From my vantage point, the cups looked to be holding spoiled cottage cheese. I brought the cup to my mouth, but the smell caused a gagging sensation and I sacrificed protocol and immediately placed the cup back on the tray untouched. We finally made it back to the bus, where I took a seat by a window, closing my eyes and letting the breeze blow across my face. The next stop was at a sausage factory, which would ordinarily have been of interest, but the smell was worse than the dairy farm and I knew my rough morning would continue. Miraculously I kept my breakfast down, which was more than I could say for two of my colleagues.

I was still confused about Holly. At times we seemed so close that I felt it inevitable that we would hook up, but then moments later her nonchalance toward me would make me think that our connection was solely in my own head. This confusion ended on the bus ride home, when she mentioned that she had started dating a student at the university from the Republic of Georgia. My stomach dropped as she told me about him and to make matters worse, she told me about his love letters to her and that, since he didn't speak English and her Russian wasn't progressing as well as others in our group, they spent their time together in bed. It couldn't get any worse. I pretended to fall asleep with thoughts of betrayal filling my head. But she didn't owe me anything and I was a fool.

In the rational way that a man's mind deals with matters of the heart, I came to the conclusion that the only solution would be to make her jealous. I sought out one of the translators accompanying us on the trip. She wore too much makeup, sported a miniskirt that was too short to be appropriate, and was quite flirtatious. She was someone who would never meet the family, but was perfect for my intentions. I flirted unabashedly with her and we arranged to meet the following day for a drink at a hotel bar in Vladivostok. Meeting a woman at a hotel bar in Russia meant only one thing.

Our date proceeded and she seemed to have the same thing in mind as I did, since she showed up wearing a dress that was more of a negligee along with a pair of fuck-me pumps. We had a couple of drinks at the bar and then I signaled to the bartender for the bill and keys to a room.

Living with my host family I had zero privacy, and the thought of bringing a woman back, much less this one, was out of the question. I had limited funds, but the cost for the hotel room was part of a release that I needed for my mental health.

On the walk back to my host family's apartment, I analyzed my actions and again felt foolish for thinking that banging another woman would make me feel better about Holly or that she would even care.

The Peace Corps announced that our site assignments will be announced next week. I am hoping for a position in Vladivostok, as I don't want to live in a smaller city or be too far from the comforts of my host family. There isn't much to do in Vladivostok, but it is far larger than any of the other cities in the Russian Far East. John and Gary have also expressed a desire to stay in Vladivostok, so we are all tense waiting for the decision.

One of the things I miss most from home is the lack of access to current news. It is rumored that our proximity to North Korea prevents any foreign television signals from being broadcast, but it might just as easily be the Russian government that wants the likes of CNN and the BBC blocked. There is one local Russian news program, but the newscasters speak too fast for me to understand and I end up focusing solely on the accompanying video footage. There is a new English-language newspaper called the "Vladivostok News," but it focuses primarily on local issues, with the occasional mention of US politics. The latest edition told about President Clinton's battle with Newt Gingrich and the Republican-led House of Representatives and the possibility of a government shutdown. The paper also mentioned that there was an ongoing major league baseball strike, which might interfere with the World Series. The stories focusing on local news brought to reality just how much mafia-related carnage was occurring: the pages were filled with stories of vicious assassinations, car bombings, and endemic corruption. If that wasn't enough to give me nightmares, there had been another Siberian tiger attack on the outskirts of the city.

We are given periodic language proficiency exams to test our communication skills, which in turn are used to determine our job place-ment and fitness to serve. I received a formal progress report from the Peace Corps staff saying that they were satisfied with my progress and they encouraged me to keep up the good work. Despite my problems under-standing the news, I feel more comfortable speaking Russian and can now tell jokes. An integral part of learning a foreign language is to rid yourself of any embarrassment when trying to communicate, which allows for greater freedom to experiment with new words and phrases. Spending time eating and drinking with Russians has also enabled me to practice in a much less stressful environment than under the watchful guise of my teachers.

OCTOBER 1, 1994

The phone roused me from a cognac-induced sleep, followed seconds later by Mama bursting into my room to tell me that the call was from America. I stumbled to the phone, hoping that it wasn't a family emergency. I brought the receiver to my ear and heard my mother's voice. This was my first conversation with anyone from home since my arrival and I hung on every word. For twenty minutes I listened to updates about my family and friends and even my cat Hendrix, becoming imbued with a sense of homesickness that had been lost under all the excitement and the stress in my life. After hanging up, I stared up at the ceiling thinking about all that I had left behind. I had wanted to tell them about my new experiences, tell them how much I had changed in the past six weeks, but the words and sentiment sounded strange and I ended up saying only that I was healthy and enjoying the experience.

Holly's host family was only a few buildings away from mine, so we often walked back and forth to the university together. This was one of the only times during the day that we got to speak English and vent about our living conditions. I would leave my family's apartment and pick her up, although being on time was not one of her strengths. This often led to me sitting down to a second breakfast with her host family while waiting.

I get along well with her family and my appetite is quite healthy, so I don't mind the extra meal. Holly's family is large by Russian standards, with five daughters ranging in age from ten to eighteen years old. It is unusual for a family to have more than two children, due to the housing shortage and the small size of the apartments. But the small families have raised the concern of the Russian government as they watch the much more populous nations of China, Korea, and Japan nearby. In an effort to encourage larger families, any woman having more than three children is given a "Hero's Medal" from the government. Both of Holly's host parents are employed at the university, with her host father working as a history professor and her host mother as an administrator. They are solidly middle class and far more financially secure than my host family, where there is constant stress about how to pay for Timofey's education. Before Perestroika, education was free to all Russians. Now universities are expensive, and the only people who can afford to pay are the mafia businessmen or those parents who get a discount due to working at the universities.

Our host families take great pride in our successes, regardless of how insignificant. We laugh when hearing how they brag to the other host families about our being able to wash our own clothes or make breakfast on our own. They seem to have such low expectations, likely based on years of Communist propaganda and the perception that we're unable to complete the easier tasks that have been automated back home. During one of my late-night tea-drinking sessions with Mama, I asked her what she had thought of Americans before meeting me. After pausing for a few seconds, she replied that Russians see Americans as spoiled by our reliance on high-tech gadgetry and the easy life we live in our big houses and fancy cars. This was understandable, since their only sources of information were the Russian press and Hollywood movies. When I think back to what my thoughts had been of Russians prior to coming here, my opinions were also colored by Hollywood: I envisioned James Bond villains, conniving seductresses, and athletes pumped up on steroids.

OCTOBER 2, 1994

One of the most positive outcomes of my moving to Russia is the amount of exercise I am getting every day. Not having a car means that I either walk or take public transportation, so I am out and about and feeling much healthier than I have in years. Losing my independence and privacy was a culture shock, but the health benefits of being here can't be ignored: I have lost twenty-five pounds since my arrival. This week was the second time that I have had to punch an additional hole in my belt, despite eating huge breakfasts, sometimes twice a day, as well as the enormous dinners that Mama prepares each night. The more weight I lose, the more Mama tries to feed me; she doesn't want the Peace Corps to think that she isn't feeding me. On the flip side, Mama's incessant bragging about my cooking, particularly pizza, has spread among the other host families, leading to Holly's family insisting that I cook dinner for them. Pizza is a relatively new concept in Russia, and requests from the other volunteers that I write down the recipe for the dough and sauce have become a daily routine.

On the day of the dinner at Holly's house, I wanted to impress both Holly and the family. I stopped at the market for fresh mushrooms, scallions, peppers, onions, kielbasa, and a kilo of the local farmer's cheese, which although not exactly mozzarella is better than resorting to Velveeta. I arrived with two bags of groceries and a bottle of Russian Champagne. It took a few minutes to acclimate to their kitchen, but once I had figured out the oven, and where the knives and cutting boards were located, I recruited the two youngest sisters as my assistants. We filled a bowl with yeast, along with a touch of sugar and warm water to activate it, and then mixed in enough flour to make several large pizzas. While the dough rose atop the oven, we prepped the toppings and made a pot of homemade pizza sauce using fresh tomatoes and a handful of dry herbs that I had brought from home. When the dough had risen, we rolled out several pie shells and spooned our homemade sauce in circular motions just like I had seen at Tony's Pizza growing up in Morristown, New Jersey. Next, we added a generous amount of grated cheese to each and invited the rest of the family members to top each of the pizzas as they saw fit. They were excited and there was great discourse on how much of each ingredient to put on each of the pies. I kept glancing over at Holly hoping to notice a change in her perception of me as I engaged with her family. This is what you are missing, I thought. I yearned to have a connection, ease my homesickness, and replace the emptiness that sometimes enveloped me when missing my friends and family.

I pulled the pizzas from the oven and left them on the countertop to rest while the family oohed and aahed as they fawned over the melted and bubbling cheese and the slight char of the toppings. The aromas of garlic and oregano permeated the air. After we had finished eating and congratulating ourselves for a job done well, I said goodbye to the family and asked Holly to walk me down to the courtyard. We were a little buzzed from the Champagne and subsequent vodka shots and made small talk as we walked down the stairwell. We were greeted by a beautiful full moon as we entered the courtyard. The moment seemed right and I embraced her. Our mouths found each other's and three months of pent-up yearning culminated in our first kiss. We made out like teenagers for several minutes before she pushed away. "You need to leave." She backed away from me toward the doors. "Who knows where we will be living next month? We could be a thousand miles from each other and I don't want to get involved. I'm sorry." With that she turned and ran up the stairs, leaving me in shock. In two minutes I had gone from emotional euphoria to a hollowness quickly permeating from head to heart. I was stunned and didn't know whether to chase her up the stairs or to wait and see if she would return. I waited a few minutes, and then turned toward the road leading back to my family's apartment. I wasn't ready to sit down with Mama, who I anticipated was ready to drill me with questions on how the pizzas had turned out, so I dawdled on my walk home, thinking about past relationships and trying to pep myself up.

OCTOBER 4, 1994

Mama was stressing out as she prepared for Timofey's birthday dinner. He had asked for mussels, which are not sold in the markets and have to be caught or, more appropriately, collected from the sea. Papa invited me to join him for this endeavor and, not knowing what was involved but wanting to enrich my remaining time with the family, I smiled and nodded my head in the affirmative. We drove to the docks and met his friend, who had a small fifteen-foot sailboat. It was a chilly morning with a chop in the water. Throwing our bags aboard, we jumped in and began our seaward journey off the coast of Vladivostok, where a series of small islands led out to the Sea of Japan. Most of the islands are uninhabited and used solely as recreational sites during the summer, abandoned during the colder months. Although Papa's friend looked like a captain, his actions portrayed something entirely different as we zigzagged our way out of the marina, coming within inches of other boats and buoys. Once outside the harbor, the sails caught the breeze and we seemed to glide across the water, allowing me to sit back and enjoy the setting.

Despite the cold breeze and forty-degree water temperature, Papa was in his element. He bravely stripped down to a Speedo and it was hard not to laugh at him as he kneeled at the edge of the boat in his goggles and snorkel. His belly hung over the tiny swimsuit and his eyes bulged from behind the thick glass face mask. He flashed a thumbs-up and then jumped in with a huge splash. I didn't want to be a wimp, so I stripped down to my underwear and jumped off the bow. Immediately my testicles shot up into my body and a fear of hypothermia set in as every organ felt like it was shutting down. I clawed feverishly in a doggy paddle until I made it back to the ladder and scampered up on deck, shivering like a wet rat. I am a soft American!

Papa had no issue with the cold and after what seemed like an eternity, his snorkel sliced through the choppy water alongside the boat. He pushed up his mask, flashed a toothy grin, and climbed up the ladder while tossing a mesh bag full of black mussels on deck. His hands were bleeding, but he didn't seem to notice as he proudly stood over his catch. The captain handed over a bottle of vodka, and Papa brought it to his lips and took a deep gulp, followed by a second. Where was the vodka when I came shivering out of the sea? I sat on a milk crate watching as Papa dumped the bag onto the deck. Among the black shells were several brown turds. These turned out to be sea cucumbers, a delicacy the likes of which I had never seen, much less tasted. Papa separated five of them from the mussels, grabbed a knife, and deftly sliced one open, holding it over the side of the boat to release the guts and innards into the sea. He rinsed the flesh in the water and then cut three slices, handing one to each of us.

The flesh was slimy and almost translucent in color. I held it squeamishly, dreading the thought of putting it into my mouth. Papa tossed his piece into his mouth, followed by another generous swig of vodka. He smiled blissfully and I closed my eyes and followed suit. The texture was similar to raw squid, but the taste was exquisite. It had the fresh sea taste of an oyster, but a sturdier flesh. My mind immediately raced to come up with a way to introduce these to the American populace. How easy would it be to raise and sell these sea cucumbers in the States? Then again, I couldn't quite picture anyone in my family getting over the appearance.

When Papa had dried off and dressed, the captain pulled up anchor and let out the sails so that we picked up speed and jumped over the small waves. We continued for twenty minutes before approaching one of the islands. We tied up to a makeshift pier and then jumped ashore, Papa grasping the mesh bag now once again packed full of the mussels. Papa issued orders and the captain and I stomped off through the underbrush to collect driftwood to make a fire while he arranged rocks around a deserted campfire pit. Once the kindling had been lit, the larger branches began to catch and soon a nice fire blazed away. I huddled as close as the smoke would allow, rubbing my hands together for warmth. Papa placed a dozen of the largest mussels atop flat rocks placed around the flames, still smiling ear to ear. Within minutes we heard water sizzling on the rocks as the shells opened and a wonderful aroma emanated from the meat.

It was my responsibility to grab the shell and carefully pour the juices and the mussel into a plastic container. The most difficult part was sneaking one into my mouth without getting caught. It was a magical setting. The smell of the sea, the roasting mussels, and the burning driftwood brought forth a feeling of being in an exotic locale. Gulls screamed overhead, diving into the surf and casting shadows under the fading rays of the sun. I felt relaxed, at peace.

OCTOBER 5, 1994

Tomorrow our job assignments will be delivered. The tension is incredible as we all wonder and fight the suspense of not knowing where we will be sent for our job assignment as well as whether we will be sent out alone or with other volunteers. Mama is as nervous as I am, fearing that I might end up far from Vladivostok. We have become close and I love them for taking me in and making me part of the family. I too want to remain close and cherish the feeling that coming to their apartment every day after class was like coming home.

The Peace Corps has also scheduled a party to celebrate our officially becoming volunteers and as a farewell prior to our being sent out to our sites. This would also serve as a thank-you to the host families for supporting us, teaching us, and accepting us into their lives. Despite my good intentions, I managed to hurt the family's feelings when Mama found out through the grapevine that I didn't want to attend the party. I had anticipated taking the family out privately and I should have been more sensitive to the pride Mama took in being a part of the group. They interpreted my wanting to avoid the party as being embarrassed to be seen with them, which was the opposite of how I felt. I apologized repeatedly after ensuring them of how fortunate I felt that I had been given the opportunity to live with them. After wiping away the tears, Mama was beaming as I told her how jealous the other volunteers were of me for being assigned to live with such a great family, which was indeed true.

Another issue that required a bit of diplomacy was my weight loss, which had now exceeded thirty pounds. I felt healthy and was pleased, while Mama had convinced herself that I wasn't eating enough and that it must be reflective of her cooking. This was ridiculous considering how much I had shoveled down my throat over the past few weeks. I explained how sedentary my lifestyle had been prior to coming to Russia and that the weight loss was a result of getting my fat ass off the couch and actually walking. I also explained that in America, I spent quite a bit of time eating pizza and consuming large quantities of beer. I thought my explanation was satisfactory until I realized that Mama understood it to mean that I wasn't getting enough pizza and beer. The next night, and for each of the five nights following, Papa brought home a six-pack of beer for us to drink with dinner. Russian beer does not contain any preservatives and is a hefty 10 percent alcohol. It is made with honey and packs a pretty nice buzz, so I have certainly slept well as a result.

OCTOBER 6, 1994

My hands shook as I opened the envelope and began to read:

Richard Sayette - Manager of the Business Center in Artyom

General duties: To provide business information and resources, provide business assistance and advice, organize business seminars given by other business centers. This center serves clients in Artyom and the surrounding area. The current PCV also speaks regularly at high school business and economics classes and assists with the local Junior Achievement program. It would be great if you can continue in this role.

I read the slip of paper a dozen times, allowing the words to sink in. I would be stationed thirty miles north of Vladivostok, which was close enough to my host family, but far enough away to allow me to establish a fresh identity. I would also get some semblance of privacy back, although I would miss being able to pop by for a quick meal and a reassuring hug. As for my work assignment, I had always assumed that I would be in a business center, but hadn't thought of the responsibility that this would entail. I was concerned that Russians would expect expert business advice and that they'd challenge me; I wasn't sure whether I had the knowledge to be of actual help to them. As I regained my composure, I looked around to see how my colleagues were reacting to their assignments. John and Gary were high-fiving each other: they had both been assigned positions in Vladivostok, as had Karl. I would have three friends living within an hour of my post, which was good since I would have a nearby escape, but bad in that I wouldn't be able to rely on these guys for my daily social network. Holly had been assigned to a position in a business center in Khabarovsk, twelve hours north by train. Despite having held out hope that we would have an opportunity to take our relationship further, I am relieved to be rid of the tension.

Having visited Artyom during the earlier field trip, I wasn't as nervous as the other trainees were; they had no idea what was in store for them. We were scheduled to spend two days next week visiting our sites before returning to complete our training. The purpose of the site visit was to meet our Russian sponsors and colleagues and to glean additional information about their expectations for us. For the past two and a half months, the similarity of our situations had brought the remaining fourteen of us closer together. We shared the same emotions and frustrations as we adapted to our new situation. Now our support network would be spread out over an area one-third the size of the United States with little, if any, access to telephones. We would either develop new friendships within our communities or end up as loners in a foreign land. I felt fortunate in that I was somewhere in the middle and would be close enough to visit John,

Gary, Karl, and my host family, but far enough away to establish myself on my own terms.

OCTOBER 17, 1994

The Peace Corps driver maneuvered the Toyota Land Cruiser as if he were playing a video game. Cars headed right at us, swerving at the last second as if playing Chicken, while he dodged large potholes and pedestrians in his race against time. My head repeatedly slammed into the ceiling of the car while he shouted to me over the thumping Russian rap music that blasted from the speakers. I couldn't understand a word. I tried to hide my fear behind a smile; I didn't want to seem like a pussy. We arrived in Artyom in a record-breaking forty-five minutes, according to my driver, while my new dress shirt was drenched with sweat and stuck to my back as if it had been painted on. There were indentations in the leather arm rest from my fingernails, but we had arrived in one piece and for that I felt fortunate.

We stopped in front of the main government administration building, stoically guarded by a giant statue of Lenin. Two women came out to meet our car. They had a brief discussion with our driver before I was directed to follow them. I tried to look dignified sitting in the back seat like a VIP; I felt anything but as I slid out of the car. One of the women introduced herself in English as Tanya, telling me that she had been sent by the mayor to welcome me and that we would be working together in the business center.

I followed Tanya into the building, which had the same gray décor in the hallways as it did on the outside of the building. We walked down a long empty hallway where the only sound was the echo of our footsteps on the linoleum. Eventually we reached a teak door that stood out like a sore thumb. In the Communist era, nobody was supposed to stand out, but in reality, power wants to be recognized. I assumed that the man behind the door wanted everyone to know he was in charge. This was the mayor's office and he was to be my new boss.

Tanya held the door open and ushered me inside, where a hulk of a man leaned back in a chair while barking into a telephone. He acknowledged our presence by raising his hand an inch off the desk and nodding, flashing a metallic smile in my direction. He stepped around the desk as he hung up the phone and offered a giant hand, which I instinctively shook. He squeezed my hand like he was trying to pop a tennis ball. My eyes stayed locked with his until I felt him ease and then we both smiled. He slapped me good-naturedly on the back and pointed toward a chair in front of his humongous mahogany desk. When I looked to Tanya, she appeared as nervous as I was as she took the seat beside me. The mayor began speaking and she quickly translated everything to English. I had been told that the current volunteer, Linda, had limited Russian-language abilities, so I wanted to start out on the right foot and impress the mayor. I quickly answered in Russian before Tanya had translated one of his questions and he smiled. I may have lost some points on grammar, but my effort to communicate seemed to have worked in my favor as he responded by commenting that he was glad to have me and looked forward to getting to know me better. I felt proud and concentrated even harder. After ten minutes of small talk, he invited me to join him for dinner when I returned to Artyom, indicating that our meeting had ended. "That went very well!" Tanya exclaimed as we walked back down the hall. My cheeks flushed and I smiled.

My role as manager of the business center will consist of working for the city administration within its economics department. I am the only male other than the mayor, and Tanya is the only other English-speaker. Linda was scheduled to depart right around the time of my arrival, so there would be limited opportunity to overlap. I was asked within minutes of each introduction whether I was married, and each of the women in the department felt compelled to set me up with someone they knew who would be perfect for me. At the end of the day, Tanya walked me back to meet my driver and told me that I had done very well. "Russians judge people by their eyes and because you have friendly eyes and a nice smile, everyone feels comfortable with you." She mentioned that Linda was a very private person and thus the Russians felt that they didn't really know her. I'm sure that there were people that she did know well and that Tanya's statement was probably to encourage me to be more open, since there was great curiosity about America as well as us as individuals. Linda had been living in Artyom for a year and had announced that she would be leaving Russia on December 7. There was only one apartment set aside for foreign workers and she was currently living in it, so I would spend my first weeks as a guest in the city's only hotel. Linda had not seemed enthused by my assignment to Artyom, but she was cordial. We hadn't hit it off at our first introduction when I'd arrived with John, Chuck, and Holly on the site visit, but since we were in similar situations, I hoped to develop a friendlier relationship. Linda was significantly older than me; while not outwardly unfriendly, she made few attempts to connect and it seemed like more than the age difference was at play.

The only time I saw Linda during this visit was in passing and I received little more than a quick hello before she trudged off in the opposite direction. I was disappointed that she hadn't been more welcoming or offered to be of more assistance. Fortunately, the fast pace of introductions and the generosity of Tanya had eased my sense of discomfort. Tanya, as one of only a handful of English speakers in the city, had been assigned to the business center despite not having a business background. She was incredibly friendly and we hit if off immediately. She was quite chatty and told me all about her life. She is married to a newspaper editor for one of the national papers and had two young children. Everyone we passed smiled at her, which not only helped put me in a positive light by association, but made the thought of living here and working with a happy person seem more attractive. Vera, who will be my assistant, does have a business background and was pleasant, but seemed incredibly shy and she spoke zero English. The third and most powerful of my co-workers is Anna Gregorovna. She is the deputy mayor and head of the economics department. She too was pleasant and seemed eager to make me feel comfortable. The three of them have taken me under their collective wing and actively tried to make sure I was comfortable.

The first group of volunteers to Russia, including Linda, had been disappointed with the Peace Corps' preparedness when they arrived and the majority of the fifty total volunteers had left within a few months of their arrival. Most of those that stuck it out treated my group, the second wave of volunteers, as if we had something to do with their initial troubles, and they wanted little to do with us. As a "pioneer" group, they had to deal with little infrastructure in place and a complete lack of name recognition and understanding of what the Peace Corps hopes to achieve. The local Russian Peace Corps staff tried as best they could to find positions for them, but the concept of accepting humanitarian aid from a former enemy was hard for the average Russian to stomach: many of the locals looked at us with a combination of suspicion and mistrust.

The city hotel is located across the street from the business center and is owned by the city. Artyom is not exactly a tourist destination, and the only hotel guests are the infrequent visitors to the government building. There is little focus on comfort. The rooms are bare, without a kitchen or desk, the shower is small, and hot water is sporadic at best and only runs between the months of October and March. The décor is similar to the city building and can best be described as Early Soviet. The lone bright spots are the women who manage the hotel. They were initially shy, but have since warmed to the fact that I'll be staying until Linda leaves and have been quick to offer me coffee in the morning, especially since I am the only guest.

The majority of my fellow trainees were not due back to Vladivostok after their reconnaissance trips for a few days, since their travel times far exceeded my own, so upon my return I had the luxury of having two days free to explore Vladivostok. Instead of meeting up with my Peace Corps colleagues, I reached out to one of the Russian students at the university, who's named Masha. We had met at the cafeteria and had gotten along well enough that we would chat in passing. She had studied English and enjoyed the novelty of having an American friend. I asked her if she would like to show me around and, to my surprise, she accepted. I liked her; she was a very cute twenty-year-old with long blond hair, green eyes, and a nice figure—there wasn't much to not like. She was studying business and worked part time at one of the city's art museums. She eagerly began planning where we would go. She spoke English with a sexy Russian accent and was exactly what I was looking for in a local girlfriend. My status as an expat boosted my prestige and confidence level and I likely seemed quite the catch to her.

Strolling hand in hand with this gorgeous Russian woman through the streets of Vladivostok gave rise to the surreal feeling that I was acting a part in a movie. Her father was a local artist who had spent time entertaining foreigners in his role as a curator, so she had fewer inhibitions about spending time with a foreigner than most of the local Russians. Few had any contact with foreigners, since Vladivostok had been a closed military city and the home of the Far Eastern Soviet navy (now the Russian navy) and had been off-limits to foreigners and non-resident Russians alike. As we passed various buildings, she would point out her father's paintings in the lobbies and atriums. At the end of the day, she scribbled down her address and invited me to stop by—her family didn't have a phone—and then gave me a kiss. An electricity flowed through me as we embraced and my mind wandered, imagining us together. I walked her back to the tram station and waited for the tram. I was happy and optimistic, but I had the realization that I would be living in another city and that, with no telephones, it would be a struggle to maintain any type of relationship.

Most Russian women are married by the time they are in their early twenties, so the single women tend to be either in their late teens or divorcees with children. As a foreigner, I am an exotic entity and it has taken some time to get comfortable with my upgraded status. Having beautiful women and local politicians desirous of my attention is addictive. It feels like a dream and I catch myself acting in ways that would make me laugh at myself if I were back in New Jersey. Living overseas immersed in a culture far different from your own allows you to reinvent yourself.

OCTOBER 22, 1994

Being an American has its advantages. The women get a kick out of my accent and innocent vocabulary mistakes, which leads to frequent approaches in the university by the female students. The Russian men aren't as keen to strike up a conversation, unless there is vodka involved to loosen their tongues. Many Russian men want to test the Americans by enticing us to match them on a drink-for-drink basis. This isn't necessarily done with malice, but since they can't compete with us for the attention of women from a novelty perspective, they feel confident that they can drink us under the table. Once the drinking starts, the Russian men become more generous and hospitable, often inviting us to dinner or trips to the countryside to visit their dachas.

A few of my male colleagues make the cultural mistake of clinging to the Russian women in an attempt to avoid the drinking. This often backfires, since the Russian women have grown up in the same culture and see this as a cowardly act. Russian culture is paternalistic and the roles between men and women are more finely delineated than in the US. Men are generally less helpful in the home than their American counterparts are, and are seen as the breadwinners, regardless of whether this is in fact the case. With high unemployment, the psychological impact of unemployment among the husbands combines with an even higher rate of alcoholism, often leading to domestic abuse. I have gotten several nasty looks when I stand to clear dishes after a meal or make an effort to help out in the kitchen.

When I told Mama that I would be living in Artyom and staying in a hotel for my first six weeks, she adamantly proclaimed that she would not permit it. "You will continue to stay with us until your apartment is ready." She continued saying that I could commute to Artyom each morning by train. This was a generous offer, but I was ready to be on my own and to establish my life in Artyom. I yearned for a bit of privacy and the ability to entertain guests. In addition, waiting for a train while fighting bitter Siberian winds, freezing temperatures, and my obsessive fear of a tiger attack further deterred me. Mama was also concerned about my falling victim to the cunning Russian women who would try to seduce me so that I would buy them things and take them back to America. With a straight face, I told Mama that I would be careful. I couldn't make eye contact with Papa for fear that we would both burst into laughter.

Taking the train from Vladivostok to Artyom exposes me to a side of Russian life that is impossible to experience in the classroom. It is harvest time and the morning trains are full of men and women carrying shovels, hoes, and picnic baskets to their dachas. They return at dusk with the baskets and burlap bags bursting with tomatoes, squash, cucumbers, and potatoes. These are not poor families, but middle-class Russians hoping to supplement their winter diets by canning and drying healthy products; the food distribution systems prevalent in Moscow or St. Petersburg don't exist here. There are no supermarkets and if you haven't prepared properly, you may find yourself in a dire situation. The dacha is a traditional aspect of Russian life, as much so as drinking vodka or reading Pushkin. The routine is so ingrained in the Russian soul that it would seem strange not to plant in the spring and harvest in autumn. The newly formed Russian middle class may have larger dachas then the pensioners and poor, but food security is a concern regardless of income. I eagerly helped the family can tomatoes, peppers, and cucumbers, and string dried mushrooms and eggplant slices on sewing thread over the weekend, not fully understanding the importance.

OCTOBER 25, 1994

Four of the volunteers were given assignments in Komsomolsk, a city twenty hours to the northeast of Vladivostok, and they returned from their site visit with nasty colds. Within two days, the rest of us were coughing and blowing our noses and generally feeling miserable. I awoke gasping for breath and sporting a temperature of 101 degrees. Mama heard my whimpering and came in with a worried look. I asked for a glass of water so that I could swallow two Tylenol pills. She brought the water, but not without giving me a lecture explaining why American medicine wouldn't work on a Russian illness. Russians are skeptical of pharmaceutical products since those available here are cheap Chinese imports with limited efficacy. Instead, Russians rely on herbal remedies and potions that have been passed down for generations. Mama couldn't bear to leave my health in the hands of Western medicine and immediately returned with an apron full of bottles, leaves, and ointments. It had been five minutes since I had swallowed the Tylenol and she asked if I was feeling any better yet. When I shook my head no, she triumphantly declared that it was time to give Russian medicine a chance. I felt too weak to argue.

Before I could protest, she forcibly inserted garlic cloves into each of my nostrils while holding my head down with the other. "What are you doing?" I whispered with fear in my eyes. With one hand holding my head to the pillow, she told me that she was responsible for getting me healthy and she wasn't about to let the Peace Corps think that she was an unfit caregiver. The garlic burned my virgin nostrils, but remarkably, within seconds my nasal passages opened and the overpowering aroma of garlic filled my head. Mama stood guard for ten minutes to make sure that I kept the cloves in place. I must have fallen asleep, because the next thing I knew she was jostling my shoulder. She held a small jar of Tiger Balm, which she vigorously massaged into my chest, neck, and throat, and then after I fearfully allowed myself to be rolled over, my calves. The mixture of the menthol and garlic made me nauseated and my mouth filled with saliva. It was at this moment that Papa appeared smiling from ear to ear, apparently not wanting to miss the fun. He removed one of the garlic cloves, which gave me a sense of hope, although this quickly faded when he returned holding a teaspoon of onion juice. He took over from Mama and placed a hand on my forehead, holding me down against the pillow.

"Hold still," he almost giggled while pouring the spoonful of onion juice into my exposed nostril. I gagged. Vomit worked its way up my throat. I wanted to jump up and run into the bathroom, locking the door behind me, but Papa's hand on my forehead kept me in place. When they were convinced that I wouldn't blow my nose, they returned to the kitchen and made a cup of tea from local herbs and berries. They brought that to me along with a bottle of black liquid that was poured into another spoon and held out to me. At least Papa wasn't trying to pour this into my nose, but the taste was a horrible mixture of Robitussin and motor oil. He waited for me to swallow the entire spoonful and then ushered Mama out of the room to let me go back to sleep, but not before winking at me.

Several times over the next few hours I would hear them approach my door and I would pretend to sleep so that I could avoid further torture. Mama would lean over me and check to make sure that the garlic gloves were still firmly implanted into my nostrils. During one visit they woke me, holding a pot of steaming water and pinecones. I followed orders to sit up and they placed the pot on my lap and a towel over my head so that I could inhale the menthol-scented steam. This was much better than the garlic or onion juice. I had snuck two more Tylenols and was able to tell them that I was feeling much better. I dressed and joined the family in the living room, asking Mama if there was anything to eat. Instantly she jumped to her feet, smiled, gave me a quick hug, and stormed into the kitchen.

I spent the next few hours napping, drinking soup, and allowing them to stick more garlic in my nostrils. I was successful in avoiding another dose of onion juice, despite Papa's badgering. I had survived an entire day of Russian medicine, or at least thought I had, and felt on the road back to good health when they cornered me and forced me to remove my shirt and lie face-down on the sofa. I prepared for another round of Tiger Balm, but instead watched in horror as they brought out a dozen mason jars, a bottle of rubbing alcohol, and a pack of matches. I tried to sit up, but Papa pushed me down. They poured a capful of alcohol into each jar before holding it at an angle close to my skin so that Papa could light a match next to the opening. As soon as the alcohol caught fire, Mama slammed the jar against my skin. The flame used up the oxygen, creating a vacuum that was supposed to suck the poison out of my system through the pores in my back. They repeated the process twelve times, leaving my back a mass of large purple welts. I returned to my room and locked the door. The next morning I feigned perfect health so that I could avoid another day of torture.

OCTOBER 26, 1994

Trying to maintain our focus during our language lessons is proving difficult now that we have received our assignments. The material is tedious, repetitive, and exhausting. We have less than a week before we ship out across the Russian Far East. I have been spending more time with Masha and look forward to seeing her on weekends, envisioning weekends together in Artyom. Finding time alone with her is difficult since she lives with her parents. The university allows the Peace Corps volunteers to pay for dorm rooms when they're available, but most have no bathrooms and they are not the most romantic place to have a tryst. In addition, they frown upon overnight guests and I resent the feeling that I must sneak around the authorities. Masha was not pleased when I told her I was moving to Artyom and she has become a bit distant. I'd assumed she was aware of this possibility, but instead of being glad that I would only be an hour away, she acted as if this signaled an end to our relationship. I explained that I would still come out on weekends or that she could visit me, but it would be difficult to stay in touch since she has no phone. My concept of mobility is different from hers and despite her speaking English, there is a cultural divide that is hard to bridge. I didn't effectively navigate this and ended up failing in setting her expectations.

OCTOBER 27, 1994

Several of the host families offered to throw us going-away parties to send us off on a high note. The first took place at Charlie's house, and they had a two-fold reason for celebrating since it was also Charlie's birthday. It was a beautiful autumn day with a bright, warming sun and cloudless sky. We had completed our final language test earlier in the morning and each of us was ready to celebrate. Gift options here are limited to booze or chocolate, so I arrived with a bottle of vodka that had a picture of Arnold Schwarzenegger on the label and was called Terminator Vodka. I was late and had barely removed my jacket when I was offered a succession of vodka shots. I should have been patient and made a single toast with everyone, but instead I ended up toasting individually and was well on the way to a wild afternoon. Soon an accordion was brought out and in typical Russian fashion, the singing and dancing kicked off, adding to the festive mood. Every few minutes another bottle of vodka appeared, sparking off more toasts. We toasted everyone and everything and by 2:30 in the afternoon we were all staggering around the apartment, bumping into each other, enthusiastically high-fiving and hugging. I would have been fine if I could have excused myself and gone home to sleep, but Mama had organized a party later in the afternoon as a goodbye party for Chuck, who had failed the final language sufficiency test and would be sent home at the end of the week. He was a security risk due to his lack of survival skills. John, Karl, Holly, and Gary were all sloppy drunk and together we began the trek to the apartment, stumbling up the mountain and singing, with our arms laden with bags of alcohol and snacks picked up from the kiosks we passed along the way.

We made quite an entrance, flushed from the exertion it took to climb the mountain and the seven flights of stairs. Papa greeted us with a big smile, which grew even larger when he noticed how much alcohol we had brought. He passed out the glasses before most of us had removed our shoes. The euphoric feeling of having finished three months of laborious training led me to continue drinking on a dangerous pace, eagerly accepting each toast with gusto. I hadn't eaten much at Charlie's party because I knew Mama was preparing a feast, so I should not have been surprised when I stood up and felt the room spinning. Holly must have seen my expression because she grabbed my hand and walked me to my bedroom where she told me to lie down. I did as instructed, and closed my eyes only to feel not just the room, but the whole universe spinning.

Moments later, Gary and John found me half in bed, half hanging over the side as I tried to keep one foot on the floor. "You should come back out and not be rude to your family." Like an idiot I allowed them to march me shirtless into a room full of my family's dearest friends. I stumbled around dancing to a rhythm that nobody else could hear. Everyone except Mama began to clap, egging me on like a Russian circus bear. Mama had seen enough and was unwilling to let me embarrass her or myself any further. She sat me down in a chair while sending Timofey for my shirt.

I awoke the next morning thoroughly humiliated with a major-league hang over. I dreaded facing Mama and knew that I had let her down. I was embarrassed because she had put so much effort into preparing for the party and I had not only failed to support her, but made her look foolish to boot. The sound of footsteps and pots and pans being jostled in the kitchen pushed me out to face the music. My eyes were focused on the floor when I entered. Instead of the berating I expected, Papa's laughter filled the air and soon I had no choice but to smile. Mama forgave me, putting all of the blame on Papa for getting me so drunk; she was unaware of how much we had consumed at Charlie's party. I gladly threw Papa under the bus, falsely explaining that I wasn't accustomed to drinking so much in America. I gave Papa a wink and he just shook his head, acknowledging that he was taking one for the team.

We had a few more nights of goodbye parties with the last being at Karl's house. It was all the more heartfelt because of the realization that once we left Vladivostok it would be several months before we would reunite. As I started to leave, Holly grabbed my hand and whispered drunkenly into my ear. I wanted her badly, but was pissed at the way she was manipulating me. I didn't want to hook up under this type of condition, but I also really wanted to spend the night together. I pushed back, mumbling something about having promised to spend the night at my host family's apartment, and then stepped out in the frigid night.

OCTOBER 28, 1994

I drove with Papa to one of the local farmer's markets on the outskirts of Vladivostok. As we neared the end of the harvest season, most of the city dwellers had finished up at their dachas and were now engaging in their own version of hunting and gathering to top off their pantries. We were chatting casually as we passed bushels of cucumbers, peppers, mushrooms, and potatoes when I stopped dead in my tracks in front of a wheelbarrow full of basketball-sized pumpkins. These were the first pumpkins I had seen in Russia and since we were only a few days from Halloween, my mind whirled as I envisioned a great way to share my culture. I approached the vendor and pointed at the four largest pumpkins, forking over about two dollars' worth of rubles. Papa shrugged his shoulders and helped me carry them to the car, waiting for an explanation, but I told him that it was a surprise and he would have to wait until dinner. When we returned to the apartment Mama and Timofey peppered me with questions as well, curious as to my secretive plans.

After the dinner plates had been scrubbed clean and placed in the cupboards, I gathered the family around the kitchen table and grabbed ahold of the smallest pumpkin. I was excited to share my American culture with them and what better way than to introduce them to my favorite holiday? I sliced through the top, scooping the stringy guts into a bowl. Next, I began the delicate knife work, carving first the eyes, a crooked nose, and finally a toothy grin. They kept quiet, curiously admiring my work. When I finished, I asked Mama for a candle and, with a little maneuvering, placed it inside the pumpkin and lit the wick. I turned off the lights and the glowing face brightened up the darkness of the kitchen to a chorus of oohs and aahs. When the lights were turned back on, each grabbed their own pumpkin and began to carve away. I told them that we would have a contest with the winner of the best-looking jack o' lantern getting to be the boss of the house for the remainder of the week. We also agreed that we would invite the neighbors over to serve as impartial judges.

With gusto, they turned their backs, each staking out a workspace on the kitchen table. The following minutes were filled with an eerie silence, broken only by the sound of serrated knives cutting through pumpkin flesh. When Papa finished, he set his jack o' lantern on the table, then ran to the closet to gather some accoutrements. These included a scarf and cap. Mama, not wanting to be outdone, grabbed her makeup and applied a touch of lipstick and blush to hers. Timofey, guarding his work from our prying eyes, worked fastidiously as well, although he felt his jack o' lantern was fine without any of the add-ons. Candles were placed inside and the neighbors were called in to cast their votes. I appreciated their enthusiasm and hoped that this would better allow them to understand how I felt experiencing their culture. Mama was the winner, as it seemed that the neighbors were as wary of upsetting her as were the three of us.

OCTOBER 30, 1994

We were finally sworn in as Peace Corps volunteers after a grueling three months of language and cultural training. We were exhausted and proud of our accomplishment. We had persevered and were eager to get through the swearing-in ceremony and begin the next chapter of our adventure. We had lived in drastically different conditions from what we had left behind in the US. We had lost our independence and our privacy and had become dependent on people we had just met. The ceremony was a big event, not just for us, but also for our host families, teachers, and the Peace Corps staff. The event was held in one of the nicer Vladivostok hotels with invitations sent out to our host families and to our new sponsors throughout the Russian Far East.

The décor of the conference hall was typical 1970s Russian with thick red carpets and shiny red and gold-leafed wallpaper that sparkled under grandiose chandeliers. A haze of disinfectant and cigarette smoke hung in the air, but did little to diminish our excitement.

Like almost every other building in the Russian Far East, it had no air conditioning and the ballroom was stifling. I stood on the stage along with twelve of my colleagues, waiting for the speakers to begin, dripping with perspiration, and fighting off nervous energy. There were thirteen of us out of the original eighteen and we were now on the precipice of taking an oath to represent the United States of America. Quiet chatter ensued as we watched the guests file into the auditorium. They too were overwhelmed by the stagnant heat and they fanned themselves with the event programs, restlessly waiting for the American consul general to take the stage and kick off the festivities.

Every few seconds one of our host parents would stand up and snap a photograph of their American. Mama and Papa were dressed in their nicest clothes and were smiling from ear to ear. They sat next to the mayor of Artyom, his wife, and Anna Gregorovna. I was pleased that they had driven out here to pay their respects. My host parents beamed with satisfaction, knowing that the other host parents would see them sitting next to the mayor and, hopefully, be overwhelmed with jealousy. I was disappointed by Timofey's absence, but not surprised; I recognized that the attention spent on me had previously been spent on him. I regretted that I had been unable to connect better with him.

Finally, Desiree Millikan, the US consul general, approached the podium. The US consulate here was officially re-established, after a seventy-year gap, within months of the "opening" of Vladivostok. Desiree cleared her throat and then dove into her speech. She spoke fluent Russian, not always the case with American State Department representatives. She exhibited a strong presence and spoke of how times had changed so much since the end of the Cold War and how both Russia and America were safer now as a result. She spoke first in Russian and then in English. Following the short speech, she turned to us and instructed us to place our right hands over our hearts. We did as we were told and then repeated the oath of service. We were now no longer trainees, but official Peace Corps volunteers! We hugged each under the flashing lights of a thousand flashbulbs. The noise level became deafening with each host family screaming out the name of their American in hopes of getting a hug of their own.

Waitresses handed out glasses of wine and trays of appetizers were offered and rapidly snarfed down, as if none of us had eaten in a week. It was a festive environment with our Russian teachers and the Peace Corps staff intermingling with our host families and future employers. The families and Peace Corps staff recounted humorous tales at our expense, but nobody seemed to mind since we had made it. I spent the first hour with the mayor, who was under an onslaught of Mama's bragging about my accomplishments. I finally stopped her when she began telling him how I was able to wash my own clothes. I could only imagine the mayor recounting this scene to the women in the economics department amid a chorus of laughter.

Earlier in the day we had received our first monthly stipend, as we were now volunteers. We were also given a moving-in allowance, so that after having the equivalent of $2 per day for our first two months in Russia, we now had the equivalent of $650 burning holes in our pockets. I no longer had to live like a backpacker, and could afford lunch or dinner with friends or to buy gifts for my host family without breaking into my savings. The money was intended to cover the cost of stocking our apartments with blankets, tableware, canned goods, and other necessities as well as for paying any bills during the month. The Peace Corps has different pay scales for every country, based on the local cost of living indices and the availability of necessity items. Our program was so new that the Peace Corps wasn't sure exactly how much was necessary to cover our costs adequately, so they started out with $400 per month. Some volunteers had to put this stipend toward their rent in addition to the staple goods, while others like me had apartments or hotel rooms provided by our sponsors.

Due to rampant inflation, sometimes as high as 20 percent a month, our stipends were based on the ruble equivalent of $400 instead of a fixed sum, to protect our buying power. It was difficult to watch the effects of the inflation on our host families; their life savings were diminishing by the day. The effects were particularly harsh on the pensioners and seniors who lived on fixed incomes and had to decide whether to spend their money on heat, medicine, or food.

Even with the Peace Corps adjusting our pay each month to reflect Russia's soaring inflation, we still lose equity if we don't spend our entire allotment by the end of the month. This didn't seem smart to John and me, so we sought out a way to exchange our rubles into dollars which, although not exactly legal, would limit our losses considerably. It was easy to exchange dollars for rubles, but finding a bank to sell us dollars was more challenging. The first four banks we visited refused, ushering us out as if we were gangsters trying to launder money. Without federally enforced guidelines in place, Russian banks are free to establish reserve ratios, interest rates, and foreign exchange fees as they see fit. There is also a fear of dealing with foreigners, which further diminished our chances. Eventually we found a bank that would sell us dollars, but at a rate several percentage points below the official rate.

With time getting short till my move to Artyom, I am trying to figure out how to handle my relationship with Masha. We have had few opportunities to talk and when we do, she comes across as distant and hurt. Masha, like most Russians, finds it difficult to understand why I joined the Peace Corps when I had so many opportunities available in the United States. We met for lunch and spoke for twenty minutes before she suddenly made an excuse to run home. It is frustrating that her family doesn't have a telephone and that my schedule is at the mercy of the Peace Corps; making plans is difficult. It takes me an hour to get to her apartment, all the while not knowing whether she will be home. Two weeks earlier I'd showed up at her apartment and ended up spending an hour drinking tea with her mother, which was awkward as we struggled to make conversation and neither of us wanted to be rude. There is a Russian custom that if a neighbor shows up unannounced for a visit (most people don't have access to a telephone), it would be rude not to invite them in, at least for a cup of tea. The custom is that if the timing is not good, the host will serve a cup of tea filled to the rim of the cup as a signal, allowing the guest and host to stave off an embarrassing situation. Once that cup of tea has been consumed, the guest leaves and all is fine. Masha's mother either didn't think I would understand the culture or assumed that Masha would be returning shortly, so she didn't follow form, making it more awkward for the both of us.

On a positive note, the head of the Peace Corps Russia desk in Washington, D.C. came to visit us. Kim is friendly and had developed a rapport with my grandmother via her frequent calls to the Peace Corps desk to ask about mailing packages to me. Kim is also African American, which made her a highly sought-after guest since few, if any, of the local Russians had ever met a black person before. My host family was particularly eager to meet her and insisted that I invite her to dinner. Kim's acceptance created envy among the other host families, which brought great pleasure to Mama. Because Kim was only in town for three days and had received many invitations, Mama acquiesced and invited Karl's host parents, my Russian-language instructor Natasha, and a few of my fellow volunteers to join the party. Mama took the honor of entertaining seriously and spent every waking moment fussing to make sure the food would be deserving of the event.

While Mama jumped head-first into a flurry of activity in the kitchen, Papa went out shopping to buy Kim a Russian memento to remember her evening with us, per Russian custom. A scowling Timofey spent the day vacuuming and dusting. I was proud of my host family's generosity and interest, and at the same time felt awkward that this was predicated entirely on the color of Kim's skin. The Russian view of American race relations was based on Hollywood movies and the occasional snippet on Russian news that focused solely on five-second clips of social discord, most recently pertaining to the Rodney King incident in California.

Kim's relationship with my grandmother had started with an initial call to check up on my well-being and soon led to weekly calls. The Peace Corps had provided us with an emergency phone number and an address in Washington D.C. where mail from our families would be collected and then sent via diplomatic pouch to the local Peace Corps office in Vladivostok. The Russian postal service is ridiculously slow and unreliable, so we were encouraged to use the diplomatic pouch. When Kim arrived, I wanted to thank her for her kindness toward my grandmother and hosting this party seemed like an appropriate means to do so. On the night of the party, I brought her to my family's apartment a few minutes early so that the family could have some individual time chatting prior to the arrival of the other guests. Mama and Timofey had decorated the apartment in a festive manner and the most amazing aromas permeated the apartment and stairwell. This was nothing compared to Papa's swooning over Kim like a love-struck teenager. He handed her a glass and filled it with Champagne—he continued to try and fill it up after every sip. He pulled her chair out before she sat, which was something I had never seen him do for Mama, and he followed her from room to room, dragging me along as his personal translator.

Papa was not alone in his fawning and I hoped the whole scene wasn't overwhelming. The Russian guests openly scrambled to sit next to her, and then immediately tossed me their cameras. Kim was a good sport and seemed flattered by the good will. After the party, both Mama and Papa couldn't stop talking about her beauty and intelligence, but more importantly, the fact that she had eaten every bite of food on her plate. After we had cleaned the last of the dishes, I made the mistake of wiping my hand across my brow and pushing the hair out of my eyes. I mentioned that I needed a haircut and before I could take it back, Papa sprinted out of the room to retrieve his barber's kit. He held my head between his hands and began murmuring as if he were a sculptor surveying a block of marble. "I used to cut all of the students' hair at the university," he bragged. Mama and Timofey nodded their heads in agreement. A shudder shot up my spine as I struggled to come up with a reason why this would be a bad idea. An evil grin momentarily slipped across Timofey's face as he egged on Papa.

I was ushered into the bathroom and given the seat of honor on the toilet while the three of them prepared for the attack. Mama and Timofey shouted instructions from the doorway while Papa stepped around my towel-covered torso and clipped away. I closed my eyes, hearing only the sound of the scissors and the suppressed murmurs from the doorway. Clumps of hair cascaded down my chest and back while I prayed, for the first time in my life, for a positive outcome.

After ten agonizing minutes, Papa brought the shaving brush across my neck and helped me stand so that I could look in the mirror. I didn't know whether to laugh or cry as any thought of ever getting laid slipped to the floor like the clumps of hair now covering the tile. I knew how important this was to Papa, so I dug down deep and found a smile. "It looks great," I stammered. Papa beamed and Mama stared at me while holding my shoulders and repeating the Russian word for *handsome*. Tim smiled at me with a hint of schadenfreude.

I was greeted the next morning by derision from both my fellow volunteers and the language instructors. At first they just grinned, noticing that something was amiss, and then after a second glance, they burst into laughter. With rapidly reddening cheeks I brushed off their quips and pretended not to be bothered. In the morning language session, my classmates made my appearance the subject of every sentence using our new vocabulary. "*Reclama*," our teacher said. We all repeated this word meaning *advertisement*. "Who wants to use this word in a sentence?" the teacher asked. Karl's hand shot up. "Go ahead, Karl." Karl followed with "Rich's haircut is an advertisement for birth control." Everyone laughed, including me. I dreaded the thought of sitting through eight hours of ridicule and wished that I had worn a hat. Just when I didn't think I could handle another comment, Nadezhda, the Peace Corps secretary, knocked on the door and asked me to follow her back to the office. I feared the worst, imagining a family emergency. When I stepped into the hallway, Nadezhda smiled and explained that she worked part time as a hairstylist and would be glad to fix my haircut. She expressed her sympathy and complimented me on my loyalty to Papa. My look of relief was answer enough. She pulled a pair of scissors from her purse, sat me down on a stool, and began sniping and trimming. I don't even know how to describe what she did, but it was enough to improve my appearance more than I could have hoped. I feared that Papa would realize that someone had touched up his handiwork, but the relief I felt looking in the mirror removed any lingering guilt. When I returned to class I received a standing ovation from the other volunteers. Upon my return home that evening, Mama asked whether I had received any compliments on my haircut. "Everyone noticed," I replied.

NOVEMBER 10, 1994

The mental anguish of saying goodbye to my life in Vladivostok, combined with the stress of starting a new job for which I fear I am entirely ill-prepared or unqualified for, has left me emotionally drained. I arrived in Artyom on a Wednesday and spent the day with Tanya going from office to office introducing myself. This entailed dozens of cups of tea and several trips to the men's room, an experience in and of itself. The men's bathroom consisted of a sink with a perpetual drip that left a rust-colored stain around the drain. A dozen large black flies competed to see who could annoy me the most as they welcomed me with a concerted aerial attack, making it hard to focus on my target. The two stalls were without doors or even a toilet, leaving one to squat over a fecal-splattered hole in the floor. With no toilet paper in sight, the only available alternative was a stack of newspaper squares that made wiping one's ass more like an exercise in finger painting.

I was mentally and physically exhausted when I arrived at the hotel at the end of my first full day in Artyom. This was where I would spend the next six weeks while I waited for Linda to depart. With no hot water with which to shower or even a coffee pot, I felt exasperated and wondered whether I had made a mistake in not accepting Mama's offer to live with them for the short term. I had hoped that Linda would invite me to dinner on my first night in Artyom, considering that there was only one restaurant in the town and it was currently closed for repairs. I struggled to understand Linda's lack of hospitality, since she most certainly understood what it was like being alone in a new city. I couldn't figure out if her treatment was a reflection of hostility or shyness, but either way I was left to eat the last of my Snicker bars for dinner as I lay in bed reading a spy novel.

With little in Artyom to hold my attention over the weekend, I returned to Vladivostok to attend John's house-warming party. I had wanted to establish myself in Artyom and make friends, but no invitations had come forth and there wasn't an option of inviting anyone over to my hotel—I had no way to cook and there were no places to dine out. I took a train to Vladivostok after work on Friday and arrived at John's apartment a little after 6:00 p.m. John looked flustered as he prepared for up to twenty guests. He put me to work in the kitchen, cleaning two kilos of shrimp that he had picked up at the market. I shelled and seasoned them before sautéing them in his one and only pan. His only other food offering consisted of two loaves of bread and a block of Velveeta cheese that he had found in a local kiosk. Velveeta is a big deal, since any cheese, even this cheese-like product that I avoided like the plague back home, was a lucky find.

A steady stream of volunteers, Russian friends, and even some of our host families strolled in wearing their party clothes. Our Russian friends come to our parties with high expectations and are often disappointed as they expect Russian-style sit-down dinners and end up with a few appetizers and ton of alcohol. Few of us had plates, silverware, or any of the kitchenware necessary to cook a meal and there were no catering options, paper plates, or other items that would ease the burden of entertaining.

The food was depleted within an hour, leaving only a handful of vodka bottles. Most saw this as a sign that the party was over and soon there were only a handful of drunken American guys questioning why the other guests had departed. John had a fiancée back in the states, so his focus was on getting drunk and trying to set the rest of us up with the women in his office. With goofy grins and a will for adventure, Karl, Gary, and I hit the street looking for an open bar. John remained home with the stragglers and wished us well. Too impatient to wait for a public bus, we flagged down a rogue taxi for the drive into the city. We didn't consider this dangerous, since there were three of us, although we had been duly warned against traveling in this manner. When a car finally stopped, it took us several minutes to explain that we wanted to go to a bar where we could meet some Russian women who weren't prostitutes. This was difficult, since single Russian woman did not go to bars. The driver took us to a place called the Green Lantern, telling us that this was the "in place" for good food and live music. We should have gotten the hint when he dropped us off in front of a shabby building with an unlit "BAR" sign, but having come this far, we walked into the building anyway and climbed up two flights of creaking stairs. At the top of the second landing, we ran into a locked glass door. The place was closed.

We returned to the street, cursing our bad luck while watching Gary blow smoke rings into the sky. Two Russian sailors passed and we asked them about the bar. They told us that it had been fire-bombed earlier in the week and was now closed for repairs. As we stood on the sidewalk contemplating our next move, a man I recognized walked past us. I had met him several weeks earlier while with Masha at a university dorm party. I called out his name and he stopped to chat, telling us that he was a musician and that he was on his way to play at one of the best nightclubs in town. Katya invited us to split a taxi with him and soon we were heading out of the city. We drove for thirty minutes and ended up in a warehouse area on the far side of the port.

As Katya paid the driver, the four of us piled out of the car in front of a bar with the silhouette of a flashing, neon-lit woman in the window. Katya had failed to mention that his gig was at a strip club, but since we were here and rapidly sobering up, we followed him inside. We were greeted with a blast of high-volume techno music and a smoky haze that narrowed our visibility to a few feet. A scantily clad waitress led us to a table alongside the stage and took our drink order. Sitting at the table next to us were two waiters from a restaurant called Nostalgia that many of the American expats in Vladivostok visited. They recognized us and invited us to push our tables together. They were halfway through a bottle of whiskey and immediately instructed the waitress to bring over three more glasses. The warmth of the whiskey triggered a second wind and soon we were laughing and offering to buy the next bottle. This led to alternating shots of vodka and whiskey, a certain recipe for trouble. The dancing girls saw us as easy prey, but after failing to entice us to deposit any rubles into their G-strings, they gave up and returned to the dimly lit stage. Two hours passed and suddenly we realized that the bar was closing and both Katya and our two waiter friends had disappeared. The surprise didn't end there as waiter brought us a bill for a staggering US $550. This supposedly included cover charges, the bottle of whiskey ordered by our waiter friends as well as the bill for the rest of their meal, our own bottle of vodka, and twelve bottles of beer. We didn't mind paying for the vodka and beer, but we hadn't been advised of a cover charge nor agreed to pay anyone else's tab.

Gary and Karl stared blankly out of red, glassy eyes. This was more money than we could afford on our Peace Corps stipend and it was significantly more than the combined amount of cash we had in our pockets. Very few Russian establishments accepted credit cards, so we were in a bit of a bind. I grabbed the bill off the table and in a bit of New Jersey attitude stormed out of my chair so quickly that I bumped into one of the dancers. "*Gde nakhoditsya menedzher?*" [Where's the manager?] I yelled in my most commanding voice. The woman pointed toward a door directly in front of me. I nodded and then knocked briskly before pushing the door open.

The stereotypical strip club manager sat behind his desk: fat, balding, and wearing a scowl that should have intimidated me into backing out of the room. I knew it was vital to keep my tough-guy image or I would end up with an ass-kicking and little else to show for my false bravado. Not knowing what else to do now that I had his attention, I laid the bill on his desk, reached for a pen, and crossed off the cover charges and the whiskey, explaining that we were friends of Katya and that we were only going to pay for the drinks we ordered. I didn't know what to expect even after he smiled at me. I smiled back. He shrugged and then said, "OK," sliding the bill in front of him and writing down the new amount. He then drew a circle around it. I thanked him and with the bill in hand, returned to my colleagues. We dug into our wallets and each of us put down a third of the new amount. It was hard to suppress my giddiness, especially since it had happened so quickly that I wondered whether we being set up and would end up going home with empty pockets anyway.

I think Gary and Karl felt the same, which led to our prompt exit from the club. We found ourselves outside in a frozen night without a clue for how to get back to John's apartment. The streets were deserted and lined with concrete warehouses as far as the eye could see. We walked aimlessly, drunk enough that the reality of our situation failed to register until Karl began to repeat, "We are so fucked." It was at this point that I caught sight of dim headlights a few blocks away. I began running at full speed, slowing only when I came within ten feet of the car, as I feared the driver would think I was attacking him and come out shooting. I walked the final distance with my palms held up, praying that I wouldn't be interrupting some pissed-off mafia schmuck getting head from a street whore. Fortunately, the driver was alone and seemed drunker than we were. He stared at me for a few seconds as if sizing me up, then rolled down his window tapping his cigarette on the edge of the window. I am not exactly sure what I said, but it was something like "My Russian brother: boy, am I glad to see you. We need a big favor!" I told him that we had been brought to the strip club by a couple of Russian sailors who left us with the bill and no way to get back to Vladivostok. He offered us a ride if we would pay to fill up his gas tank. This sounded a lot better than freezing to death in the middle of nowhere, so I responded with an enthusiastic "Da."

I ran back to Gary and Karl, explaining that I had found us a ride back. They stared at me as if I were speaking in tongues as I pushed them along back toward the car. Ivan, our driver, stepped out of the car and as

I made the introductions he staggered and fell against the side of the car. He gathered himself and tried to assuage our fears by saying that he was fine to drive—considering our other options, we went along with the plan. Ivan had difficulty getting the key in the ignition, so I offered to drive, but neither Ivan nor my buddies thought it was a good idea. I sat in the passenger seat while Gary and Karl crouched in the back, their eyes closed with hands gripping the armrests. We drove down darkened roads, some barely paved, swerving and bouncing until I began to wonder if I was going to puke. The longer we drove, the more suspicious I was that we were going to be robbed. I realized we outnumbered Ivan three to one, so that even if he tried something, we could overpower him, unless of course he had a gun. Just as I was gauging our situation, we stopped in the middle of a dark alley. Ivan honked the horn with a series of short beeps before stepping outside. Within seconds a garage door opened and a man appeared under a single illuminated bulb. We could see Ivan pointing at us while gesturing as if he feared that if he didn't keep his hands moving they would freeze.

I didn't want to turn toward Gary and Karl for fear that they would sense my anxiety. After a few seconds Ivan approached my window and motioned for me to hand him the money. I handed him enough to fill the gas tank up twice, but at this point I just wanted to get on the road and back to John's. He took the money and returned to the garage, where the other man was fiddling with some type of hose. A minute passed before Ivan and the stranger returned to the car, awkwardly straddling a large barrel hoisted between them. They positioned the barrel so that they could pour the gas into a funnel that led into the gas tank of the car. We waited in the cold silence as the alcohol and the late hour sapped our energy. We finally got back on the road, and within minutes the lights of Vladivostok appeared on the horizon. I gave him directions and soon we were standing outside of John's apartment. I slipped Ivan an extra twenty dollars because I was so thankful that we had made it back. We staggered up the steps to the apartment and it took five minutes of heavy knocking before a pissed-off John opened the door.

After hearing our story, he could only laugh and say how happy he was that he had stayed behind.

NOVEMBER 13, 1994

After a wild weekend, I was ready to settle down and get my bearings in Artyom. Tanya, my interpreter, had taken it upon herself to introduce me to everyone within the administration as well as every shopkeeper within walking distance of my hotel. "I am amazed at how the city has taken to you," she remarked after a lively discussion with an old woman selling vegetables at one of the open-air markets. Linda and I have different personalities but since were the only two foreigners most people had met, we were often compared to each other. This may not necessarily have been fair to Linda, but since she had shown little empathy for my situation of being stuck in a hotel with no cooking or dining options, I didn't feel obliged to defend her. Tanya remarked that I had met more people in my two weeks than Linda had during her prior year in Artyom. This was partly due to the attention I received from the local newspaper: they published a front-page story about me illustrated with my photograph, which led to passersby pointing at me wherever I went. The article mentioned that I was living in the hotel without a kitchen, and immediately dinner invitations began to fly in from people within the administration. I accepted every invitation and my network increased accordingly, as did my language skills. It is definitely easier to be a man coming to a stranger's apartment, since safety is not as much of a concern, but personality also plays a part. Russians don't exercise the same reserve that Americans do with asking personal questions, particularly concerning whether a guest was married, had been married, wanted to find a Russian partner, etc. As a young single man, I was excited about being set up with local women, while this Russian matchmaking tendency likely did not have the same appeal for Linda. The more willing I was to open up my life to them, the more they shared with me. In contrast, Linda was perceived as being unfriendly for turning down the invitations, the word about her spread, and few Russians wanted to extend an invitation for fear of being turned down. I missed my social interactions in American and yearned to get involved with my new community as quickly as possible. I also wanted to forge a closer relationship with Linda, particularly since I had so many questions to ask her. Unfortunately, this desire wasn't mutual; I got the sense that she resented the attention I was getting and she expressed anger that I was treated in a different manner than she had been upon her arrival. After the article came out in the city paper, she grew even more distant, and our relationship became one in which we both counted down the days to her departure.

My first invitation was from Uri, a friendly forty-year-old architect who elicited a smile from everyone he passed. Tanya explained that he had become quite popular after the fall of Communism as the mafia suddenly needed someone to design and build their new mansions. The typical Russian lives in a Soviet-era concrete apartment complex or, if in a village, a small cottage likely without running water. Meanwhile, the mafioso live in huge homes surrounded by high walls and gun-toting security guards.

Uri was talkative and eager to show me the city from his perspective. We met outside the office and drove off in his Toyota to the outskirts of town so that he could show me his own home, which was under construction. Within the same neighborhood were several recently completed mansions belonging to the mayor and a few of the other high-ranking city officials, his cronies. Uri spoke only Russian, so our conversations were slow and included plenty of pantomime. The neighborhood was not too different from an upper-middle-class American version, albeit with the addition of security fences and armed guards. A vicious Doberman guarded Uri's house to protect the exposed building materials from thieves, and the dog immediately recognized me as a stranger, struggling against his chains while snapping a mouthful of teeth as I slipped past for a quick tour. The house was a four-bedroom split-level with a built-in sauna, an enormous kitchen, and plenty of room for entertaining.

We drove for the next forty-five minutes through other neighborhoods so that Uri could show off homes he had built. Finally, as my stomach started to growl, we arrived at the apartment he and his wife lived in as they waited for their house to be completed. His wife was cooking dinner when we arrived and had apparently been unaware that he was bringing along a guest, much less one who was now gracing the front page of the newspaper. This was uncomfortable—she scolded Uri before rushing into their bedroom to change out of her sweat suit before greeting me. Uri led me to the living room, handed me a can of beer, and then popped a porno into the VCR. If I hadn't already been uncomfortable, I now was extremely so. Sitting alone in a stranger's house trying to make a good impression and instead, I'm staring at a video showing a highly flexible threesome of actors engaging in hardcore sex to the sound of 1970s disco. I fidgeted, unsure of whether this video was a sign of what they expected from me or if he was just trying to impress me. I couldn't imagine that this was normal behavior in Russia ... were they swingers? My agony finally ended when I was beckoned into the kitchen. In typical Russian fashion, his wife had laid out plates piled high with delicacies on the table. We were formally introduced and I awkwardly made small talk while complimenting every bite of food. Uri had not turned off the porno and the faint moaning and groaning continued to fill the silence. Uri asked me a few questions for the benefit of his wife, to put her at ease, while tearing the cap off a bottle of vodka. Some of the vodka bottles have metallic pull-tabs on the lids similar to the lids of our yogurt containers so that once opened, there is no way to re-seal. Uri filled three large glasses to the rim, handing one to his wife and then one to me. "To our American guest!" he proclaimed, and then we clicked glasses and chugged the vodka. Immediately he refilled our glasses. I noticed that his wife brought a piece of bread up to her nose and inhaled deeply after swallowing. I asked her why she did this and she told me that this was how you could avoid the harsh aftertaste of cheap vodka, an obvious dig at Uri, who only shrugged his shoulders.

As the guest, I offered the second toast, thanking them for bringing me into their home and serving me such a wonderful dinner. They smiled and we clicked glasses before slamming down the second glass of vodka. I sniffed a piece of bread, aiming a smile at his wife. "It works," I lied. The glasses were filled a third time with Uri making a toast to his wife, and then before drinking he added, "and to the rest of the beautiful women in the world." With three glasses of vodka and the required toasts accounted for, I felt more relaxed, despite the continuation of the background noises. More toasts interrupted our meal until my cheeks burned, prompting Uri to inquire whether I was drunk or just blushing from the video.

I was wiping up the last bits of gravy with a piece of bread when the doorbell rang. Uri ushered in a man named Mikhail, and after a brief introduction, I was told that it was Mikhail's birthday and in honor of this, Uri opened another bottle of vodka. This was my first real vodka-drinking opportunity in Artyom and I wanted to hold my own in front of my new friends. I stood toe-to-toe with these two Russian men until the second bottle of our dinner had been emptied. I was pretty drunk. I tried to act like I wasn't, which meant desperately trying to stay upright in my chair and to focus on the conversation, which was all in Russian and being slurred by my drinking companions. This was an important moment, for if I carried myself well and didn't puke all over the kitchen table, I would probably continue to get invited to dinners. After the second bottle, I figured that I had represented myself well and could leave with my self-respect intact. I stood up and began to thank them for dinner when Uri took hold of my shoulders and told me that the night was not quite over as we had been invited to join Mikhail's family for a quick celebration at their house. I smiled, nodding my head in agreement while inside I cringed, trying to come up with a inoffensive way out.

Mikhail's house was one of Uri's designs and was quite elaborate by Russian standards, which in itself might not necessarily signify mafia involvement, but when that was combined with his stocky build, rugged features, and crude manner, it was obvious that he wasn't a city administrator. I was given a tour in which he made sure to tell me the price he had paid for every piece of electronic equipment or furniture that we passed.

Eventually we returned to the kitchen, where another feast awaited us. It pained me when I saw how much food was once again set out, knowing that I was in for another huge meal. This unease only increased when I saw half a dozen vodka bottles lined up on the table.

The dinner was a paternalistic embodiment of 1950s-era American sitcom values as the men sat at the table and were waited upon by Mikhail's daughter and wife, who stood ready to fill our glasses or serve more food onto our plates as needed. My head was fuzzy from what we had already consumed at Uri's apartment and now with each successive shot of vodka, I felt closer to face-planting into the kielbasa and potato salad. During the meal, Mikhail brought out his photo albums, showing snapshots of his youth as a military advisor for the North Vietnamese army. This was a delicate situation: our countries had been on opposing sides of the con-flict. But with the war twenty-five years in the past, it felt OK to discuss without assigning blame. Somehow, I made it through dinner and I must have impressed my new friends because at the end of the meal Mikhail draped his arm across my shoulders and handed me a Cuban cigar. The cigar crumbled when I tried to light it, but it was a nice gesture and I guess that was all that really mattered. Somehow, I made it back to the hotel. I woke fully clothed on the bed feeling like shit, but proud to have survived my night out with Uri.

The only guest in this ten-room hotel, I spend as little time here as possible. I appreciate having a shower and toilet, but without hot water, my showers are rapid affairs. The four women who work at the hotel have become more welcoming as the strangeness of having an American guest has faded. I have jumped at every invitation from them, whether to join them for a cup of tea or to watch television in their office since I don't have one in my room. I have shared my photo albums with them, showing pic-tures of family and friends back home. They are extremely interested in this, stopping me with questions about the homes and people as well as about life in America. As have most of my Russian acquaintances in Artyom, they have been patient with my language abilities, gently correcting my grammar and often teaching me new words. They seem genuinely interested in hearing about life in America, and we pass the hours discussing the differences between our two cultures. All four of the women are married, and since they work twelve-hour shifts, I have spent time with their families also, who often visit in the evenings.

My sudden celebrity status in Artyom has boosted my confidence as the dinner invitations come in and the women in the city administration, including Tanya, try to set me up with Russian women they know. The Russians have a problem pronouncing my name and after three months, I have stopped correcting them: I just smile when they call me "Reech." Tanya and I have been getting along very well and since she is seen as my social gatekeeper, she too gets bombarded with questions about my availability. She often chides me on nights when I return to the hotel after work, saying, "The poor American has nowhere to go to eat tonight!" Most of the dinner invitations have also been extended to one of the single women. Not having my own apartment and feeling it incredibly rude to subject a guest to the stares and attention of the hotel staff as there are no room keys and I must ring the bell to get let in.

NOVEMBER 14, 1994

I took the train to the Peace Corps office yesterday for the first time, which required a bit more savvy than just going to Vladivostok, since my stop to visit my host family had been the one at the end of the line and so I'd never bothered to pay attention to the train's loudspeaker announcements. The Peace Corps office is located halfway between Artyom and Vladivostok, so it is a short trip and an easy opportunity to check for mail, visit the Peace Corps library, and chat with other volunteers. Each step toward becoming more self-sufficient increases my comfort level and gives rise to the feeling that I will succeed. Visits to the Peace Corps' office provide a chance to relax, speak English, and visit the medical office for vaccinations, medicine, and free condoms.

Last night I was lost in thought on the train returning from the Peace Corps office when three Russian teenagers began to hassle a young woman. They were loud and obnoxious and despite not understanding what they were saying, I could tell it was rude and threatening. I was not sure how to react since I am a foreigner with poor communication skills, but I couldn't sit back and wait for something bad to happen. I moved closer, pretending to look out the window, all the while keeping an eye on the woman. As I debated with myself whether to get involved, a babushka got up from her seat and walked up to the group, pointing her finger in their faces while angrily gesturing. A small child ran to her side and clutched her free hand. The teenagers laughed and responded with obscene gestures. Her face turned crimson and the volume of her yelling rose until she was screaming. Everyone openly stared as the old woman suddenly stopped yelling and collapsed.

I jumped to her side, untied her scarf, and checked her breathing. A circle of faces peered down and then a hand appeared with smelling salts. The babushka coughed and her eyes gradually came into focus. I lifted her into an empty seat: she had lost all mobility in her left leg, which I assumed was the result of a stroke. I had no idea what to do and everyone else in the train returned to their newspapers once she had regained consciousness. I offered to get off the train with her when she indicated that we had reached her stop. I held her up by her shoulders while uttering reassuring words to her grandson that everything would be OK. Once on the platform I looked around for a taxi and when one pulled up, she accepted my offer to pay the cabbie in advance of her ride. I could see the pain in her face and felt guilty that I hadn't stepped in sooner. When her taxi pulled away, I realized that I now had to find a way back to Artyom. Eventually another taxi pulled up and after a few seconds of haggling, the driver agreed to take me home for the equivalent of $10. This was double what it should have been, but I was tired and eager to get back to the hotel.

NOVEMBER 20, 1994

Friday afternoon I was summoned by Valentina Constantinova's office. She serves as the local representative in the *Krai Duma*, a position similar to that of a US congresswoman. Her dress and manner indicated both wealth and power. After a brief introduction, she invited me to join her the following afternoon to attend the local harvest festival. I had no idea what a harvest festival was, but was honored nonetheless, and gratefully agreed. I had assumed that we would be walking through muddy fields and shaking plenty of hands, so the next afternoon, I dressed in a flannel shirt, jeans, and my work boots, and returned to her office.

I stuck my head through the doorway to announce my presence and was shocked to see that she was wearing a fancy dress and high heels. Her hair was coiffed and her jewelry sparkled. Oops! I stuttered trying to explain my appearance, but she interrupted my mumbling with a great burst of laughter and told me to run back to the hotel and put on something more appropriate. I sprinted back through the building and across the street to the hotel, returning moments later in my finest—and only—suit and tie.

I expected a Lada sedan, as featured in the old spy movies, to be picking us up. But instead a shiny white Toyota Land Cruiser pulled up to the door. We drove down country roads bordered by naked fields and the occasional farmhouse before finally coming to a stop in front of a one-story school building constructed of brick and concrete and surrounded by a large parking lot full of small pick-up trucks. Valentina's driver quickly jumped out and opened her door, leaving me to exit on my own. She was greeted by several distinguished men, including an older, well-coiffed man who kissed her on both cheeks before leading her toward the entrance. I half-jogged to catch up with them, which eventually led to my introduction. He was the Russian minister of agriculture. We shook hands and he asked me how I was enjoying Russia and then, without waiting for my response, he took Valentina's arm and walked inside.

We entered a large gymnasium that had been converted into a reception area and were met with the aroma of freshly baked bread. There were a hundred tables lined up in front of a small stage. In the typical style of a Russian feast, each table was adorned with bottles of vodka, Champagne, and baskets of bread along with platters of sliced kielbasa, leaving barely enough free room for the silverware. There was a stage in the front of the room with a single table wrapped in orange crepe paper and a sign welcoming the agricultural minister and Valentina Constantinova. Cigarette smoke rose like a hundred factory stacks from men who stood haphazardly around the gymnasium floor in groups of three or four. I felt awkward tagging along behind Valentina, pretending to be a part of a conversation in which my participation was clearly not wanted. The volume of chatter grew louder and the air continued to thicken as more people filed in clutching cigarettes.

Eventually the minister of agricultural nodded to me and indicated that I should follow the two of them to the VIP table on the stage. A chair was pointed out for me to the right of Valentina and then the two of them went back to their conversation, leaving me once again to stare out at the crowd. I scanned the other tables, hoping for a familiar face while trying to act as though I wasn't surprised by my position. Being on stage and in view of the entire room made me self-conscious and very aware that I was an outsider, especially given the fact that, without Tanya, I was left to fend for myself. A few other men and women joined our table and I stood and shook hands before returning to my seat. When everyone burst out in laughter, I chuckled quietly without a clue as to what was so funny. Many of the men in the crowd were dressed in military fatigues, while the women donned more formal attire. A nervous energy permeated the room. The minister grabbed the microphone and cleared his throat before addressing the crowd, which had now grown to several hundred people. He spoke for ten minutes, nine minutes and fifty seconds of which went in my right ear and out my left. Suddenly there were two words I recognized: *American* and *Reech*. He stopped speaking long enough for a round of applause and my heart skipped a beat as he motioned for me to join him at the microphone.

He put his arm around my shoulders and said something to the audience. Clapping again erupted. I wiped my hands on my pants, smiling back at the crowd, trying to conceal my nervousness.

I had been in Russia for less than three months and had little confidence in my language abilities and was now being asked to speak in Russian to several hundred people! The microphone felt cold in my hand. "*Zdravstvutay*" [Hello] I said, trying my best to smile. Silence. I cleared my throat and was about to speak when the Minister handed me a glass of cognac so full that the trembling of my hand caused it to splash over the rim and run down my wrist. The silence was now deafening, as everyone except me anxiously waited to hear the American speak. I was one of the first, if not the only, Westerner in forty years to visit this rural area and there was great curiosity about my presence. I took a final deep breath and started speaking in my best Russian.

"Thank you, Mr. Minister," I began, since I had forgotten his name. "It is a great honor to be invited here to celebrate this holiday with all of you. I apologize for my poor language skills, but I promise to study hard during my time here in Russia." I looked at the crowd and felt my cheeks redden. The audience was leaning forward. Beads of perspiration rolled down the side of my face and I fought the urge to brush them away. I held the glass of cognac up in the air to take their eyes away from my face and continued. "I would like to toast to the great friendship between Russia and America and hope that there will always be peace and warm feelings between our two great countries. I hope that our children and grandchildren will work together to make the world a better place for everyone. Thank you for your hospitality and generosity." With that, I brought the glass to my lips amid another round of applause and drained the cognac so quickly that I didn't feel it go down. Everyone clapped and a smile returned to my face as I took my seat, eyes slightly out of focus. Valentina reached over and gave me a one-armed hug as the minister told everyone to begin eating. There was a thunderous ovation and then a chorus of corks popping and glasses being clinked. My glass had been refilled, this time with vodka and only slightly less full than the prior glass, and I drained this one just as quickly as the first. The minister gave a more personal toast to our table, working his way around so that he mentioned each of us by name. He winked at me as he said my name and then shouted "*na zdorovie!*" I learned something from him as I saw that he had made eye contact with each guest, giving all of us the impression that we were welcome and important.

The meal continued in this fashion, with one guest after another making a toast and the rest of us downing our glasses, including Valentina, who showed no signs of slowing down. My nervous apprehension receded, replaced by a state of being pleasantly buzzed. As the feeding frenzy slowed, the band joined us on stage and assumed positions in front of the table. They held accordions, French horns, saxophones, and trumpets, and set into a series of Cossack ballads that had the crowd swaying. I was so full that I relished the thought of standing up and loosening my belt when the music stopped. Thirty young women were led out to the middle of the dance floor facing our table. It felt as if they were all staring at me because they were in fact staring at me. A few started giggling and soon most were covering their mouths with their hands. I looked to Valentina for some manner of understanding and she smiled and told me that these were the single women in the audience and that as the guest of honor and a single man, I was expected to select the most beautiful one to be my dance partner. The nervousness I felt when making the speech was nothing compared what I was now experiencing as Valentina and the Minister led me down the steps and onto the dance floor.

I was led up and down the line of smiling women while Valentina spewed out a steady commentary declaring the beauty and intelligence of each. The entire gymnasium was silent except for the drummer who kept a steady beat. Many of the babushkas had come down to point toward their granddaughters in the hopes that they could sway my vote by their incessant badgering. I was in a no-win situation: I would be living among these people for the next two years and any selection was bound to offend those not chosen. Finally, an idea came to me and I walked over to one of the grandmothers standing off to the side. Her toothless grin and weathered skin gave her an endearing look, so I grabbed her hand and led her onto the dance floor. The crowd burst into laughter and the band kicked into a swinging melody. I made small talk as we waltzed awkwardly with everyone watching. Her garlic-tainted breath burned my eyes and she seemed to have consumed as much alcohol as I had, since she tripped over my feet. I smiled, feeling like I had outsmarted my hosts and avoided an awkward situation. Other couples joined us on the dance floor and I was in the midst of congratulating myself when Grandma began groping my buttocks. I thought that I must be dreaming, but then I heard laughter all around us as I moved her hands back up to my back. For five minutes I fought with this elderly woman as she cupped and squeezed my ass like she was trying to pick out a melon at the market. Finally, someone pulled her away and I backed up, hoping to find the restroom. She was yelling and fighting to get back to me, spittle flying out of her mouth like birdshot.

Men sitting at tables along my route stopped me to ask that I join them for a drink, which I politely accepted. Within twenty minutes I had traveled fifty feet and was no closer to the bathroom, but had finished off five hefty shots of vodka. My head was beginning to spin, so was I trying to excuse myself from the latest group when I felt a hard push in the middle of my back. I flew forward, stumbling over several empty chairs before regaining my balance. I turned around and saw a man in a Russian military uniform staring at me with a look of intense hatred. He swayed from side to side, taunting me in a singsong voice. I could only understand the word "American." My body tensed. He stepped forward and took a swing at me, missing wildly. I took a quick step backwards and dodged his second punch. This time his momentum caused him to stumble forward and I grabbed his shirt and pushed him to the floor. Three men who had recently been sharing a toast with me jumped from their seats and grabbed him as he came back at me.

A large man forced his way through the crowd and grabbed the military man by the neck, dragging him out of the room before any more harm could be done. People were apologizing and I shook it off as if it were no big deal. This was my first experience with anti-American sentiment. I was ushered back to my original seat at the table and accepted what I hoped would be my final glass of booze, since I was already quite drunk and had yet to make it to the restroom. The night ended shortly afterwards with twenty minutes of hand shaking. I was tired and drunk and ready for bed.

NOVEMBER 24, 1994

Being an hour from Vladivostok allows me to escape to my host family's comforting apartment and the camaraderie of my American friends. I get overwhelmed at times speaking and actively listening to Russian so that I understand the gist of what people are saying. As such, I was excited when John called my office to invite me to a party. As if I needed further encouragement, he explained that Gary needed a wingman because he had invited a few of his female Russian colleagues over, and had promised to set them up with his friends. Since John's fiancée was back in Florida, he lived vicariously through us, frequently trying to play matchmaker. American women seldom came to our parties, partly because they resented having to compete with the Russian women for our attention and partly because they had little interest listening to us mangle the Russian language in our attempts to seduce the Russian women.

I arrived at John's apartment to find Karl, Gary, and John already several drinks into the night. I grabbed a beer and had barely taken a sip when the doorbell rang and six Russian women entered. They had been to a few of our prior parties and enjoyed hanging out with us, if not for the free food and drink then for the amusement of listening to us flirt in Russian. They understood that we were nice guys and that they would be safe.

Under dimmed lights we danced to cheesy disco music, stopping only to make toasts and guzzle vodka. It was a great night and we laughed non-stop. I spent most of the night with Anna, who was training as a ballerina and had a decent command of English. She thought that by improving her language skills she would improve her chances of joining an international dance troupe. I liked her, but often caught myself comparing her to Masha. I hadn't been able to get in touch with Masha since moving to Artyom, and although I could take the tram to her apartment, the thought of getting stuck chatting with her mother again was off-putting.

Anna left with her friends at nine o'clock; Vladivostok isn't the safest place to be out after dark. In fact, Vladivostok had been ranked as one of the three most dangerous cities in the world in a recent report on violence and crime. With the women gone, the four of us were sitting in the living room with a rapidly diminishing bottle of vodka, complaining about the drawbacks of celibacy, when we were interrupted by a woman's scream from the courtyard. I ran to the window and saw a woman surrounded by several men, all yelling and pointing at each other with exaggerated animation. A man's body lay on the ground and the woman seemed to be physically fighting with at least one of the other men. Without thinking I grabbed a kitchen knife and ran out the door assuming that my friends would follow. "Police, *Militizia!*" I yelled as loud as I could in an effort to scare them off and avoid a confrontation. Unfortunately, nobody moved or showed any fear in my arrival. Their attention shifted to me: out of breath and trying to hide the kitchen knife behind my back. It was at this point that I turned around for support and realized that I was alone. I slid the knife along my forearm, realizing that to approach with a weapon could start something ugly and I definitely didn't like the odds. Suddenly my sense of chivalry was replaced by my instinct for survival. I asked the woman if she was injured. She pointed to one of the men and said that he was her brother and that he and his friends had beaten up her boyfriend. That was enough to assure me that she wasn't being raped, so without a word I turned and walked as fast as I could back to John's apartment.

NOVEMBER 25, 1994

Thanksgiving is a few days away and—as I had on Halloween—I want to share my culture and traditions with my host family. I had been telling them about Thanksgiving for the past few weeks and as the date neared, I felt the same excitement as if I were back in New Jersey. I was faced with the impossible task of finding a turkey, cranberries, yams, and stuffing to make a meal that would resemble a real Thanksgiving. Shopping is a treasure hunt in the Russian Far East, since there are no supermarkets. What is available in a local kiosk every day for a month may disappear on the day you decide to purchase it and then not return for another two months. This leads everyone to stock up on things like canned soup and Velveeta to barter for items that someone else has found. Like most Russians, I carry a small mesh bag at all times called an *avoska* (meaning "just in case") bag. Almost every conversation between volunteers inevitably leads to a discussion of our shopping successes and failures. Two weeks earlier I had stumbled across a can of sweet potatoes, but everything else for my big dinner would require trading with other expats and substituting locally available goods. As the day approached, I had secured a bag of cornbread stuffing, a can of small white onions, and even some cranberry sauce, but alas, no turkey.

The most difficult part of locating a turkey turned out to be my efforts to explain what a turkey was. My explanations and drawings drew strange looks and suggestions that I was referring to a chicken, duck, and even dinosaur. I can say with a high probability that there are no turkeys in the Russia Far East. With only one day left, I gave up and settled on a large chicken. On Thanksgiving morning, I packed up my ingredients and took the train to Vladivostok. When I arrived at the apartment, I took out each item individually so that Mama could see them in their pre-cooked state. She had never heard of sweet potatoes, and after a small taste still wouldn't admit that these were potatoes, insisting that they were large carrots cooked in sugar. Russians take their potatoes seriously and the thought that there were sweet, orange potatoes was just too strange to comprehend.

Buying quality poultry or meat proved to be almost as difficult as finding a turkey. Farmers park their trucks near the markets, unload a tree stump to use as a cutting block, an axe to cut meat, and a scale to determine the weight. The heads and hooves of the animals are often displayed on the hoods of their trucks as evidence of the meat's origin. In recent months arrests have been made since dog meat and even human flesh taken from the morgue have been sold at the markets. If this wasn't enough to convince one to become a vegetarian, then nothing would be. Buying meat takes skill and effort: you must arrive early and find a farmer with a fairly intact carcass so that you can direct him where to cut. If you aren't specific, the butcher (and I use this term loosely) will swing his axe down and hack off the easiest chunk, often leaving you with as much bone and gristle as meat. During the summer months, it is even more important to arrive early because the markets don't have refrigeration and the stalls become inundated with flies by mid-morning.

My family appreciated the time and effort as well as the food that our Thanksgiving meal provided, but it lacked the shared excitement and football that I had grown to expect.

I returned to Artyom the next morning for a meeting with a representative from the local Internet provider. In the United States, this would not seem like such a big deal, but with Russia's limited and outdated telephone infrastructure, it is close to impossible to get a reliable connection. Linda had been trying to get a vendor from Vladivostok to come to our office, but their promises had come to naught. Linda had vowed that this would be her final project for the business center, as she wanted to be able to send one email before heading home. With her departure less than a month away, the last thing I wanted was a confrontation. But this seemed inevitable, since I'd spoken with Gary, Karl, and John, and they had all established connectivity within days of getting to their sites. I decided to go around Linda and called one of the service providers in Vladivostok. After a little bargaining, he agreed to set up our business center in exchange for the official price, plus an additional 10 percent "private charge" to cover his trouble. Paying an outright bribe was forbidden, but in Russia, the law is like a tree: hard to knock down or go through, but easy to get around. The service man came on his day off and had everything installed in less than an hour, so that I was already sending out messages when Linda strolled into the office Monday morning. She looked over my shoulder, saw me typing, and walked out without saying a word. I wanted to gloat to pay her back for the way she had been treating me, but I also pitied her and understood her isolation and her feelings that she hadn't been treated with the same hospitality that I had. She continually blamed her isolation on her status as a woman. She often proclaimed, "You get the attention and invitations because you are a man," whenever she overheard my conversations with Tanya regarding a dinner out with a new friend from the city administration.

DECEMBER 1, 1994

Andrew, a volunteer from New York, was given an assignment on the border between North Korea and Russia. Three days before his scheduled move, a local mayoral election took place and a hard-line Communist was voted into power. His first act as the new mayor was to negate the deal, forbidding Andrew to move to his city. Despite Moscow's and Washington's desire for cooperation, at the local level many of the older politicians weren't keen on giving up the Cold War theatrics. Andrew's situation made it clear that we had to be extremely careful in what we said: the slightest misstatement could provide ammunition to those that didn't want us here. Russia looked to the world like it had embraced democracy immediately when Gorbachev loosened control of the press, but unfortunately this wasn't really happening overnight.

The day after being told that he didn't have an assignment, Andrew got in a car accident that left him with a broken neck. The US navy had to send in a special military plane to evacuate him, which required a great deal of negotiation by both the Peace Corps staff and the American Consulate, since the Russians were paranoid about allowing an American military plane to land on Russian soil. Once the plane landed, they refused to allow any of the American doctors to disembark to help with the evacuation. The sobering effect of losing yet another volunteer gave rise to a feeling of fragility.

On a happier note, two of Papa's friends from Tomsk, a city in central Siberia, came for a visit and the family invited me home to join them in a celebration. The friends were anxious to meet an American, since their only experiences with us had occurred during the Vietnam War. I met Papa at the airport in Artyom to greet them and then drove back to Vladivostok for the party. They were burly Siberians with accents that were difficult for me to comprehend. Once at the apartment, sensitive to my language deficiencies, they began to speak slowly, which coincided with the opening of the first of many bottles of vodka. One of them had been an advisor for the North Vietnamese, and we had a few difficult moments when discussing the war. He recounted how he had shot down an American plane early in the war and how during the final months before the American troop withdrawal, he had been wounded and captured by two American marines. He had heard such awful things about Americans that he was sure that he was going to be shot, but instead they bandaged his leg and set him free. After telling me the story, he poured two glasses of vodka and we toasted to the US Marines who had spared his life. It was difficult for me to hear about American casualties without getting angry, but I understood that soldiers didn't start the war and for the most part, only did as instructed.

We were getting pretty drunk despite Mama's trying to stuff enough food in us to absorb the alcohol. We toasted to each other multiple times and then I listened while they exchanged stories of their childhoods. Toward the end of the night I was about to excuse myself when the doorbell rang. Quan, a Vietnamese friend of theirs, arrived to a succession of bear hugs. Quan was a frequent guest who stayed with the family whenever he was in Vladivostok on business, but this was my first opportunity to meet him. Quan's arrival led to another bottle of vodka and several more toasts. Our conversation became philosophical and at times emotional. Russian men have no qualms showing emotion and if a tear is shed during a toast, it is seen as a strength of character and not as a weakness as in America.

DECEMBER 3, 1994

Early this week a quirky man in his late sixties stepped into my office, gave the place a quick once-over, and declared that he would talk to me later since he was hesitant to speak inside. It seemed strange, but I didn't think much of his visit, since Russians were often curious about what I was doing in their city and wanted to see the American for themselves. My office had formerly been the Communist Party library and there were certain people within the city who felt that having an American capitalist occupying this area was as close to blasphemy as an atheist could get. Later that afternoon the man returned, only this time he explained that he was nervous to be seen talking to me. He mentioned that he feared that the Communists would eventually regain power in Russia and punish all those who had ventured into capitalistic endeavors. It was protocol to require all visitors to sign a registry before we provided any services, supposedly to enable the administration to judge how busy we were and whether the costs of keeping the center open justified the traffic. He thought that the truth lay in the administration's desire to keep track of those with capitalistic aspirations, so he politely refused to sign his name and asked that I not make mention of his visit.

His name was Vitaly and he eventually switched from Russian to a heavily accented English, explaining that he had not spoken my language in more than fifty years. He had brought along his friend Alex, and together they crept around my office looking at the maps and photographs I had on the walls, as if they were searching for cameras or listening devices. Alex didn't speak English, so Vitaly explained that Alex was a local doctor interested in learning more about America. It was close to the end of the workday so I agreed to meet them outside and join them for a cup of tea at Vitaly's house. I didn't feel that they represented a danger, although their sense of paranoia was a bit unnerving. We piled into Alex's beat-up two-door Volga, driving a few miles down the main street before turning off onto a dirt road that rose steeply to the top of a hill overlooking the city. Gullies formed where rainwater from the monsoon season storms had cut into the reddish dirt, leading to a very bumpy ride. Vitaly's house was at the crest of the hill. We passed dozens of ramshackle homes constructed with bits of wood, metal, and plastic, leading me to believe that his neighbors were the miners, factory workers, and farmers who were struggling to survive during these economically difficult times. Vitaly's house stood out in contrast: his yard and structure were well-kept, with vegetable gardens flanking both sides of the house. In the back, there was an outhouse and a chicken coop.

Once inside, Vitaly lit a coal-burning stove and almost immediately the chill evaporated. My eyes roamed, taking in the furniture, the knick-knacks on the shelves, the photographs and the art on the walls. A small black-and-white television with a rabbit-ear antenna perched on a shelf directly across from a sink that had been harnessed to a water tank balanced precariously on the opposite wall. There was no plumbing in the village, so all water was pumped from a communal well and hand-carried to the home. Unexpectedly, Vitaly placed a bottle of vodka along with a jar of pickles and a loaf of bread on the table. "So much for tea," I thought, as he filled three glasses before toasting "*Za Droojzba*—To friendship!" We touched glasses. I felt the slow burn in my throat, but had little time to recover because Vitaly wasted no time refilling the glasses. Recognizing that he was a pensioner on a limited budget, I felt guilty consuming too much, but I also didn't want to seem ungrateful. After the second glass of vodka, he began to tell his story, in English so that he could make sure that I understood what he was saying. Sometimes he would stop abruptly, asking for a word in English, and once I gave it to him, he would continue.

He began by telling me that he was a pensioner, having moved to Artyom from Central Siberia a few years earlier to start a new life after his wife had passed away from cancer. Then he began a brief history lesson, taking me back to the early 1900s. "I was born in China in 1920, in the city of Tianjin, as my father had emigrated—or more accurately been chased—out of Russia following the 1912 revolution. He was an officer in the White Russian army and was forced to flee, along with thousands of others, officers and soldiers, to northern China to avoid being shot. He escaped with little more than his family and a small amount of clothes. Tianjin, a seaside town south of Beijing, was where we ended up living for the next twenty years. While in Tianjin I attended a missionary school where I studied English, Chinese, and Russian along with math and science. During the early 1930s, there had been simmering unrest between Japan and China, because Japan was aggressive in their policy to secure raw materials and other resources like coal, going so far as to enslave Chinese workers to work on their projects. In 1931 the Japanese invaded Manchuria, which was followed by several small-scale intrusions leading up to the 1937 Marco Polo Bridge incident that led to a full-scale war between the two countries. The Japanese achieved success with victories in Shanghai, and by the end of 1937 they had captured the Chinese capital of Nanking. After failing to stop the Japanese in the regional capital of Wuhan, the Chinese central government relocated to the Chinese interior. By 1939 the war had reached a stalemate, with China turning the tide with victories in Changsha and Guangxi using guerrilla warfare tactics. Battles and life in general were less clear with Japan enmeshed in World War II and fighting the US, until the eventual surrender on September 2, 1945 following the two horrific atomic bombings of Hiroshima and Nagasaki and the Soviet invasion of Manchuria."

After another round of shots, he continued. "I was captured by the Japanese army during the initial invasion of Manchuria by Japan in 1937. I stood out from my fellow Chinese soldiers with my big mess of red hair, six-foot frame, and huge nose. And as such, I was singled out by the Japanese and given the choice of going to a prison camp with the Chinese prisoners or agreeing to return to Russia as a Japanese spy. Japanese prisons had a horrifying reputation, but I also considered Russia my homeland and did not want to betray my roots. I asked for a day to think it over and when they agreed, I escaped to the forest, where I joined Mao's Eighth Army."

Again, he stopped speaking long enough to fill our glasses with vodka. After we drank, he continued. "Over the course of the war I was shot five times." With this, he pulled up his shirt and pointed to faded scars on his chest and back. "In October 1934, Chiang Kai-Shek and his troops surrounded the Communists and were prepared to declare victory. Mao led his army of farmers and peasants on The Long March which led to an eight-thousand-mile chase across the country. Many of the troops on both sides were severely malnourished and poorly clothed. Communist mythology celebrated the Long March as a great victory solidifying Mao Ze Dong's leadership, but it was those soldiers themselves—who made it to the end of the march, overcoming rugged terrain and sub-zero temperatures, dangerous river crossings, attacks by various warlords, and the continual pressure from the Kuomintang—who should be seen as the heroes. It took ten more years of fighting before Mao secured control of China, chasing Chiang Kai-Shek and his supporters to Taiwan. As a Caucasian, I stood out from the Chinese—there were few foreigners in Manchuria. I loved the adventure of living in the forests and mountains and formed an incredible bond with my fellow soldiers. We had little food and we suffered through terrible weather. During the winters, we would drink water flavored with chili peppers to give us energy and keep us warm. With the help of the United States, the Japanese were eventually driven out of China, which should have been a happy time for us. Instead, due to the civil war that had been brewing in China before the Japanese invasion, the killing and violence continued as Cheng Kai-Shek again focused his troops against the us, issuing arrest warrants for all of Mao's supporters including a tall red-headed white man. I hid, hoping to avoid the Chinese prisons, which were as frightening as the Japanese camps. Since I was so easily recognized, it was hard for me to hide, and with few options, I went to the US embassy in Peking and asked for asylum. The US was in a precarious position because they were allies with China and didn't want to get involved with an internal conflict, so unofficially they allowed me to stay with a Marine barracks until a solution could be found." He took a breath and poured another round of shots. We toasted to world peace and I was silent, immersed in his story.

I wanted him to continue, but wasn't sure how long he could: the difficulty in speaking English was wearing him down. He often stopped and said a word in Russian, which led to me shrugging my shoulders as my grasp of Russian was far inferior to his grasp of English. He would either come up with another word or move ahead. After several minutes of small talk, he returned to recounting his past.

"It was a crazy after the war. Rumors circulated and people ran off to the port in the hope of getting a ship out of the country. Some were luckier than others, and soon every foreign embassy was packed with Chinese families, documents in hand, waiting in line to request a visa. Despite having lived in China for almost thirty years, my family was threatened and we remained in hiding. Three of my brothers, my sister, and my father were with Chinese friends in Tianjin, but since I was in Peking it was too dangerous to reach out to them. I heard afterwards that my father had immigrated to San Francisco and that a few of my siblings had found passage to Canada and Europe, but I had no way of knowing for sure. The US Marines treated me well but I could tell that they were eager to move me to avoid problems with the Chinese government. I was introduced to the finer aspects of American culture, like baked beans and the Glenn Miller orchestra. It was at this time that I heard rumors that Russia was offering citizenship to any Russian exiles. I made the fateful mistake of giving up my dreams to go to America and instead chose Russia."

His eyes glazed over at times as if he didn't even realize there was anyone else in the room. It must have been hard to talk to other Russians and garner any sympathy about his past; so many had similar tales of despair and hardship during the war years. I was fascinated but I was also conscious that Alex didn't understand a word of English and had sat for the past two hours drinking the shots of vodka and waiting for Vitaly to finish.

Vitaly continued. "I had an unrealistic view of Russia's past, due to

the glorified history I'd been told by my father, and this led me to be
excited about the potential of beginning a new life in Russia. My visa
arrived via the Marines and the Americans escorted me to a Russian ship
leaving for Nakhodka in the Russia Far East. I didn't have much to pack,
considering that I had been living on the run for the past two years, and
seeing this several of the Marines donated extra pants and shirts. I took
down their names and addresses and promised to write once I got settled.
Unfortunately, immediately upon arriving in Nakhodka, I was searched by
the Russian secret police and arrested as a spy when they found the address
book filled with names of American soldiers. Without a trial I was led off to
the gulag. Do you know the word *gulag*?" he asked. I nodded, quietly men-
tioning that I had read Aleksandr Solzhenitsyn, as a knot rose in my throat.

"I was sentenced to twenty-five years of hard labor and taken to a
Siberian prison camp. The temperatures averaged -40 degrees in the winter
and the life span of most prisoners was less than six months due to the
poor conditions and brutal treatment. There was no way to prove your
innocence and the more you tried, the worse you were treated. The gulag
was full of prisoners whose only crime had been to disagree with the ruling
Communists and we were all accused of being an enemy of the state. Society
had slipped to a point where anyone overhearing someone speak against
the government was required to report it immediately or they would suffer
the same consequences as a traitor would. Everyone was afraid to open his
mouth for fear of getting into trouble. Children turned on their parents,
brothers turned on each other. It was terrible. If you spent an evening
with friends, you would return home and wonder whether you had said
anything that might be against Stalin or the Communist Party. If you did,
you would run to the militia and report yourself before someone else. This
destroyed our humanity." We lifted our glasses and drank another shot.

I was tired but didn't want him to stop talking. It was as if I had opened
a novel and was unable to put the book down. Vitaly asked me if I wanted
Alex to drive me home—it was getting late—but I told him that I was in
no rush to go back to the hotel. As long as he wanted to talk I was happy

to listen. His talking seemed to be therapeutic, since he had an eager listener and was able to express his sorrow. After a few mouthfuls of food and another shot of vodka to wash it down, he continued. "My job in the prison camp consisted of chopping down trees with an axe. Guards directed us to cut the trees no higher than twenty-five centimeters off the ground and since the snow was sometimes three feet high, we would have to shovel it away before we could swing the axe. If a guard found that a tree had been cut at a height greater than twenty-five centimeters, the prisoner would be denied his daily 200 grams of bread. We had threadbare clothing and my shoes were scraps of cloth tied around my feet. I felt fortunate since some prisoners had nothing on their feet at all. I dropped more than 50 percent of my weight in only six months and was barely surviving.

"When I finally collapsed I was brought to the infirmary, where I waited for death. Fortune must have been watching: I woke from a semiconscious state to overhear the Russian nurses trying to read the English instructions on a bottle of medicine. None of the nurses had any English-language skills and I was able to summon up my strength to tell them that I spoke English and had studied medicine. They handed me a bottle to see if I was telling the truth and when I read it to them, they asked if I would like to be transferred to the nursing staff. They nourished me with hot soup and porridge so that I was soon able to assist them. Once I regained some strength, I was given other duties that included inspecting the food served to the prisoners and serving as an office clerk. I am not sure why they needed an inspector since the food consisted primarily of hot water mixed with sawdust and bits of rotten vegetables and potatoes.

"I couldn't complain or even try to help the other prisoners for fear that I would be returned to the fields doing hard labor. I served ten years before Khrushchev freed large numbers of political prisoners. I was thirty-two years old and furious that I had been wrongly accused and deprived of ten years of my life."

Alex had waited patiently for his chance to talk and as the hour grew late, he finally interrupted to tell me his story. He spoke slowly in Russian, as if to make certain that I caught every word. Vitaly interrupted with translations when I looked confused, but I understood that Alex wanted me to help him write a letter to a Russian church in Alaska that had offered visas for Russians wishing to immigrate to America. I suspected that this was a scam; many Russians seemed naïve about schemes promising wealth, visas, and business opportunities, but I agreed to write the letter for him and send it off via one of the Alaska Airlines pilots. As Alex and I prepared to leave, I told Vitaly that I would like to visit him again. I knew he was uncomfortable coming to my office, convinced as he was that the Federal Security Bureau was watching it. Vitaly and Alex weren't the only suspicious Russians; Tanya had mentioned that people within the administration speculated that I was a spy. Uri had told me of rumors circulating that I was actually fluent in Russian and just playing dumb.

DECEMBER 5, 1994

Tanya introduced me to several of the local English-language teachers and I find it hard to believe that we speak the same language. The Russian curriculum for learning English is based on British materials that appear to date from the 1940s. Since many of the teachers have never had the opportunity to speak with a native English speaker, I will continue with the goal of visiting elementary and high schools to allow the students to practice their English, as well as working on the Junior Achievement program. I enjoy talking with the students, since provides the students with a chance to deepen their insight into America by letting them interact with a real American. I begin my presentation with my background and a description of the Peace Corps and our goal of promoting understanding between America and other countries. Then I open it up to questions. The students, initially shy, require some prodding to speak up, but eventually become quite animated, leading to a deluge of questions—few of which are related to the work at hand. Surprisingly, most ask about my marital status and whether I think Russian girls are as pretty as American girls. The girls dress more provocatively than my recollection of American girls of their age and they apply such brightly colored lipstick that they resemble circus clowns more than the magazine models they hope to emulate. The most mind-blowing aspect comes when the students line up and ask for my autograph at the end of our session. I doubt anyone will ever ask for my autograph again, so I happily oblige.

The Russians are incredibly curious about my life in America. Since international news is limited, many Russians' primary means of learning about America is through Hollywood movies, sitcoms, and in particular, the soap opera "Santa Barbara," which runs daily on Artyom's only television station. Students often ask me about the characters and, much to their dismay, I am unable to provide any information since I have never seen the show.

My social life in Artyom has been active, with a steady stream of introductions to the single women. These women have been friendly and on the shy side when first introduced, but if in a social setting and with vodka flowing, they open up quite a bit. There is a housing shortage and, with high unemployment, there aren't many eligible women with their own places. Since I am still in the hotel, opportunities for a rendezvous have been less prevalent than I would prefer. The Peace Corps medical office provides us with condoms as needed, which is their way of minimizing situations down the road. Strangely, Russian women react poorly when I bring out a condom, expressing hurt that I think that they are whores and unclean. Most Russian women use IUDs or similar devices, since the local condoms are imported from China and of dubious quality.

The more time I spend building a network of friends, the more I have learned about local politics. Artyom's biggest industry is coal mining and the big story at the "water cooler" is the prospect of a miners' strike to protest unsafe working conditions as well as an arrear of pay lasting for five months. This all came to a head after a mine collapsed, killing two local men. Almost everyone in Artyom has a relative or friend who works in the mines and there is little respect for the mine owners. Also at issue is the fact that, despite having the mine in Artyom, there are electricity shortages. All of the coal is shipped off to South Korea, Japan, or China in exchange for hard currency, which likely ends up in the pockets of the politicians.

Health conditions are also of concern due to poor sanitation and limited education on what constitutes a healthy lifestyle (diet, hygiene, and exercise). This has led to warnings of tuberculosis and other viral outbreaks. The Peace Corps has made sure that we have been vaccinated against everything from tuberculosis to encephalitis, but many of my Russian colleagues are not as fortunate. Officials declared a state of emergency in a neighboring city after an outbreak of diphtheria claimed forty-three lives.

DECEMBER 8, 1994

While riding public transportation I keep my facial muscles tensed, my teeth clenched, and I avoid eye contact, to fit in with the Russian commuters. When waiting at a bus stop or on a train platform, I let my arms hang down, hands at my side and out of my pockets, contrary to the Western posture. Being anonymous has its advantages, since I am free to observe without having to engage in small talk or fear of becoming a target. Today I took the train to Vladivostok. The scenery ranged from absolutely beautiful to utterly depressing. During the summer, views along the coast are spectacular, with shimmering blue water and rocky cliffs. In the winter there is a lack of color: the only things to see through the train windows are the occasional ice fishermen who appear like polka dots on the frozen ice. If you want to see the negative effects of living in a mining area, all you have to do is look at the soot-stained snow or blow your nose: the particles of coal dust are everywhere. What you can't see is the poisoning of local waters from the nearby nuclear submarine base. Unsafe radiation levels are well known and so severe that we were lectured by local environmentalists during our training to avoid swimming at most of the local beaches and eating any locally caught fish. As you near Vladivostok, you pass the naval headquarters where hundreds of rusting ships sit in dry dock; a sad reminder of what had once made Vladivostok the envy of the rest of the Soviet Union.

I got off the train in the heart of Vladivostok and walked ten minutes to Masha's apartment, eager for a cup of hot tea to warm my frozen hands and a kiss to warm my heart. I waited five minutes in the dark stairwell, stomping my feet to keep the circulation going, before giving up and leaving a note. I then walked back to the tram station to catch a ride to my host family's apartment. I should have worn a hat—my ears were burning and I could anticipate Mama's unmerciful scolding—but it is hard to look sexy with hat-head. It took an hour before I stumbled into the apartment and I tried to remove my coat and gloves quickly, hoping that Mama wouldn't notice my hatless head. No luck. I suffered a ten-minute lecture while Papa smiled at me from behind the doorway. To add insult to injury, they told me that Masha had called five minutes before my arrival and had not left a number for me to call her back. I had no way to call her back and didn't want to spend another hour in transit without a promise of seeing her at her house.

Most nights at my host family's apartment end with drinking tea with Mama in the kitchen and talking about our dreams for the future. Now that I lived alone, I missed these talks, and when I mentioned this to Mama, tears came to her eyes. I told the family about my new life in Artyom, leaving out the drunken nights with Uri and my occasional tryst. They laughed when I told them about the harvest festival and smiled with pride when I told them about my evenings drinking with the mayor and his friends. I was so comfortable at the apartment that I fluctuated between going to a party at Karl's apartment or staying in with them. The lure of a party was too strong and at 8:00 p.m. I left. Mama forced me to wear a homemade woolen hat and then gave me such a strong hug that I almost coughed up my dinner. Three months ago we had been strangers and now I really felt like I was part of the family.

It was so cold that I actually kept the hat on until I got inside Karl's building, and then spent several minutes trying to comb my hair with my fingers. On the way there I'd stopped at one of the kiosks when I noticed another bottle of "Terminator" vodka with Arnold Schwarzenegger's picture on the label. This was too good to pass up. Anybody with a bathtub and a distillery could make vodka and sell it at the markets; there isn't much of a regulatory system in place. Illegal vodka is so common and dangerous that the papers are full of stories of people dying or going blind from drinking the poorly made alcohol. I was instructed shake the bottle vigorously and check the size of the bubbles to determine whether it was safe to drink.

When I got upstairs, the party was in full swing with a Dire Straits song on the stereo and several couples dancing in the living room. Before arriving in Russia, we had been advised to bring as much music with us as possible since there were few radio stations and no music stores selling tapes or CDs. To help relieve the monotony of listening only to our own collections, we traded with each other whenever possible.

I had just opened a beer when Masha and two friends came through the door. They had braved the weather and made the journey across town after receiving an invitation from Karl. Masha looked beautiful. It was an awkward few minutes as I voiced my frustration at not having been able to get in touch earlier in the day. She told me that she had tried reaching me for the past three weeks at my office number, but kept getting the answering machine. Answering machines are a novelty in Russia and, as silly as it sounds, most people don't understand how to leave a message. Anyway, I never received a message and had no idea how hard she had been trying to reach me. We spent the night dancing together. All of my apprehension about continuing our relationship faded as we drank more and became increasingly intimate. I kept thinking how surreal this would seem to my friends back home, watching me dancing with a beautiful Russian woman to the Bee Gees while drinking vodka by the bottle.

DECEMBER 12, 1994

I had promised to visit Vitaly this afternoon and at exactly five o'clock he showed up outside my office and together we walked the two miles to his house. Thanks to all of the walking I had done in Vladivostok, this trip barely made me sweat. After a welcoming glass of tea, he brought out a bottle of vodka, setting it down on the table with a thud. We talked about my work for the administration, of which he was incredibly suspicious, believing that either I was a spy or they were using me to gain some sort of political advantage. I promised him that I wasn't a spy and that I wasn't providing any information on my clients to any agency, Russian or American. He believed me to be a bit naïve, but decided to continue with our relationship despite any misgivings. After a few more glasses of vodka he continued his story.

"After my release from the gulag, nervousness set in: I suddenly had to come up with a plan for my life. I had never lived in Russia outside of a prison camp and the Soviet government required us to seek permission to leave Siberia. They worried that there would be a great influx of freed prisoners to the cities, which would be unable to accommodate us. So they were encouraging us to move to the smaller rural towns since they were in need of labor to maintain the agricultural and mining industries. I had no friends and no idea if any of my family remained in Russia. In addition, all Russians were required to carry identity cards and on the top of my card in big letters there was the word *convict*, despite the fact that all of my charges were dropped due for lack of evidence. Just because I was no longer in the gulag didn't mean that I was a free man."

We drank another shot and I stared into his eyes. It was inconceivable to imagine living this way and it made me sad to think how much we Americans took for granted. I wanted all American teenagers to hear Vitaly's story so that they would understand what our parents and grandparents had fought so hard to protect. Vitaly went on to tell how he had eventually found work in a photography shop and then met his future wife, a war widow who was living alone with a young son. There were so many widows in Russia because of the war and Stalin's purges that any man, even a former prisoner, was considered a good catch. Vitaly told me of rumors that as many as forty million Russian men had died in Stalin's purges and that another twenty million died fighting the Germans. Vitaly eventually married this woman and adopted her son. Within a year she got pregnant and they had a son of their own, naming him Oleg. It was then that he was contacted by a brother who had also immigrated to Russia and was living in Moscow. Vitaly was unable to get permission to move to Moscow, so his brother joined him in Siberia. His dream of having a real family life had finally come true.

All went well for several years until everything crashed five years ago. In a span of three weeks, his brother died in a car accident, his wife died of cancer, and his adopted son was killed in a work accident. Vitaly was beside himself with sorrow and decided that the only way that he could continue to live would be get permission to move away from his Siberian city where there were so many memories. He wanted a fresh start in a new place to free himself from the pain. He applied for permission to move to the Russian Far East where he hoped that he could use his Chinese language skills to earn a living. The government granted him permission to move with his son Oleg, who was now eighteen years old. For a while, things appeared to be going well for them: they found a house and Vitaly had begun to make contacts with local businessmen. Unfortunately, after little more than a month in Artyom, Oleg got arrested for stealing a car. He had been spending time with a group of teenagers, whose parents had mafia connections. When they got caught, the other kids shifted the blame to Oleg and he received a five-year jail sentence. I could understand why Vitaly had so much sadness in his eyes.

DECEMBER 13, 1994

The highlight of my week was watching Linda leave for the airport on her way back to America. Besides getting my own apartment, I will now have full control of the business center and can coordinate with Tanya and Vera , my two assistants, without having to argue about every decision. I am particularly eager to have a kitchen again so that I can entertain and repay the hospitality that has been lavished upon me since my arrival. As I gleefully expressed my excitement, Uri warned me to be careful as the FSB, formerly the KGB, was responsible for the remodeling of the apartment and I should take the necessary precautions—nothing I said or did in my apartment would be private. Uri has become a close friend and it surprises me that even he has doubts about whether I am a spy.

The mayor formally appointed Anna Gregorovna as my official sponsor within the administration. Since my assignment and subsequent move to Artyom, she had been cordial but distant, as if she resented having to spend part of her day babysitting the American. Now that Linda is gone, she's opened up and seems more eager to develop a relationship with me. On the afternoon of Linda's departure, Anna stopped by the office and invited me to her home for a birthday party. I was unsure of what to bring and didn't want to break protocol on my first visit, so I played it safe and brought a bottle of Champagne and a box of chocolates. As a foreigner, I am not held to the same standards as the locals and since the Russians have no idea what to expect from American culture, I have a free pass to do as I please as long as I avoid any major faux pas. Even so, I felt a little nervous as I approached her door and more so once she invited me into the room, where I noticed that I was the only man in a group of sixteen.

Anna introduced me to each of the women and amid a jumble of hand-shakings and mumbled greetings I took stock of the situation. I spent the first thirty minutes answering questions about my life in America and about how I was enjoying my time in Russia. Russian custom dictates that at a party, the men are responsible for opening all liquor and wine bottles, which became a full-time endeavor for me. In between bites, I would be handed another bottle to open. I didn't mind doing this, but as I was a novice when it came to opening Champagne, I feared that I would end up spraying half the bottle across the table with each pop of the cork.

The meal progressed well until, as I watched in horror, the table and chairs were pushed aside and a boom box was brought into the room. Anna inserted a cassette and immediately Russian pop music burst from the speakers. Two women grabbed my hands and I was thrown into a gyrating circle of perfume-scented women. I did my best to avoid stepping on anyone's toes while forcing a smile. I was about to pretend an injury when in walked Louba, Anna's eighteen year-old daughter. I was dragged from the dance floor and we were formally introduced. Louba, a student at the Technical University in Vladivostok, spoke English well—a pleasure after spending so much energy speaking Russian during the party. As a teenager herself, she recognized the discomfort I felt being surrounded by older women and she invited me to join her in the kitchen. We talked about what she was studying and she advised me that she was preparing to take an English-language proficiency exam to qualify for an American study-abroad program. My invitation suddenly made sense as Anna joined us in the kitchen and asked if I would tutor Louba over the next few months prior to her taking the exam.

It was after nine p.m. when I returned to the hotel and I was ready to catch up on some much-needed sleep, but instead loud music and a haze of cigarette smoke greeted me at the door. A party was in full swing in the reception area, with the mayor and his friends drinking vodka and munching on an assortment of appetizers. Before I could sneak into my room, the mayor caught sight of me and shouted "Reech!" over the music. The mayor shoved a glass of vodka into my hand while wrapping his arm around my shoulder. It would have been disrespectful not to join him and his friends, so I smiled and said, "Just one drink," which caused an outpouring of laughter. The mayor asked me to bring out my photo albums, and soon I was hooked into a night of drinking while showing pictures of my friends and family to a dozen drunken mafioso. It still amazed me when I would look around and see that I was completely surrounded by non-English speakers and was able to communicate in full sentences, when only three months earlier I was unable to read the Russian alphabet much less pronounce any words. The mayor appreciated my going along with him and it highlighted the symbiotic nature of our relationship as we both benefited by being in the company of the other. It made him look like a progressive to be on good terms with the American and I benefited by being treated like a VIP.

The following morning, I got to the office early and turned on the computer, fixed a cup of instant coffee, and began to check email. John had sent me a note saying that Holly was coming to Vladivostok for the weekend and that there would probably be a party somewhere, so I was welcome to stay with him. I was eager to catch up on the volunteer gossip; I was isolated in Artyom and it had been a few months since our swearing-in ceremony and the subsequent separation of our group.

I had trouble focusing on work and by two o'clock I decided that I may as well play hooky. I had yet to walk up to visit Vitaly on my own, but since the sun would still be shining until 4 p.m. I would be fine. I knew he would be excited to see me, so I made an excuse to Tanya and headed out. Aware that Vitaly was on a limited budget, I stopped off at the outdoor farmer's market, buying much more than we could possibly eat so that he would have leftovers during the week. I didn't know where to go to get specific items that I needed and ended up walking past every kiosk in the hope that I would find something interesting. On this trip, I felt fortunate to find a can of salmon, a loaf of bread, an assortment of vegetables, as well as the ever-important bottle of vodka. There is a Stolichnaya distillery in town and the cost of a bottle is the equivalent of one dollar, which is less than it costs to buy an imported can of soda.

Vitaly opened the door with a big smile. I reached out to shake hands and he stepped back, admonishing me never to do that. "In Russia it is considered bad luck to shake hands across the entranceway because in the olden days family members were buried under the thresholds of the door to protect the living. It was said that if you greet someone while standing over the threshold, you will soon quarrel with him. Once inside, you can greet in any manner you like," and with that he offered a warm handshake. "I hope you don't mind my just stopping by," I started. He cut me off before I had a chance to finish my sentence, telling me that I was always welcome and never needed an invitation. Together we unpacked the groceries and then he put a pot of water on the stove to boil for tea, which required shoveling coal into the stove that served as both a range and heating furnace. Once the tea was ready, I joined him at the kitchen table and he brought out his photo albums, which helped put faces to the people in his stories. I was shocked at how much he had aged during the past five years. His hair had turned from orange to white and his once-proud shoulders now stooped. I asked him if he had been able to use his Chinese language skills to his advantage, but this was apparently a sensitive subject and required a glass of vodka prior to my receiving an answer.

For the next half hour, he told me how he had gotten mixed up in a get-rich-quick scheme with a local businessman who said he was looking for a Chinese-speaking Russian to work with a group of Chinese merchants. The man convinced Vitaly to put up his life savings as a down payment on a shipment of Chinese goods, promising to pay him back half of the profits plus his investment once the goods were sold. The man ended up taking all of the goods and the money, leaving Vitaly with a big debt to the Chinese merchants and the loss of his entire savings. The legal system is inept, as were the police in following up on the theft, since Vitaly had no way of bribing the police to do anything. Vitaly's business naïveté and inexperience led to his trusting the man, which cost him his reputation as well as his money. Vitaly, like many other Russians, was unprepared for the dog-eat-dog world of a capitalist society. Most seniors had lived under the care of the government, but now that the government was broke they were forced to fend for themselves and had little savings or monthly pensions with which to do so.

DECEMBER 17, 1994

Papa's birthday was on December 10, and to celebrate Mama had arranged a party. I wanted to express my appreciation for all of the family's hospitality but had trouble coming up with an appropriate gift. I settled on a deep fryer so that he could make French fries, a use of potatoes surprisingly absent in the local cuisine. I also gave him a framed photograph of the two of us taken on our trip to collect mussels. He liked the photo and loved the fryer. Mama invited the other Vladivostok-based Peace Corps volunteers, including Holly, visiting from Khabarovsk. I felt guilty that they were spending so much money on the party, so I helped out with the shopping—I didn't want to offend their dignity by offering them money. Everyone brought birthday gifts, which gave Papa a permanent smile as he paraded around in the shirt Gary had given him while pouring shots of the cognac brought by Karl. One of Papa's friends had brought his accordion, which led to Karl running home to get his guitar. By the end of the night the Americans were teaching the Russians Beatles songs and the Russians were teaching us their favorites.

DECEMBER 18, 1994

I returned to the hotel on Sunday afternoon despite the promises that I would be able to move in by the end of the prior week. I was frustrated that the repairs had not yet been completed, leaving me to sleep on the thin hotel mattress that is as bumpy as the blankets are itchy. To make matters even worse, the pipes leading to the hotel had frozen and burst, leaving me without running water. This morning I woke with a nasty hangover, making the entire situation unbearable. I had worked late yesterday trying to finish a report for Anna and when I finally got outside, all of the food kiosks were closed. Without a refrigerator or even a hot plate in my room, I was stuck. Fortunately, the only restaurant in town had reopened after a six-month remodeling period. The restaurant is considered Chinese because the chef is from China, but the food is typically Russian: plenty of potato dishes, salads, and fatty sausage similar to what you would find in any of the Russian cafeterias or city restaurants. The chef had occasionally stayed at the hotel when he wasn't sleeping at the restaurant due to his fear of being robbed. Being the only two foreigners created a mild sense of camaraderie between us. He could barely say hello and goodbye in Russian, and didn't speak a word of English, so our communication came down to a combination of hand signals and grunts. The women at the hotel howled with laughter when they would see us chatting or making hand signals to each other. His name is Won Mil Yon, which sounded like "one million" to me and was therefore easy to remember and pronounce. He has as much trouble pronouncing my name as the Russians do.

The restaurant was empty when I arrived and Won Mil Yon sat me at a table by the front window, trying to use my presence to entice others to come in. I had brought a book along to ease the discomfort of dining alone, and after ordering a glass of vodka, a loaf of bread, and a plate of Russian ravioli, I opened "The Brothers Karamazov." I was on the first page when the door opened and in walked Uri's friend Anatoli, known locally as the mayor's "muscle." He looks every bit the enforcer, with a pugilist's face and matching physique. He flashed a metallic grin while shaking my hand, telling me that he was hosting his goddaughter's birthday party in the back. I offered my congratulations and wished him well before returning to my book. I was tired and frustrated by my living arrangements and feeling a bit homesick to boot. I missed the comfort of having old friends or the mindlessness of sitting in front of a television with English-language programming. I poured myself glasses of vodka and toasted a friend back home with each sip, engaging in imaginary conversations.

I was about to pay my bill when I remembered Anatoli and his guests in the back room and decided to send them a bottle of Champagne. I had been invited to several meals at his house and thought this would be a nice way to return the hospitality. I wanted to leave before the wait-ress delivered the Champagne so that they wouldn't feel obliged to invite me to join them. This plan collapsed when I went to get my coat and ended up talking with the coat-check girl. I had a nice buzz and since she was cute and flirtatious, we ended up laughing together as I complained about my homesickness. I had all but forgotten about sending the bottle of Champagne when Anatoli's goddaughter grabbed my sleeve and insisted that I join them for a toast. I didn't want to offend her or Anatoli, so I agreed to have just one drink. I returned my jacket to the coat-check girl and winked back at her as I allowed myself to be led into the back room.

Under a dim light, I squinted through the smoky haze. Fragments of conversation echoed against the mirrored walls. "Reech!" Anatoli bellowed, pointing toward an empty chair. Fourteen people sat squished together around a table covered with plates stacked with rice, potatoes, chicken, pork, mushrooms, and others dishes that I couldn't identify. In addition to the food, there were at least twenty bottles of vodka and Champagne wedged in between the dishes. In America the excess would seem beyond comprehension, but here to overindulge was a sign of having "made it." The plates were huge with Russian delicacies including Beluga caviar. I sat between Anatoli's wife and goddaughter and blushed as I was introduced as the most eligible bachelor in Artyom. Anatoli worked introductions around the table, giving me each guest's name and their relation to him. Then the toasts continued in a staccato of shots that barely allowed me time to put my glass down before it was refilled. I must have had a dozen before the music started and I was dragged onto the dance floor. My "few minutes" had turned into an hour and I was thoroughly drunk.

Eventually I excused myself, claiming to have an early morning meeting. While retrieving my coat, I again flirted with the coat-check girl and, since I was getting such good vibes, asked her to join me for dinner at my apartment. She said yes, but enquired how drunk I was and whether I would remember inviting her. I sheepishly promised that I would, while struggling to zip up my coat. It was so cold outside that my body convulsed the second I stepped outside the door. At night the temperature often dropped to forty degrees below zero, which interestingly enough is the same whether in Fahrenheit or Celsius. The five minutes to walk to the hotel were the longest five minutes of my life. I went straight to my room and collapsed on the bed still wearing my coat and gloves and shivering uncontrollably.

RECIPE FOR RUSSIAN RAVIOLI

There are three kinds of Russian ravioli: *Vereniki, Calduni* and *Pelmenyi*. *Vereniki* is a Ukrainian version, which is often stuffed with cottage cheese (*Tvoroke*). Other popular fillings are cabbage and mashed potatoes. The cabbage can be fried or salted and mixed with onions and peppers. *Vereniki* are eaten with sour cream/*Smetana*. In the Primorski region they are often eaten with melted butter or vegetable oil instead of *smetana*. When cooking *Vereniki*, if you run out of stuffing, you can cook the dough by itself and the Russians call this *Galooshki*, which means naked. One local tradition is to stuff one of the *Vereniki* with hot peppers and garlic. The unlucky person who bites into this bundle of pain will be ridiculed while being praised for their good fortune.

The second version is called *Calduni*, which is derived from the Russian verb *coldavat*, which means to bewitch, or to work as a sorcerer or magician. This supposedly came about due to the appearance of a cook standing around a large boiling pot and scooping up and serving delicious little packages as if by magic. These are found frequently in Siberia, and are stuffed with meat and cabbage.

Pelmenyi, in contrast, are usually stuffed with a mixture of pork, lamb, garlic, onions, and peppers. The *Pelmenyi* dough is similar to the dough for *Vereniki* and *Calduni*, except it is made without eggs, using only flour and water. I cook and mix all of the meat ahead of time before stuffing the pasta so that there will be no worry about undercooked meat. The word *Pelmenyi* means ear and bread in an ancient Siberian dialect, which explains why *Pelmenyi* are ear-shaped. According to Russian tradition, *Pelmenyi* should always be served with vodka, not Champagne, wine, or god forbid, something without alcohol! I have been told to visualize a frosty, windy Siberia outpost with a group of soldiers huddled around a small fire in a security hut drinking vodka and eating hot *Pelmenyi* to stay warm.

Due to the large geographic footprint of Siberia and diversity of the inhabitants, many variations have evolved. Russians feel quite strongly about the protocol of eating these, reminding me of the way Italians feel about the appropriate time to drink a cappuccino (only in the morning on an empty stomach). Russians traditionally will only serve *Pelmenyi* at suppertime. A true sign that you have been accepted as a friend by your Russian neighbors is to be invited over for *Pelmenyi*. I have been fortunate to spend entire evenings sitting around a kitchen table, rolling out and stuffing the dough before cooking *Pelmenyi* in between toasts of ice-cold vodka. This is a communal effort and reminds me of family game night back in America, with the addition of vodka. *Pelmenyi* are served with butter, sour cream, vinegar, or even mustard. Some people cook them in bouillon with bay leaves, parsley, pepper and dill. They should be put into boiling water for 3 to 5 minutes when fresh and a few minutes longer when frozen. Some people make hundreds at a time and freeze them for a later date. *Pelmenyi* should always be served hot. As Mama says, "a cold *Pelmenyi* is not a *Pelmenyi*."

The dough for *Vereniki* and *Calduni*:

Ingredients:
1 egg
2 cups warm water
Pinch salt
2 cups flour (although you will add until dough is hard)

First put the water, egg, and salt into a large bowl. Mix well and then add flour until the dough is not sticky. Knead with your hands in the bowl until no longer sticky, then transfer to a floured surface and knead roughly for several minutes. The grandmother's way is to roll into a tube, as thick as a sausage, and then slice off circles which will then be rolled out and stuffed. Tanya's way is to divide the dough into two parts and roll out onto a well-floured surface. Then take a large glass and cut out circles. Whichever way you choose, you will then have to stuff with your choice of meat, potatoes, or cabbage. To stuff, place a spoonful of the mixture into the center of the dough and fold in half. Pinch the edges so that a good seal is formed. The *Vereniki* or *Calduni* should be cooked in boiling water for three to five minutes. After removing from the boiling water, mix well with butter so that they will not stick together.

DECEMBER 21, 1994

Yes, I finally have an address that doesn't include a room number and the word *hotel*. It took me all of twenty minutes to unpack my belongings as my entire wardrobe barely filled two duffel bags. I had half-dragged, half-carried the bags from the hotel, through a parking lot and then up four flights of stairs to my new apartment. I have an actual kitchen where I can cook my own meals, entertain with a degree of privacy, and above all, have a place to escape from the rigors of being a foreigner. The apartment consists of a living room, kitchen, and a bathroom the size of a telephone booth. There is also a separate area with a small bathtub and sink. I have been warned to keep the toilet lid closed and secured with a brick to prevent rats from pushing their way into the apartment. I fucking hate rats! In the living room, there is a couch serving as both my bed and a place for guests to sit. Unfortunately it doesn't pull out into a sleeper, so I have to sleep in a fetal position or hang my feet over the edge and the fabric is so abrasive that it tears at any exposed skin. As for the kitchen, only inches separate the table and chairs from the oven and refrigerator, but this place is my own and for that I am thankful. A small balcony is accessible through either the kitchen or the living room, but is so narrow that the only practical use is to hang laundry across it.

I had purchased a metal bucket and heating coil at the local market and this proved to be my most important possession. If you want to bathe with hot water, you need these two items: there is no hot tap water, despite the government's repeated promises. To bathe, I fill the metal bucket with cold water and then insert the electric coil, forgetting everything I have ever learned about sticking something electric into a bucket of water. Next I plug the coil into an outlet and hope that I won't be electrocuted. It takes about twenty minutes to heat the water to an acceptable bathing temperature so that I can use a coffee cup to scoop and pour water over my body.

The second most important item in the apartment is the telephone. Only 5 percent of Russian households have their own phone, so I am fortunate, although this doesn't mean that I can just pick up the phone and call home. I have to call the operator and put in a request to make an international call. After providing the number, I hang up and wait for them to call me back once the call has gone through. I can receive calls from America without having to do anything, which allows my family to contact me provided they remember the twelve-hour time difference. The view from my apartment is a bit on the depressing side: my windows face the gray concrete government buildings. But the proximity to my office and the consequent two-minute commute more than make up for the view, especially considering the winter temperatures and my ability to walk home to use the toilet.

I didn't have to wait long to take advantage of having my own place, as tonight was my date with the coat-check girl. I shopped at the kiosks until I had purchased enough ingredients to make a pizza and a tray of brownies. I also picked up a bottle of Champagne and some juice, not knowing what to expect from Sasha—this was our first date and my recollections of meeting her were a little foggy. She arrived a few minutes late and was so nervous that she had trouble speaking. I tried to put her at ease by turning on the stereo and offering her a glass of Champagne. After a few minutes of awkward small talk, I had her join me in the kitchen while I prepared the pizza. When I finally put the food on the table and we began to eat, she picked at the pizza as if she thought I was trying to poison her. She spoke no English and I questioned whether she really spoke Russian, for when she did speak it was in such a quiet tone that I had trouble understanding her. I ended up drinking most of the Champagne and had to force myself not to look at the clock every five minutes. After dinner she went into the living room and turned on the television. A Tom and Jerry cartoon was on and she became so fixated that it made me wonder whether she had ever seen a television. She laughed and clapped like it was a live performance, smiling at me during the commercials. When the program ended, she picked my photo album off the table and began flipping through the pages while I pointed out family and friends. When we had gone through all of the photos, we were again stuck in an awkward silence. With a Champagne-inspired approach, I leaned over and kissed her with the sound of Tom and Jerry in the background. It felt forced and uncomfortable and within a few minutes, we both eased away from our embrace. I told her that it was probably time for her to catch the bus back to her home, which seemed to provide her with as much relief as it did me. She had been seduced by my apparent local fame: she remarked that she had seen my photo on the front page of the paper and then later that night watched as I was invited to dine with Anatoli, a well-known if not well-respected "businessman." This may have clouded her judgement and resulted in her agreeing to join me for dinner, but her nervousness at going to a foreigner's apartment alone for dinner was probably too much for a village girl to process. I should have been more aware of the gap in our life experiences and the shock she would feel. I had been living in a hotel or at my host family's apartment for several months and the thought of having a girl over for dinner and sex struck me as an incredible opportunity—I selfishly thought only of my own desires. Spending time alone with her had not turned into the wild passionate evening I had fantasized about and instead was an awkward failure. I hoped that there would be no discomfort when I returned to the restaurant, particularly since it was the only restaurant in town.

Monday morning I was sitting in front of the computer with a cup of coffee when Olga, Tanya's best friend, walked in with her boyfriend and his sister Natasha. I was still excited at having my own place, and without thinking immediately invited them for dinner. Since moving in I had yet to do any real shopping and now that I was having guests I wanted to impress, a sense of urgency set in to stock my refrigerator and cabinets. I had gained confidence with the shopkeepers and was now able to order food and groceries, which sounds easy but isn't quite so in Russia. First you wait on line to order from the shopkeeper. They add up the cost on an abacus (no, I am not kidding) and give you a piece of paper with the amount. Then you wait on another line to pay and get a receipt. With the receipt in hand, you wait in a third line to exchange the receipt for the goods you have already picked out. Not the most efficient and a bit difficult when you are struggling with the language and have a line of impatient customers urging you on.

After years of scarcity, many Russians have developed an affinity for fat that far exceeds that of Americans, and therefore, it is a good idea to tell the butcher that you want just a minimal amount, to avoid spending time and money cutting away at your roast. During the summer months, I recommend arriving very early to the market since there is no refrigeration and the chance of contamination rises with the temperature and arrival of flies. For those who would order meat cooked to rare or medium rare back home, it is best to "tough it out" and have it cooked to at least medium well to save yourself from a bout of food poisoning.

When setting up your pantry here, the essential products are flour, yeast, salt, powdered milk, baking soda, pasta, rice, bags of onions and potatoes, bouillon cubes, tea, sugar, and any spices you come across. There is no consistent supply of foreign products, but chances are you will always come across something interesting. Living in America, I would have been embarrassed to be seen buying Velveeta cheese, much less having it in my house, but when I stumbled across a five-pound block in a kiosk, I immediately bought it and actually bragged to my fellow volunteers about my good fortune.

Possibly the greatest difference between Russian and American cultures is the Russian use of and need for family dachas, which supplement the winter diet as I have already explained. According to one of the pioneer Russian Peace Corps volunteers, they survived their first winter in 1992 on what was generously called the "White Diet," which consisted of flour, sugar, salt, potatoes, and cabbage. Now, two years later, the amount of goods available has increased, although it is still a far cry from what we expect in the West.

The art of not only surviving, but thriving in our new surroundings depended on our ability to develop relationships with our neighbors. Since I was comfortable cooking, I had no qualms inviting Russians to my apartment for a meal. And after spending so much time in the hotel, I had quite a few families whose hospitality I wanted to return. Some Russians were nervous about inviting Americans into their homes, so offering to host them first also eased their nerves. My initial dinners in Russian homes lasted five hours or longer, so I wanted to make sure that I was well prepared to host my first dinner.

I assumed that my Russian guests would be interested in sampling American dishes, but also knew that they were hesitant to try new things.

Russians also drink significantly more alcohol than most (non-college student) Americans and it is often seen as a source of pride for Russians to show off their prowess in drinking. Many foreigners, myself included, feel compelled to try to keep up. It is part of the culture. Over the past few months, I have learned a few tricks to avoid an embarrassing incident. When offered a drink, it is considered rude to cover your glass with your hand or to say no, but it's completely understandable if you raise the glass to your lips and take a tiny sip in lieu of draining the glass. To refuse to drink is considered an insult. Several of the volunteers advised their host families that they didn't drink alcohol, which was fine, but you need to be consistent because if the families see you drinking with others, they will be offended. Russians also tend to drink very little water or non-alcoholic beverages. I don't know whether this is due to the poor quality of the tap water or to the relative scarcity and cost of bottled water or foreign soda, but at many dinners, if you aren't drinking the booze, you aren't drinking at all.

One drinking tradition takes place when Russians meet a new acquaintance. The ritual begins with the cap or lid of a bottle of vodka being symbolically thrown away immediately upon opening as an indication that the bottle must be drained in honor of the new friendship. If you fail to finish the bottle, you are sending the signal that you aren't interested in developing the friendship. Russians are also incredibly serious about their toasting. Some toasts last several minutes, especially at the start of an evening. With my poor command of the language, I feign comprehension and stare back, nodding my head, waiting for the moment to down the glass. As an honored guest, I am expected to offer a toast. To offer a short toast to my hosts would be seen as uncultured, so there is great pressure as I run through my prepared words. I start by thanking my hosts and toasting to friendship, good health, and to success: all easy phrases to learn. The person or people toasting always stand and look toward the recipients of the toast. The first toast of the night is made by the host, in which the guests are thanked for coming. This is immediately followed by a toast in unison from the guests in honor of the host. This is then immediately followed by all the men standing and toasting to the women in the room. So, if you are a man, you will consume three large shots of vodka within the first five minutes. These aren't wimpy college bar shots, but juice-glass sized drinks that the Russians swig down without a hint of discomfort. Again, you can get away without finishing the glass as long as you make the motions of raising the glass to your lips.

At the end of the meal, coffee or tea is usually served along with cakes, cookies, or candies. These are good gifts to bring to a home in addition to a bottle of Champagne, which is widely available in kiosks. Any gifts that you offer from America, such as souvenirs from your home city, are also well received. When entertaining at your apartment, picture albums and magazines from home make great conversation pieces.

DECEMBER 25, 1994

There were no religious holiday celebrations, not even Christmas, while the Communist Party ruled the Soviet Union. Thanks to the new openness, many of the older traditions and rituals are once again becoming fixtures in Russian society. The reopening of churches, along with revival of rituals and traditions that had been dormant or hidden behind closed doors for seventy years, now had mass support and participation. Many churches had been converted to other uses and were now being restored to accommodate the growing number of churchgoers. During the Communist times, Christmas had been changed to a winter solstice celebration with Santa Claus replaced by "Father Frost" and his elves with "Snow Angels."

Father Frost is a Merlinesque figure with a flowing white beard, pointed conical star-covered hat and a multicolored robe. The Christmas tree is called a New Years' tree. I had become a little merrier as the holiday approached, caught up in the general excitement of holiday parties and gift-giving. I planned on celebrating with my friends in Artyom prior to traveling to Vladivostok to spend time with my family. This all changed when Tanya stormed into the office, begging me to volunteer to dress up as Father Frost for the local children. It sounded like fun and a good opportunity to improve my ties with the community, so I agreed, receiving a tremendous hug in return. As Father Frost, I would visit children in homes throughout the city. The children are required to dance, recite poetry, sing, or do magic tricks in exchange for gifts. The parents would buy the gifts and secretly give them to Father Frost, who would then hand them out to each of the children. In the past, the parents paid Father Frost to visit their homes, but I felt strange accepting money and offered to do it for free. If they persisted, Tanya recommended that they send a donation to the local orphanage. About two dozen families had signed up and Tanya was ecstatic: she was to dress up as the Snow Angel and accompany me on the visits.

Feeling in the holiday spirit, I returned to the hotel with a bottle of Champagne and a homemade pizza to thank the staff for taking such good care of me during my six weeks in their company. After listening to my complaints about not having a kitchen and the occasional bragging about what I could cook, they were anxious to see if I had told the truth. They would laugh at me, saying that it was very unusual for a Russian man to help out in the kitchen, much less plan and prepare a whole meal. They often repeated the saying "the only thing more foreign than the stove to their husbands was the vacuum," after which they would burst out in laughter. None of the women had ever tasted pizza, so I had little pressure: I wouldn't be disappointing them. I made the dough from scratch, rolled it out, and lovingly applied a coating of homemade sauce and an ample amount of grated cheese before topping it with a sampling of local mushrooms and smoked kielbasa. It was almost too beautiful to cut into slices. They applauded my efforts, begging me for the recipe so that they could surprise their families. As I had been the only hotel guest during most of my stay, they had grown as fond of me as I had of them.

DECEMBER 26, 1994

One of the perks of being the volunteer in Artyom was automatic assumption of the English Club presidency. Linda had started this group with some of the local English-language teachers and now that I was at the helm, I was able to impart my own style. I had attended one of Linda's meetings and felt it too formal and impersonal. The first thing I did was to lighten the mood, hoping to make the club fun for both those coming to improve their English-language skills and for me. And what better way than to include alcohol? With the first meeting scheduled for the week before Christmas, I asked each of the teachers to bring in pastries and I volunteered to supply the Champagne. For two hours we talked about stereotypes from both the Russian and American viewpoints. I told them to feel comfortable asking me anything or saying anything, since I didn't want them to feel restricted. I told them about my preconceptions of Russians prior to coming here. Since Linda and I were the only Americans most of them had ever met, it was interesting to hear how our behavior contrasted with their expectations. Linda had been adamant about restricting all questions of a personal nature, which was strange for the Russians who had so much curiosity. I didn't have any of Linda's concerns and welcomed the give and take. I felt that my openness was more in line with developing friendships and would hopefully enrich my time here. It took a little time (and Champagne) before they lost their timidity and our dialogue grew from questions about work and business to those of life and personal experiences.

After the meeting I ventured up to see Vitaly with a basket of food and drink. I wanted to make something impressive, but the only meat I could find was a package of chicken legs. So, along with these I picked up a few cans of vegetables and a bottle of vodka. The Russians call the chicken legs *Bush Nogi* or "Bush Legs," due to a humanitarian aid package that had arrived in the winter of 1993: then-President Bush had donated a million tons of frozen chicken legs in response to the opening of ties between the two countries. Russian chickens are more natural than the American versions, because there is no money to inject steroids, antibiotics, and hormones into the animals. This leads to the Russian chickens being more muscular and smaller in weight than the American chickens, so when the Russians saw these big juicy chicken legs it created quite a shock. I also brought Vitaly a paperback novel so that he could practice his English. His vocabulary had improved greatly since our first conversation and I hoped that if I gave him books, mostly American and British spy novels, his memory would continue to strengthen. While skimming through the first book, he looked up with a puzzled expression and asked me what a "redneck" was. I tried not to laugh. During Communist times, certain books were prohibited, including most written by American authors. Russian writers had to receive government approval prior to publication. One of the books that I had brought detailed a sexual encounter in a way that so flustered him that, he told me, he had to re-read the section several times.

During one of our prior dinners, Vitaly mentioned that he had received a letter from a distant relative in Moscow saying that they had located his half-brother in Montreal, Canada. It had been fifty years since he had seen his brother and Vitaly was pained that he didn't have an address to write him. Finding an address seemed like an achievable task for me, so I sent an email to my family in New Jersey and asked them to look up the Montreal White Pages to see if they could find Vitaly's brother's name. A few days later I received a response that included his address and phone number. Vitaly seemed incredulous that I was able to get this so quickly. Astonished and overjoyed, he couldn't stop smiling as he recounted childhood stories of their coming of age in China. He was so excited that he asked me to help him write a letter before starting our dinner. We camped out at the kitchen table with a samovar of strong tea and a note pad. I wrote fast to keep up with his words, constantly re-reading sections to him and allowing him to make corrections. For two hours we reviewed and edited the letter until he felt it accurately portrayed his thoughts. He had many questions about what had happened to the rest of his family and hoped that a response would bring closure. I also transcribed Vitaly's portrayal of his own life following the end of the war through to his current situation in Artyom.

During the visit, Vitaly invited me to spend Christmas and New Year's Eve with him. He had assumed that we would be together, since neither of us had any family in Artyom. When I told him that I had plans to be in Vladivostok, he looked crestfallen. To make up for it, I promised to celebrate the Russian Orthodox Christmas with him. It would come on January 8 according to the Orthodox calendar, and we would prepare a huge meal. He accepted the offer, but throughout the night and on my way home, I couldn't get his look of sadness out of my mind. The only salvation was that I had the letter he had written to his brother and that I would make sure it got sent out. I was emotionally drained and needed time alone to think and relax. I also wanted a break from the heavy drinking that I have endured. Everywhere I go, there seems to be a party and numerous toasts. I have been fooling myself that I need to keep up with the Russians in order to earn their respect, but inside I know I enjoy it, particularly the attention lavished on me. Every morning I wake up with a headache and lie in bed waiting for the fog to lift as pieces of the night unfold. I know this is destructive behavior, but I am young and invincible. I also feel that if it were not for the bonding during these vodka binges, I wouldn't have established such close relationships with Uri, Vitaly, and even Papa. The non-drinking volunteers, including Linda, often complained that they felt excluded and were often angry when they heard us laughing about the long nights we spent drinking with our Russian counterparts. They didn't receive as many invitations as we did, which they blamed on their abstinence. It is no surprise that getting drunk loosens both our and the Russians' inhibitions so that we are freer in our attempts to communicate and to ask more personal questions. Most women are expected to participate during the two initial toasts and can then beg off, politely declining. Some just take a small sip and put the glass back full without making a big deal of it, but to refuse outright comes across as an affront to the hosts.

DECEMBER 28, 1994

My first acting role in Russia, assuming the identity of Father Frost, turned out to be more of an adventure then I had anticipated. "They didn't just steal the Father Frost costume, they stole our driver too!" Tanya sobbed as she strode into the office. There had been some discord within the administration about the fact that an American was playing Father Frost, so I wasn't too surprised when I heard that some character had usurped the costume and driver. We didn't want to disappoint the children who had already signed up for the visit and had been fervently practicing, so Tanya went out to locate another Father Frost costume. A half hour later she returned with an old costume found in a storage closet and within minutes she was sewing, taping, and somehow making the robe respectable. This included gluing the long white beard to my face. It was a far cry from the new costume we had purchased earlier in the week, but it was better than nothing, and hopefully the children wouldn't notice the difference. Tanya's foresight in bringing her Snow Angel costume home had saved her from a similar predicament.

It was a typical Russian winter day with a fierce wind and temperatures dipping well below zero. Without a driver and with a route that traversed several miles, we had no choice but to stick out a thumb and hitchhike, hoping that our costumes would inspire a bit of philanthropy from the citizens of Artyom. We stood alongside the main avenue, my laundry bag—which was serving as Father Frost's gift satchel—clutched between my gloved fingers. I stomped my feet to keep the circulation flowing while Tanya waved her arm desperately at the passing cars. Several cars slowed, eying us with a mixture of suspicion and amusement, but none stopped. Eventually a car stopped and after hearing our story, agreed to take us to the first house on our list.

I knocked on the first door and shouted "Father Frost" when asked who was there. A chorus of squealing children scampered about as the locks were frantically unlatched. Once the door opened, I strolled inside bellowing a deep, "Ho-Ho-Ho!" I had failed to ask what Father Frost was supposed to yell, so I hoped that it would be the same as in America. While I held the children's attention, gifts were dropped into my laundry bag and instructions whispered to Tanya so that she would know which gift to went to each child. In the meantime I commented, in Russian no less, on how cold it was and how tired my feet were from traveling all the way from the North Pole. I finished my little speech by asking for some entertainment. The children were so excited that they talked over themselves and it took a parent's stern voice to keep them in line. They wiped their hands nervously on their best Sunday clothes waiting to recite poetry, dance, or sing to me. Once each had performed, I struggled to stand with all of the padding stuffed in my costume and waited for Tanya to hand me a gift. I took one gift so that Tanya could call out the child's name and so that they could come forward for their present. The parents beamed as the little ones unwrapped their gifts; laughter and smiles covered their faces. After the gifts had been distributed, the parents offered me a glass of cognac as well as a plate of kielbasa and bread. Since I had refused to take any money, I didn't mind accepting a small token of appreciation. I spent twenty minutes eating and drinking before Tanya pushed me toward the door whispering that we still had many more children to visit. By the time we had completed our route, encompassing twelve apartments, I needed a nap. I had been rewarded with at least one drink at each stop.

DECEMBER 29, 1994

John called me this morning to say that he is thinking of quitting in January. Being separated from his fiancée Mary, combined with having little to keep him busy at the office, was rough. These hardships, added to his lack of hot water, cable television, and any ability to shop for food, had him depressed. It is not unusual for volunteers to feel more homesick around the holidays, especially when we are so far north that we are dealing with twenty hours a day without sunlight. It would be a great loss if he leaves.

JANUARY 1, 1995

Late in the afternoon on December 29 I took on the challenging winter weather and rode the train to the Peace Corps office to collect January's monthly stipend before the holiday weekend kicked off. Several other volunteers had come in for the same reason, and there were several holiday parties taking place in Vladivostok. A festive mood prevailed as we regaled each other with tales of our recent adventures. It was comforting to hear that not one of us was alone in raising suspicion within our new communities and that others too experienced bouts of frustration and loneliness. Several of us worked on arranging the gatherings and getting the word out in the absence of telephones. Holly arrived as Gary, John, and I were heading out. She quickly grabbed her $400 in rubles and joined us on the train back to the city. With limited accommodations, we were forced to crash at the apartments of the volunteers in town or stay with our host families and while neither offered much privacy, it would be good to reconnect.

Gary was staying in a dorm at the same university where we had originally been housed while waiting for our family stays to begin, and this served as our central meeting and partying locale. Gary's dorm room was big by Russian standards, consisting of a large bedroom and a separate living room complete with a sofa for overnight guests like myself. The advantages of living at the dorm were the fifty-foot commute to the tram system and plenty of young coeds with whom to party. The negatives were a shared dorm kitchen and, more restrictively, a midnight curfew. The communal kitchen was so disgusting that even the rats made faces as they scurried past. Gary had purchased a hot plate to boil water for coffee, pasta, or soup, and if necessary, he had an iron to make grilled cheese sandwiches.

John and I stopped to buy snacks and alcohol on the way to Gary's and had hoped to find something special instead of the standard vodka. The thought of having a bottle of tequila or rum was a driving force, but the weather chilled our ambitions and we returned with the local varieties. Holly, Kurt, Karl, and Gary had beaten us back to the dorms and were already swilling the strong 12-percent Russian beer when we trudged in with our bulky winter clothes. As soon as we draped our coats on the back of our chairs, shot glasses were filled and Gary toasted us as his guests. We toasted again and again until we had consumed all of the alcohol. It was still quite early and we wanted some excitement, something other than sitting in a university dorm that was almost empty—all of the students had returned home for the holidays—and listening to each other's stale stories.

We needed something new to keep the flow of energy alive. Gary had invited two cute students to join us. These women spoke English well enough to supplement our poor Russian and they enjoyed hanging out with us and flirting, which was always a good start to an evening. Their names were Anna and Julia, two of the most popular names in Russia, which made it awkward as we now had relationships going with three different sets of women named Anna and Julia. Holly and Kurt had decided to stay behind, attempting to keep their budding relationship with each other a secret. Whenever I looked at Holly I thought about what could have been had we hooked up, but now I saw her through a different light and the luster had worn thin. Hooking up with another volunteer was common in most Peace Corps countries, but our group consisted of such a small number that it was awkward for everyone, particularly when things didn't work out well. That being said, I understood their desire for privacy as well as not wanting to brave the freezing temperatures to watch Gary, John, and I get drunk with a couple of Russian college girls.

It was so cold that we had to seek shelter in bars every half block to warm up. This inadvertently led to us showing up at the hotel bar much later and drunker than we had planned. We promptly ordered a bottle of vodka and several orders of fried potatoes in an effort to absorb the alcohol. After our meal, Anna and Julia had to catch a ride home; they were staying with their parents and didn't want to get back too late. We waited for them to grab a ride and then returned to the bar to continue drinking and people-watching, as the majority of guests consisted of wealthy Russian businessmen (mafia), foreign consultants (USAID), and high-end prostitutes. We made small wagers on whether the prostitutes would succeed as they preyed on the men at the bar. This was good entertainment, particularly in the absence of other options.

Not wanting the night to end but no longer enjoying the stale clientele, Gary stuffed our half-empty bottle of vodka inside his jacket and we strolled back into the night. Thoroughly inebriated, the three of us walked past the port and along a ridge of cliffs that sloped down steeply to the bay. The cliff dropped fifty feet to the beach, where the snow-covered sand and sea ice glistened under the bright glare of a full moon. During the day, fishermen would camp out on the ice sipping vodka while waiting for a fish to snag their bait, but now at night the ice was deserted as far as the eye could see.

There was a refreshing, almost sobering quality to being outside and looking out over the cliff along the coast at the flickering lights from hotels and mafia mansions. I looked at John, then Gary, and without a second thought jumped down the slope pretending to ski as I sailed haphazardly downward. My feet sunk through several feet of snow, momentarily hitting solid ground before I was tossed airborne. My arms flailed and I saw my boots silhouetted against the moon before I hit something solid with a loud whoosh as all of the air left my lungs. I had landed on the snow-covered rusted skeleton of a car. Before I could warn them John and Gary followed, not wanting to be upstaged by a crazy man from New Jersey. I yelled out and luckily both swerved, landing in snow banks only inches from where I lay. We shook off the snow and our giggles turned into full-fledged laughter as Gary pulled the bottle of vodka from his coat, miraculously intact, and took a deep chug.

The ice was thick enough for cars to drive over, but there was a sense of danger when walking over it, as scabs of thin ice covered the fishermen's holes. If you fell through, the current would quickly carry you far from the hole, making it impossible to swim back to safety. We needed to find a warm place soon and since there was no way that we could climb back up the steep cliff, we walked along the beach in the hope of finding a path back up to the road. After thirty minutes of trudging along we came to a big No Trespassing sign with the Russian military insignia, advising us that the area was off-limits. We could see a cleared road ahead of us that wound up to the street. Since it was so cold and we were thirty minutes' walk into this direction already, we decided to risk it and run up quickly to the street. We were only fifty feet from the street when headlights cut through the night, passing back and forth across the road. Immediately we dove into a snowbank, holding our breath and hoping that the snow would shield us. Without passports, a requirement for all foreigners, we would be in for a tough time. The Russian military was suspicious of Americans in general and would be even more so when we were trespassing in a restricted area. For ten panicky minutes we lay motionless as the sound of a slowly moving patrol car approached and then passed our hiding spot. "Stupid, stupid, stupid," were the only words that came to mind as I contemplated the penalty and embarrassment of being roughed up by Russian soldiers and interrogated before getting kicked out of the Peace Corps and heading home in disgrace. When the car had passed and enough time had elapsed to allow our heart rates to return to normal, we ran in a crouch up the remaining road and through the gate to the street.

The streets were desolate: the cold temperature and brisk winds discouraged most sane folks from venturing outside. Despite the wind and the cold our smiles returned and spirits improved as we moved farther from the naval base. The promise of warmth kept us moving forward and eventually the sparkle of flashing lights and the faint sound of Russian pop music signaled the onset of civilization. Red, green, and blue neon lights flashed "Vladivostok Hotel and Disco," and our pace quickened. This popular mafia establishment featured a casino and a disco, the entrance of which was staked out with women in fishnet stockings, skirts that barely passed their ass cheeks and high heels: the type of fuck-me pumps seen in porn movies. We could see several large men in crew cuts, black leather jackets, and sweat pants standing by the door, arms folded against their chests, staring at our approach. We had been walking in silence for several minutes, so neither Gary nor I had noticed that we had lost John. When we stepped up to the bouncers, they pointed behind us and we turned to see John lying in the middle of the road staring wide-eyed at the sky with a big shit-eating grin plastered on his face. "Are you OK?" we asked. A muted giggle escaped his lips. Gary pulled the bottle of vodka from his pocket and began pouring it, a few drops at a time, into John's mouth until he reached up and grabbed the bottle. "OK, OK, I'm coming," he said, getting to his feet.

The guards blocked our way, shaking their heads, as if daring us to take another step so that they would have an excuse to crush us beneath their boots. They decided that we were too drunk to enter, quite an accomplishment in Russia. We thought better of arguing. As we walked away toward the main square in the hope of catching a taxi back to John's apartment, John blurted out, "Rich shit his pants!" I reached around and touched the back of my pants—they were soaked. I walked to the street light and saw that my hand was covered in blood. I felt around and found a sore spot on my ass; I must have cut myself when I landed on the rusted car. Since there wasn't much I could do about it, we decided to deal with it when we got back to John's apartment. When we finally go to the apartment, my left butt cheek was throbbing. The second I walked inside, I dropped my pants and saw that the wound had bled considerably and had saturated both my underwear and pants. My chest tightened as I slowly probed with my fingers to see how deep the wound was and whether it would require medical attention. I wasn't particularly eager to have Gary and John inspect my buttocks, but had little choice. It was 2 a.m. and much too late to call the Peace Corps nurse. We had been warned not to go to a Russian hospital unless an absolute emergency, so that was out of the question. Based on my colleagues' medical expertise, it was determined that I needed stitches. The Peace Corps provides each volunteer with an emergency medical kit complete with needles and surgical thread, so I informed John and Gary that they had some sewing to do. Gary, being slightly more sober, seemed the better option despite his goofy grin, so I handed him the needle. How bad could it be? I took a big chug of vodka and passed the bottle to Gary before lying face-down on the couch. I felt him pour antiseptic on the wound and I clenched, waiting for the needle. After a few seconds I looked over my shoulder and saw Gary taking another chug. I reached for the bottle. We passed the bottle back and forth until he broke down. "I can't do it. I'm sorry, but I can't." John stopped laughing long enough to dig some gauze and antibiotic ointment from the kit along with a roll of duct tape. They pinched the wound closed and duct-taped it to prevent further bleeding.

I woke up the following morning, which happened to be the last day of 1994, with intense pain that spread from my ass to my head. I woke John and asked him to make some coffee; he told me to fuck off before sticking his head under his pillow. Gary hadn't moved from where he had fallen asleep on the floor and didn't look likely to be doing so any time soon. I popped a few Advils, splashed the ice-cold tap water on my face, brushed my teeth with my finger and a dollop of Crest, and then headed off to visit my host family. I prayed that blood wouldn't seep through the bandages and stain their furniture, which would undoubtedly require an explanation.

Mama wanted help in preparing for their New Year's Eve party: twenty guests were expected, most of them my fellow Peace Corps volunteers. I didn't want the family to spend money out of their own limited budget, so I had shopped ahead of time for groceries, including six bottles of Champagne. Mama had been in competition with Holly's family to see who would host a party and after much consternation, calmer minds prevailed and they compromised so that from 6 p.m. until midnight we would celebrate here and then afterwards we would move the party to Holly's family's apartment. Mama felt that it was indeed a competition, and pulled out all the stops in the hope that we would have so much fun we wouldn't want to leave at midnight. We went a little overboard in the kitchen, simmering, sautéing, baking, and sampling until every square inch of counter and table space had been filled. We baked trays of pizzas, cakes, and an assortment of dishes encompassing seafood, roasted chicken, and a variety of salads.

The family dressed in their finest clothes and I wore a shirt and tie, wanting to make up for the poor impression I'd made at—half-naked and dancing—at the going-away party. The guests, including my Peace Corps friends, also arrived well dressed and in a jubilant mood as the end of 1994 approached. The crowd was evenly split between Russians and Americans and they all mingled and seemed to be enjoying themselves. Papa named himself official pourer of Champagne and flitted about the apartment filling empty glasses, including his own. Mama was a blur, wending her way between conversations with trays packed high with appetizers. Tables set up along the wall struggled under the terrific weight of the salads, pies, pastries, pizzas, sea cucumbers, mussels, smoked salmon, caviar, chicken, pork, and pasta dishes. Each dish had been painstakingly seasoned and prepared and Mama beamed under the steady stream of accolades. Papa also smiled from ear to ear, and that might have had as much to do with his pride as his alcohol consumption. At a few minutes before midnight the tables were cleared and everyone held a glass of Champagne in the air as we counted down the final seconds of 1994. Three ... two ... one ... Happy New Year! We clinked glasses, toasted, drank, and hugged each other in celebration.

Despite knowing the arrangement we had with Holly's host family,

Mama seemed crestfallen when we immediately dressed in our winter garb and headed outside. John had promised to meet his host family for a quick celebration, so Gary and I agreed to meet him later at his apartment, where we would spend the night since Gary's dorm had a midnight curfew. Holly's host family also didn't want to be outdone: immediately upon our entrance, glasses of Champagne were thrust into our hands and the toasting onslaught commenced. As a group, we reenacted the New Year's countdown with the same enthusiasm as we had earlier in the night. Not wanting to offend Holly's family, we set in for a second humungous meal to chase down the copious amounts of alcohol. When the clock hit 2 a.m., Gary and I said our goodnights and braved the frigid temperatures to catch a taxi to meet John as promised. I would have loved to have just curled up on a sofa and slept off the mass quantities of food and booze, but I knew that John was counting on meeting us back at his place.

The streets were lined up bumper to bumper with traffic in every direction, making our attempts at hitchhiking to John's apartment futile. Our only option was to walk the four miles. Ordinarily this would have been risky due to late hour, but with so many people celebrating in the street it didn't seem dangerous. The ferocity of the winter wind forced us to stop several times along the way in bars to grab a drink and warm up before venturing back outside. The excitement and celebration was contagious and we chatted with other partiers, smiling and buying each other drinks as we slowly made our way across town. The sense of optimism for a better future spurred the partying among the younger generation, who were able to afford to be out drinking, in contrast to the pensioners who were living on diminishing state handouts and had seen their standard of living crash due to the massive inflation and privatization of most public services.

It took us an hour and half to cover the four miles, which wasn't too bad considering all of our stops. We had expected John to be pissed at us for taking so long or to be passed out drunk but worse than that, our knocks went unheeded. Our happy buzz quickly dissolved into discomfort brought on by weariness and the frigid temperature in the stairwell.

Having seen the traffic, we understood why he was late—but this didn't stop us from cursing him endlessly as we huddled together to keep warm. During a lull in our swearing we heard the sound of music and voices from a neighbor's apartment. With nothing to lose, I persuaded Gary to follow me and I tentatively knocked on their door. A rosy-cheeked woman in her fifties answered the door with one hand on her hip and an accusatory glare, as if expecting that we had knocked to complain about the noise. I explained our situation and she shrugged, stepping aside to usher us inside into the warmth of her home.

It was so nice to get out of the cold stairwell that we were overly appreciative. Surprisingly, several people were still awake and eager to party with a couple of lost foreigners. We joined the other guests who were sprawled out in chairs and on the sofa, and after explaining our predicament we introduced ourselves as they passed out glasses of vodka. This was the last thing we needed, but considering the alternative, we joined the toasting. To compensate for the awkwardness of invading their home, we felt obligated to entertain them with stories of our Russian experiences. They laughed at our self-deprecating jokes and repeatedly filled our glasses to wash down the plates of food. Since Gary was a vegetarian and most of the food contained meat, I ended up having to eat everything so that we wouldn't seem ungrateful. At 4:30 a.m. it looked as if our hosts were struggling to remain awake, so we thanked them and promised to visit again at a more proper time.

Stepping back into the cold, dark stairwell, we heard the sound of John's drunken Russian accented with his redneck twang. A carload of teenagers had picked him up hitchhiking and in appreciation he'd invited them back for a few drinks. Again, instead of being able to curl up on a bed and sleep as I craved, we ended up joining in for a few more drinks, until the sun rose and we begged to end the night.

JANUARY 2, 1995

I awoke on the first day of 1995 and stumbled into the kitchen to make a pot of coffee. My butt cheek still throbbed from the puncture wound, making me wonder whether it had become infected. I peeled off the duct tape and was pleased to see that a nice, clean-looking scab had begun to form. This was great, as I didn't want to have to visit the Peace Corps nurse and explain the injury. Starting 1995 hung over wasn't what I had planned, especially since John and I had agreed to have lunch at one of John's colleague's apartments at noon. We had already canceled on her twice, and without a phone, there would be no way to make an excuse.

Natasha, (a common Russian name) lived with her parents in an upscale apartment that was packed floor to ceiling with electronics and other assorted accessories, thanks to her father's "import/export" business. We showed up with a bottle of Champagne and some flowers, hoping to make up for our tardiness. After the obligatory kiss on the cheek, we were ushered into the apartment and promptly greeted by a large Rottweiler that crouched in the corner, its menacing eyes following our every move. When we walked by, its growl caused the hair on the back of my neck to stand on end. The dog belonged to the father, and was quite agitated by his absence; the father had been caught cheating a few days earlier and Natasha's mother had kicked him out of the house. The father had trained the dog and the presence of two unknown men in the house made it nervous.

Natasha told us to make ourselves comfortable in the living room while she joined her mother in the kitchen. I was starving because John's refrigerator had contained only alcohol and half a loaf of old bread. The dog followed us into the living room and kept watch like a secret service agent. John went to the bathroom, leaving me alone with the dog. I tried feigning interest in the television and stretched out on the couch, watching the dog out of the corner of my eye. Slowly it crept closer, so that eventually I could hear its breathing, as if it was testing my resolve. In a determination to show my toughness, I stared at the dog and forced a small laugh.

I definitely didn't scare or intimidate the dog: it immediately leapt across the room and landed with his full weight on top of me. My right arm shot up to protect my face just as its jaws clamped shut, catching my hand in a viselike grip. Everything was in slow motion. I must have screamed because Natasha and her mother ran into the room, followed by John, who was still buttoning his pants as he exited the bathroom.

I stared dumbly while the mother-daughter team applied antiseptic and gauze to my hand. The dog was now locked in the bathroom. After a series of apologies, we moved to the kitchen for lunch. I barely said a word during the meal, replaying the attack in my mind over the sound of whining from the dog and in a struggle with my incredible desire to leave. My hangover and butt-puncture wound were forgotten as the new throbbing of my hand took full stage. During lunch, I downed Champagne like water while trying to hide my shaking. Halfway through the meal, Natasha's mother, whose regard for men was apparently quite low, decided that the dog had been punished long enough and she let it out. Natasha smiled at me and said that the dog had learned his lesson and would behave. I kept my eyes glued to the table, never letting go of my butter knife. I wanted revenge so badly that I inconspicuously dropped chicken bones under my chair in the hope that he'd choke on them and then while he was gasping for air, I could step on his throat and smile. Immediately after lunch I made the excuse that I had to catch a train back to Artyom and walked out the door, vacillating between extreme anger and self-pity for my increasing number of injuries.

JANUARY 3, 1995

I forgot how good it feels to wake up without a headache! I drank my coffee solely for the taste of the beans and took my time reading a months-old *Newsweek*. After months of instant coffee, here I was casually sipping and imagining Juan Valdez atop a donkey on his Colombian plantation. You can't get actual coffee beans or even ground coffee here unless someone brings it from abroad or via a care package. I was drinking an Italian roast that was given to me as gift and was relishing how delicious it was in comparison to the slop that I normally drank. The few instant coffee variations available are imported from Korea; they taste of chemicals and invariably lead to an "instant" case of the runs.

It was too nice of a day to be inside, so I coerced John into exploring the city. A military exhibition was in full swing when we reached the central plaza, complete with soldiers posing beside newly polished tanks and aircraft. For a few rubles, you could stand alongside a soldier next to a SCUD missile launcher, or if you had a wad of rubles, you could sit in the cockpit of a MIG fighter plane. It's hard to see why the Russians get so upset when foreigners take photographs of the military equipment when any Tom, Dick, or Boris can buy his way into the cockpit for the price of a kielbasa link.

We continued walking along the pier, passing a ship called the *Vladimir*. A "Restaurant & Disco" sign on the boat piqued our curiosity, so we climbed a plank leading up to the main deck and followed arrows imprinted with the name of the disco through a series of passageways and up another set of stairs. There were no guards or sailors in sight, but a sense of unease set in as if we were trespassing. We finally reached a glass door leading to the bar, where a sign on the door stated that the club opened at 10 p.m. and had a 1,000-ruble cover charge, equivalent to US $20. This was excessive for the Russian Far East, but with few opportunities for adventure, the boat disco seemed a future possibility.

JANUARY 8, 1995

When living as an expat in a potentially dangerous foreign country, it is a no-brainer that special precautions should be taken to avoid trouble. In the Russian Far East, these would invariably include staying away from mafia bars or other places of dubious character. Somehow my internal voice of reason took a back seat to my twenty-something yearning for excitement.

This false sense of invincibility and a belief that I could talk myself out of trouble, regardless of the circumstances, led me to the humbling experience outlined in the pages to follow. Since arriving in Russia, whenever we wanted to party, we invariably spent time in the apartments of our friends and host families. The possibility that we had finally found a bar in which we could meet Russian women and drink in a new environment was exciting. We had been to several mafia bars and had always been treated with respect, although not particularly welcomed.

The night's ominous start should have been an omen: John made a beeline to the toilet just as we were about to head to the *Vladimir* for the evening. Twenty minutes of loud groaning interrupted by thunderous explosions were followed by his pale and perspiring face peering around the bathroom door to tell us to go on without him. As a Peace Corps volunteer, regardless of which country being served, casual discussion of digestive issues are common to our everyday conversations. We sympathized with John, but no way were we going to pass up on a night out to keep him company. Gary and I dressed in multiple layers of our warmest clothes along with our winter boots to face the brutal temperature, well below freezing. We left the apartment and immediately an icy wind tore through our jackets. This should have been seen as the second omen of the night. We made our way directly to the *Vladimir*, walking briskly to keep the blood flowing to our extremities. The ship's silhouette on the moonlit bay was ominous, lacking the vibrancy apparent we'd seen earlier, during the day. Taking the stairs two steps at a time, we reached the first level and, not seeing anyone, continued up to the second level where the faint sounds of the disco could be heard above the roar of the wind. There were a few women standing around the door wearing very short skirts and high heels. They were heavily made up and gave us the once-over as we walked past. We were so bundled up in our wool hats and thick work boots and still shivering while these women seemed oblivious to the cold.

We pushed open the door and soaked up the heat as well as a welcoming wall of smoke. It took us a few seconds to adjust to the dim lighting enough to realize that we were alone in the bar. Blinking Christmas tree lights sparkled across the dance floor and along the tops of the surrounding tables. We approached the bar and each ordered a beer. The bartender set two bottles before us, in addition to two complimentary shots of vodka. A few minutes passed before several tough-looking men entered, taking a seat in a far corner of the bar. They must have been regulars, because the bartender brought a bottle of vodka to their table without a word between them. Each of the men had the same style crew cut, brown leather jacket, sweat pants, and a cigarette dangling from his lips. They were the epitome of the Russian mafia: loud, intimidating, and easily recognizable. Over the next hour, several more mafia thugs and what looked like prostitutes filtered in as we continued our beer and vodka chaser routine. A surreal feeling enveloped us, as if we had stepped into a 1950s Clark Gable movie set.

The music was Russian techno-pop and loud enough to discourage conversation. Several Russian women approached us over the course of the evening, but the music was too loud to say more than a few words. Eventually several of the women ventured onto the dance floor, shaking and gyrating in their skimpy dresses, providing ample entertainment while we continued holding up the bar. By 2 a.m., the effects of a long day of drinking sunk in and we flagged down the bartender and paid our bill. We were on our way to the coat-check station when two women, wearing what looked like lingerie, asked us to dance. Wearing bulky construction boots and feeling clumsy didn't stop us from allowing ourselves to be led onto the dance floor. We must have looked horribly out of place. Our dulled senses, combined with a testosterone boost, spurred our interest and also unfortunately led to our failing to notice the glares coming from the men sitting in the back corner.

The woman I was dancing with moved in close, grinding provocatively and spinning around behind me to nibble on my neck. I looked over at Gary and he seemed similarly enchanted. I was running my hands up and down the silky material when my perfume-induced rapture was spoiled by a fist pounding into my shoulder. Thinking it was Gary, I turned, keeping the girl within my embrace. The same fist that had hit my shoulder now landed squarely against my nose, knocking me backwards. A young mafioso, barely out of his teens, stared at me with what I can only describe as hate. For several seconds we faced each other and then he turned his back and walked off to join his friends. I shook Gary's arm. "What do you want?" He seemed annoyed with my intrusion. "Some guy just punched me in the face!" I replied.

I was about to say that we should leave when a Champagne bottle came out of nowhere and crashed across the bridge of my nose. In slow motion I felt myself stumbling backwards as the bottle bounced upwards toward the ceiling. The sound of the glass shattering barely registered above the pulsating music. The teenager continued staring at me as I caught my balance and tried to make sense of what was happening. He lunged forward and instinctively I grabbed a hold of his jacket and slid behind him, grasping him in a bear hug with all of my strength. I ran in full panic mode toward the bar, hoping to slam his chest into the railing with the combined weight of our bodies. Unfortunately my aim was off and I ran directly into the Christmas tree alongside the dance floor, which then proceeded to crash down across several tables, sending drinks and ashtrays flying. There was a second of silence—the music had been turned off—and then a staccato of shouting erupted. I held onto my bear hug, knowing that it was the only thing protecting my face and chest as an onslaught of punches and kicks landed to my back, head, and legs.

Suddenly the kicks stopped and my fingers were pried apart. I had no fight left, not that it had been much of a fight anyway. I stood up and saw a look bordering between shock and pity from the Russians. Blood dripped like sweat down the sides of my face and out of my nose and mouth. My nose lay flattened against my cheek. I spit blood onto the floor. The owners may have been worried that the men had gone too far with a foreigner and didn't want any attention from the authorities; we were ushered toward the door while the manager handed us our coats. I wanted nothing more than to get outside so that I could get my bearings. I heard Gary swearing in English and felt his arm across my shoulders. As we passed the table of my attacker, he shoved it and several bottles fell to the ground. The manager stepped in immediately to usher us out before any further escalation occurred.

The cold did little to stifle the pain or staunch the blood, but it felt great to be outside in the crisp dry air. "Those mother fuckers," Gary repeated. I just shook my head, still trying to clear the cobwebs. "Fuck you! You mother fuckers can kiss my ass!" he screamed up at the star-laden sky. When we reached the street we had to walk past a series of Toyota Land Cruisers, the vehicle of choice for the local mafia. Gary's anger had built to such a state that he couldn't control himself and he ran toward the closest car and violently kicked in the headlights. As if encouraged by the sound of breaking glass, he continued to the next car and then the next. Meanwhile, the mafia guys had either followed us out onto the deck of the ship or had heard the noise and run on deck. They could hear the attack being inflicted on their cars and they ran down the stairs. We weren't aware that we were being followed until we heard the sound of feet on pavement.

We started running, but it was too late. A body leapt onto my back and together we crashed into the snow, my face shoved through the hard icy crust. A frenzy of kicks followed to my head, ribs, and legs. I rolled to my side and tried to stand, only to get knocked back to the ground. I jumped up and momentarily broke free, raising my hands in the air to surrender. This stopped the commotion and I yelled to Gary to do the same thing. Two guys grabbed my arms and held them up high so I was unable to protect myself while another unzipped my jacket and began rifling through my pockets. He took my wallet and passport before grabbing my wrist and unclasping my watch. With this out of the way, two other men, including the younger one who had started the fight, began hammering away at me while I struggled to free my arms. They took turns punching me in the face and stomach. I kept my mouth shut to protect my teeth, bracing for each blow. I looked up to see their smiling faces. The teen motioned for the others to back off, holding an empty vodka bottle in one hand while slapping me with his open hand. He brought the bottle down on the top of my head and I collapsed. I pressed my eyes closed, pretending to be unconscious.

I must have eventually passed out for real, because my next recollection is of waking up and not knowing where I was. Everything hurt. My eyes were swollen shut with caked blood. The wind blowing in off the bay sounded like a freight train, but otherwise the only thing I could hear was my own difficult breathing. I knelt in the snow and the throbbing increased. Then I saw Gary, motionless in a fetal position surrounded by bloodstained snow. I feared the worst. Then I saw his chest rise. His face was bloody and there was a wide gash across his chin. I gently rubbed his shoulder, speaking softly. My voice sounded foreign, my swollen lips muffling my words. "It's OK, man, they're gone," I whispered.

I looked around and was shocked by the amount of blood marking the snow. I helped Gary to his feet and saw the jagged edge of what had been his front teeth, all broken just above the gum line. He winced as the exposed nerves reacted to the cold air. "Let's get the fuck out of here before they come back," I whispered, trying to get his attention. I helped him zip his jacket and then, with me half pulling and half pushing him, we stumbled back to the central plaza. I attempted to flag down a taxi, but after a quick inventory, realized that neither of us had any money. I don't know how long we stood there before a Russian police car came into view. I ran toward the car and must have looked pretty scary, because they screeched to a halt and both the driver and passenger jumped out, their weapons drawn.

They yelled for us to stay put but I didn't care and just continued dragging Gary behind me. After I explained that we were Americans and had just been robbed, we were taken to a police station and asked to sit while they frantically called their superiors. I couldn't focus on what they were saying as the warmth inside the station released the tension that had gripped me since waking up in the snow. Finally we were told that they were going to take us to the hospital. This was something that the Peace

Corps administration had strictly warned us to avoid at all costs. I argued with them to call the US consulate or to drop us off at the gate. They capitulated after twenty minutes and dialed the consulate, but after a minute of ringing nobody picked up and there was no machine to leave a message. While this had been going on, a Russian doctor arrived. He began to assess our injuries, wiping blood from our faces with a damp cloth. Gary clutched a gloved hand over his mouth, his eyes glazed. I could feel his body tremble and knew that I needed to do something quickly.

With nobody answering at the US consulate, my second request was that they drive us to Ken Hill's apartment, explaining that he was the director of the Peace Corps and would be able to take us off their hands. I couldn't recall his telephone number but knew how to get to his apartment, so we were ushered into the back of a black police sedan and driven by an FSB (formerly KGB) agent to the apartment. It was 4:00 a.m. when we rang the doorbell. We looked like we had stumbled off a movie set, our faces streaked with blood and our eyes, lips, and noses swollen almost beyond recognition. Ken must have thought that he was having a nightmare as he shook his head in an apparent attempt to make sense of us standing there with the FSB. He welcomed us inside and we took seats around the kitchen table. I explained that we had been mugged, thinking it better not to mention that we had been in a bar fight before getting beaten up for vandalism; either of those events would likely get us one-way tickets back home. Ken called Gille, a Canadian nurse who worked for the Peace Corps, and then took several photographs to document our condition and justify our possible evacuation. When Gille arrived, we were given a preliminary examination to ensure that we hadn't suffered any life-threatening injuries and then taken to a Russian hospital for stitches and X-rays.

My mind was spinning as I feared that Gary was seriously injured. I was also concerned with the appearance, there at the hospital, of several Russian detectives who seemed determined to question us. Since Gary couldn't open his mouth without experiencing great pain, I volunteered to speak for the both of us. I kept to our story, stating that we had been mugged after leaving a bar. I didn't mention the *Vladimir* for fear that the owners of the Land Cruisers might have reported the vandalism, and that would have justified the damage to our bodies in the minds of the police. After I had given my statement, the detectives asked that both Gary and I report to their headquarters in the morning for further questioning. The Russian hospital, which had run out of surgical tape, wrapped our heads in gauze, leaving us like a couple of mummies, which when combined with our blood-soaked clothing didn't paint a pretty picture. I was amazed at how much blood there was on our clothes and felt lucky to be alive. Both of us had cracked ribs that ached with every breath and although my teeth were not as damaged as Gary's, there were chips where I had heroically blocked punches, bottles, and kicks with my face. My nose, although not extremely painful, looked terrible. We both were in need of additional medical care and it was up to the Peace Corps to determine whether we would be shipped back to Washington D.C. for surgery, since there was little faith in the quality of the Russian medical or dental facilities. Gary was in excruciating pain due to his broken teeth and a bruised kidney that caused him to piss blood. He also had a gash under his chin, the result of the mafia gentlemen finding Gary's Swiss army knife and using it on him. But overall, we were both quite lucky that this was all the damage done after what had happened to us.

Once at the dorm, we were given strict instructions to stay put until a car came to pick us for our second set of police questioning. We had been awake for twenty-eight hours. All I wanted was to collapse on his couch and sleep. But the Peace Corps is a small group and word travels quickly, so when we opened the door to Gary's apartment, Kurt and Holly were waiting for us. They stared up from Gary's kitchen table and waited for an explanation as to why we looked like horror-movie extras. Neither of us felt like explaining our own part in it all, so we gave them an edited version that resembled what we had already told the police and the Peace Corps. Despite having earned a reputation for partying hard, we had expected a bit more compassion from our colleagues than the "you got what you deserved" look we received. We knew we had taken a chance going out to the *Vladimir*, but we had done nothing to deserve the beating—at least the one in the bar.

I awoke with the sun burning through my eyelids. A throbbing pain coursed through every inch of my body, indicating that the healthy dose of painkillers I'd taken had worn off. If I moved, it hurt. If I breathed, it hurt. It took me ten minutes to get to my feet and walk the five feet to the bathroom. I looked in the mirror and a gruesome reflection stared back. If I weren't hurting so badly, I would probably have burst into tears. I walked to Gary's bedroom door and listened for movement and then knocked quietly until I heard him moan. He managed to mumble that he wanted a glass of water. I returned with a glass and two pain pills. Knowing how important it was to keep our story straight, we discussed our options and affirmed that we would deny any reference to having been at the *Vladimir* as well as to categorically deny kicking in the headlights, for fear that we would both be kicked out of the Peace Corps. We didn't want to lie, but saw this as our only option. The Peace Corps had an unspoken rule that any injury or accident that involved intoxicated volunteers or the commission of a crime would be grounds for immediate dismissal. Gary was going to say that it hurt too much to speak due to his broken teeth, so I would respond to all of the questions; in this way we wouldn't contradict each other.

The police interrogation room was right out of a 1950s Andy Griffin set. We sat across the desk from a burly Russian policeman with Natalia, our Peace Corps-appointed interpreter, sitting between us. She not only translated for us, but defended us whenever she felt the police were being too hard. The policeman's jowls seemed to envelop his face and when he raised his voice his cheeks would redden and jiggle as if he were holding back a cough. He would start to ask a question, and then stop to read from our file while tapping a pencil against his desk, before finally finishing. I worried that I looked nervous and figured it best to focus on my pain so as not to look guilty. He repeated every question as if trying to catch us in a lie, including asking us to state our names and why we were living and working in Russia.

I explained the series of events that led to our supposed mugging, describing in false detail our time at a bar called The Ussurisk. As long as we could create some doubt and maintain the support of the Peace Corps, we hoped to minimize any potential fallout. The policeman had mentioned a report that several cars had been damaged and asked us if we knew anything about it. I said no. Then he mentioned that he had visited the site where we were beaten up and expressed surprise at the amount of blood in the snow. This was the tricky part of the story because we had gotten beaten up directly in front of the *Vladimir*. He then questioned whether we had visited the *Vladimir* and each time I looked him directly in the eyes and said that I had never heard of the *Vladimir*. I pretended to get angry that he was spending so much time questioning us when he should be looking for the muggers. My heart was beating so hard that I was sure he could hear it from across the desk. He knew I was lying, but Natalia didn't, so each time he directed the questions in an accusatory manner she became infuriated. I felt bad for deceiving her, but I had to stick to our story. Since Natalia translated each question, I had time to prepare an answer; the detective had no idea that I could understand him. The interrogation lasted for five long hours. Stoically I repeated lie after lie until he became convinced that I wasn't going to change my story. At the end, he asked both Gary and me to sign our statements. I signed the paper with a steady hand and hoped that this would end the ordeal.

The Peace Corps' medical staff determined that both of us required medical treatment in the United States and that we would have to be medevacked as soon as possible. I needed surgery to fix my broken nose and tests were needed to assess any internal damage since we were both still had blood in our urine. I also needed some dental work and Gary needed dental surgery. My biggest problem was that my passport and visa had both been stolen and I could not return to the United States without replacements. I couldn't get a new visa from the Russians without having a new passport, which had to be processed and provided by the United States embassy in Moscow. Both required jumping over hurdles of bureaucracy, and there was only one flight to America each week; if I missed the next one in two days, I would have to wait another seven.

Brian came through like a champ. I'm not sure how he did it, but he worked the US consulate and the Russian foreign ministry like a puppet master. He arranged for a replacement passport, took me to get passport photos, he made copies of the police reports and called the US embassy in Moscow when necessary to push things forward. Our situation had drawn a great deal of attention, particularly from the US embassy and Peace Corps headquarters in Washington, who were concerned about volunteer safety in the Russian Far East. The paperwork came together in time and I was booked on the same flight as Gary. The past few days had been a whirlwind and I needed to digest what had happened and prepare for the shock of returning home. I asked the Peace Corps not to contact my parents, since I knew that if they heard I was injured and being medevacked they would assume the worst. I felt fortunate that my injuries were minor in nature and I anticipated a prompt return to Russia.

I now had a day and a half to put things in order before leaving Russia. My first stop was to visit my Russian family and explain what had happened and to make sure they understood that I would return. Mama cried and blamed Papa, since she felt too awkward to yell directly at me. They felt that the ordeal would negatively affect my opinion of Russia and that my American family would encourage me not to return. After saying goodbye to them, I was driven to Artyom by a Peace Corps driver and given twenty minutes to pack a bag for, I hoped, only a two-week stay in America. I didn't have time to inform Vitaly, Tanya, the mayor, or anyone else. I had been converting my monthly stipend from Russian rubles into US dollars, since the inflation rate was skyrocketing. I didn't feel comfortable leaving $600 in cash lying around the apartment while I was gone, and I didn't want to take it with me because the Russian customs agents could confiscate any money leaving the country. So I took my duct tape and formed an envelope of it. I stuffed the money inside before wrapping the envelope and an additional two feet of tape around one of the water pipes, making it look like a plumbing reinforcement. There were many people with access to my apartment, both with and without my knowledge. As such, I didn't want to leave anything to chance. I felt bad not having time to provide an explanation to my Russian colleagues and friends in Artyom, but I hoped that the Peace Corps would get the message out.

The following morning, Gary and I were picked up by a Peace Corps driver and taken to the airport. We were both lost in thought and spent the thirty-minute drive staring out the windows. I couldn't speak for Gary, but the shock of getting beaten up, interrogated, and then dealing with getting replacement documentation had worn me out. Now that we were about to get on our plane, I finally had time to think about going back to America. It didn't take long for visions of gourmet cheeses, ethnic food, and fine wines to fill my head. I looked over at Gary and wanted to ask him whether he blamed me for what had happened. He was in significantly more pain than I was and had seemed withdrawn during our meetings with Peace Corps staff. I knew he was dealing with the same issues of saying goodbye and preparing his office for his absence, as well as having to explain what happened to everyone. Mentally, I felt fine—I thought. But I'm not sure that I was as fine as I thought, since I often caught myself drifting into a dream-like state in which I relived the beating, snapping out of it at the point where I fell face-first into the snow listening to the sounds of Gary getting beaten. The medical staff had focused entirely on our physical well-being, possibly expecting that once we were in DC, the doctors would dig a bit more deeply into the psychological aspects of the attack.

We waited in line at the airport, tightly holding onto our tickets. The airport was quiet, with only a handful of flights out of Vladivostok during the winter, leading to even fewer passengers or vendors pushing postcards in your face. We handed our tickets and passports to the ticketing agent and, after a cursory look, were ushered into another line where we pre- sented our customs forms. This too passed quickly. The third line was for

Immigration and seemed to be moving much slower, since greater attention was paid to passenger documentation. Gary walked up first and after a few seconds and a question or two, his passport was stamped and he moved into the waiting area. I walked forward and placed my documents on the counter. I could see that the agent was perplexed by something as his eyes switched from my passport to my visa and then to his computer screen. He told me to wait and walked away with my documents in hand. My heart beat faster. What if the police decided not to let me leave because they knew I had lied during the interrogation? My stomach knotted up and beads of sweat formed on my upper lip, despite the freezing temperature inside the terminal. After a few minutes, the officer and another uniformed man returned and together they pointed at the screen while whispering to each other. The olive-green uniforms, holstered sidearms, and grim countenances reinforced the seriousness of the situation. I tried my hardest not to look nervous, pinning my hands to my sides and staring nonchalantly at the calendar and photos on the officer's desk. Finally, they looked up, and in rough English one said, "The passport number on your visa doesn't match your number on your passport. So we cannot allow you to leave Russia. Please return to the terminal."

I couldn't speak. I had to get on that plane. If only the Peace Corps had sent a chaperone to make sure we got on the plane! I began to stutter, stalling so that I wouldn't have to leave my place in line. Fuck, fuck, fuck! When Brian applied for my replacement visa they had reissued it using my old passport number instead of the new number, and nobody had caught the error. I was still bandaged and figured my best plan of action would be to play for sympathy. "There are special circumstances!" I cried. I pulled a copy of the police report and of the X-rays that the Peace Corps medial office had given me to hand over to the Washington doctors. I pushed them into the officer's hands, explaining that I had been mugged and was going home for surgery. I pointed at the X-rays, circling several dark blobs with my fingers in an effort to convince them that I had serious medical problems and had to get on the plane. I sensed a glimmer of sympathy.

They reviewed the police report and then told me to wait again while they disappeared into the office.

Gary had disappeared into the terminal waiting area twenty minutes earlier and I knew that he must have been concerned about my absence. The fear that the local police were behind this filled my head, and panic set in as I pictured the angry detective repeating his questions to me about our involvement with the Land Cruisers. I wanted to cry, scream, and stomp my feet in desperation. Minutes passed, which seemed like hours, before the two officers returned. One smiled and I knew at once that they had reconsidered and I would be allowed to pass through and get on my plane.

We landed in Washington D.C. and were checked into a special hotel near the Key Bridge that was reserved for Peace Corps volunteers who had been medevacked from their country of service. Gary and I were given a two-bedroom apartment that had a living area but no kitchen. We were specifically instructed not to ask the other volunteers why they were here so as to avoid awkward conversations for those volunteers who had suffered sexual assaults or had been sent back for psychological reasons. There was little mystery behind our presence, since we had cuts, bruises, and bandages on our faces, but on many of the others there were no outward signs of injury. I spent six weeks waiting for the Russian government to issue a replacement visa, while Gary was able to return after two weeks. We both spent considerable time with doctors and dentists, as well as with a therapist who immediately reported that we were both fit for duty and ready to return. I had a new nose and some dental work, but otherwise it was boring waiting for the call that my documents were ready. I watched plenty of movies and ate everything that wasn't available in Russia. I was told that I had to be ready at any time to fly out within twenty-four hours, which meant that I shouldn't stray far from DC. This didn't stop me from flying to New Jersey for a long weekend to visit my family or from taking another short trip to Key West with some friends. I was ready to return, though: I felt in limbo between my life in Russia and a transient life in DC. The waiting became monotonous, and the stress of being on edge about whether my new visa would arrive on any given day added to the anxiety.

John Collins had finally gotten up the courage to tell Ken that he was quitting; the time away from Mary, his fiancée, had gotten to him. He was on the verge of giving his notice when Gary and I got beat up, and for some reason he didn't want Ken to feel that we were all deserting him at the same time, so he held off on quitting until Gary returned. I was saddened—he was a good friend—but I was impressed that he had lasted as long as he had. On the positive side, I got on the internet at the Peace Corps office and tracked down Vitaly's brother in Montreal. I called him. Because he not yet received the letter, he was shocked to hear that Vitaly was still alive after fifty years and he asked me a million questions about Vitaly's life and current state of affairs. We ended our conversation with his promise to mail me some cash and a letter to bring back for Vitaly.

FEBRUARY 15, 1995

Forty-five days after getting beaten up and forty days after arriving in Washington, D.C., I boarded an Alaska Air flight back to Russia. I had expected to be gone for only two weeks and thus hadn't worried too much about contacting my colleagues and friends in Artyom prior to leaving. With all the time that had passed, I was now concerned that they would believe I had left for good without bothering to say goodbye. The thought of seeing everyone and getting back to my Russian life was exciting after spending so much time sitting around waiting. The flight was uneventful, with only a handful of passengers on the last leg between Anchorage and Vladivostok. I collected my bags and smiled my way through customs and immigration, emerging into a cold, hazy Russian night. I scanned the crowds, searching for the familiar Peace Corps face that would be driving me back to my apartment or to Vladivostok. I started getting a little concerned after walking from one side of the terminal to the other as the crowd thinned. Finally I was alone with a handful of airport staff and a lonely policeman walking the halls. How could the Peace Corps bail on me? I had been so excited and the realization that I hadn't been met at the airport felt terrible. I wondered whether it was due to how I had left the country.

I had no Russian currency and the foreign exchange window was closed, so I had no way of exchanging dollars into rubles. The only bills I had were a few singles and a $100 bill. No taxi driver would admit to having change, so if I took a cab I would end up having to give an $80 tip. I returned inside the airport in the hopes of finding an employee willing to give me a ride into town, as Artyom was small enough that many would recognize my name if not my face. But I didn't have any luck and was on the verge of giving up when I recognized someone from the city administration. Luckily she had been working late on an airport project and agreed to have her driver take me to my apartment.

It was pitch dark in the stairwell—all of the lightbulbs had been stolen. I dragged my duffle bag up four flights of unlit stairs before finally reaching my apartment. I gagged at the overpowering scent of stale cigarette smoke. When I got to my door, I felt around with the key to slide it into the lock, but it wouldn't fit. I stepped back to make sure that I was at the right apartment, then slid my fingers along the doorjamb and felt splintered wood. "Shit, I must have been robbed," I thought. The stress, fatigue, and anger came to a head and I leaned against the wall not knowing whether to scream or cry. I had been traveling for thirty hours and now I couldn't even get into my own apartment to sleep. I took several deep breaths and then knocked on my neighbor's door. We had never been properly introduced and I felt guilty disturbing them so late at night, but I didn't really know what else to do. I was too tired to drag my bags back down the stairs and to the hotel.

My neighbor opened the door an inch, with the chain still attached, while I explained my predicament. Recognizing that I wasn't a threat, he invited me inside and told me to wait while he got dressed. I heard him talking to his wife and recognized the Russian words for "American" and "police station." He reappeared wearing a heavy jacket, gloves, and fur hat.

"I will take you to the police station. They should be able to help." We walked downstairs and then five blocks to the local police station. I was too tired for small talk and other than thanking him, I kept quiet. The officer on duty told me that there weren't any reported burglaries at my apartment and as far as he knew, the police didn't have a key. In most countries you wouldn't expect the local police to have keys to private residences, but here things were different. I was one of only two foreigners in the city (the other being the chef at the Chinese restaurant) and we were deemed suspicious enough to require the local authorities to have the responsibility of monitoring us, supposedly for our own protection. The police officer on duty promised to get in touch with the mayor's office, as they were responsible for the apartment and should have a key to the new lock. The officer took my neighbor's telephone number and promised to call as soon as he had news.

We walked back to his apartment to await the call. I was very uncomfortable at the thought of keeping his family awake for what could be hours. When we returned, his wife ushered me into the living room and offered me a cup of tea and some cookies. She sat across from me and began asking me a series of questions, which I imagined she had been waiting to do since I had moved in across the hall. I tried not to show my exhaustion and answered in as friendly a tone as I could muster. Their six-year-old daughter joined us and she too began to ask me questions with the same gusto as her mother. Just when I didn't think I could take another minute of forcing a smile, the phone rang. It was the building superintendent calling to say that she was on her way with the new keys. I thanked my neighbors for their hospitality and had my bags in hand when the superintendent knocked on the door.

With the light from my neighbor's apartment illuminating the stairwell, I could see that the lock on my door had been jimmied. After inserting the key and opening my new lock, I felt for the light switch. Initially everything looked as it had when I left, but when I stepped inside I saw broken glass strewn across the floor. Two glass shelves on the far wall had fallen and shattered, but otherwise everything looked untouched. It was good to be back despite the mess. After a quick clean-up job, I collapsed onto the couch. I was angry with the Peace Corps for not being at the airport to pick me up as well as with having to deal with the new locks on my apartment. It was standard practice that every volunteer is met at the airport by a Peace Corps driver; I took their absence as a sign of either displeasure or apathy.

In the morning I put more effort into cleaning and then unpacked my bags. A good night's sleep had eased some of my anger and I was actually in a good mood: happy to be back in Russia. I was eager to catch up on the gossip, particularly since I imagined there were quite a few stories circulating about my own misadventures. I walked across the street to my office to see Tanya, but found that the office locks had also been changed, leaving me to wander the halls and visit colleagues until Tanya arrived with the new keys. The women in the administration shrieked when I entered their offices, leading to many a heartfelt Russian bear hug and wet kisses. When news of my mugging had surfaced, many people speculated that I wouldn't return and that my opinion of Russia would sour. The mayor had been advised of my return and he too stopped in to the office with a bottle of vodka and two shot glasses. I hadn't tasted vodka in almost two months and can honestly say that I hadn't missed it a bit, neither the chemical smell nor the caustic burning of my gullet. He promised that I would always be safe in Artyom, and apologized profusely for what had happened. It felt great to be back with my community!

I stood in the doorway to my office watching the sunlight stream through the windows, casting shadows onto the plants that adorned the windowsill. Before my unexpected departure, I had copied my Russian colleagues by installing a window garden to ensure that I would have fresh herbs to cook with during the winter months—there were no greenhouses or groceries to provide them. I had brought plenty of seeds from the US when I first came to Russia and had planted these in November so that I now had a blossoming garden full of mint, basil, and oregano. I was glad that Tanya had kept them alive: it cheered me up and reinforced the feeling that it had been the right decision to return. As high as my spirits were, it felt like a kick to the gut when I looked over at my computer and Xerox. The Xerox looked like a car propped up on cinder blocks with the once-neat assembly of wires now resembling a bird's nest. After poking around, I realized that someone had plugged the 110-volt monitor directly into the 220-volt power outlet instead of into the converter, which destroyed my poor Xerox and monitor. Without being able to do any work, it seemed futile to remain in the office. So I embarked on a journey to the Peace Corps office to express my displeasure at my underwhelming welcome-back party.

My first stop was at the nurse's office to say hello to the new nurse and catch up on the latest gossip. Lisa had moved to Vladivostok shortly before my departure, but we had formed a close bond from the get-go and I had a slight crush on her. She greeted me with a huge smile. Like most Canadians, she had a great sense of humor and was extremely animated in the way she would tell stories. She begged me to stay out of trouble for the remainder of my stay, since the amount of paperwork revolving around my evacuation had been incredible. I had missed several of my scheduled vaccinations, so my visit ended with me rolling up my sleeves for my tuberculosis, hepatitis, and encephalitis shots. My next stop was the mailroom, where my mail cubbyhole was overflowing with magazines and letters from home. A package from my grandmother, sent from NYC in October, had caused a bit of concern from US consulate staff and the local Peace Corps office due to the discolored stains and stench emanating from the packaging. Due to the additional month and a half without refrigeration, my grandmother's sweet gesture of sending me a couple of pepperoni sticks now seemed the opposite of sweet, oozing an oily putrid mess. At first I was surprised that nobody had thrown the package into the trash, but then again, I guess nobody had the guts to touch it.

I braced myself before entering Ken's office. I wanted to express my disappointment without seeming ungrateful for all of his and Brian's help in the aftermath of the beating. I knocked on his door and then stuck my head around the door after hearing him say to come in. Ken and Brian, both huddled over the desk, looked up with wide-eyed surprise. "When did you get back?" they said in unison. Their surprise alleviated my disappointment and as much as I wanted to scowl, I broke out into a smile. They apologized profusely and expressed regret that the Washington D.C. Peace Corps office hadn't let them know of my itinerary. It was a relief that the slight had been unintentional. We agreed to talk more during the week, since I was anxious to visit with Gary and my host family. Before leaving, I made sure to track down Natalia, who had served as my translator during the police interrogations. I gave her a big hug before presenting her with a necklace as a token of my appreciation. Most of the Russian staff had gathered around and I was overcome with appreciation for the warm welcome; I couldn't shake my grin when I walked out to take the train to Vladivostok.

I walked into Gary's office acting like it was just another day and he did a double take and then jumped up and we embraced. It had been almost two months since we had begun the nightmare and his surprise at seeing me without any warning equaled that of Ken and Bryan. With John back in the States, Gary and Karl would be my primary confidants. With Gary, our shared history had also strengthened our bond in a way that would be hard to replicate with any of the other volunteers. We picked up a bottle of vodka to celebrate our Russia reunion and it felt like only yesterday that we had set out to find the *Vladimir*. I was relieved that Gary hadn't strayed from our version of events and that our secret was safe. We had showed incredibly poor judgement, but further punishment didn't seem to make much sense: we had definitely learned our lesson. No more late nights at mafia bars, no more drinking with Russian sailors, and no more hitchhiking to strip clubs in the wee hours of the night.

Walking, or more accurately stumbling and hoofing, up the mountain to my host family's apartment the next morning, loaded down with groceries, proved to be much more of a challenge than being able to finish off a bottle of vodka with Gary. Sitting on my ass for seven weeks had drained my physical endurance much more than the absence of vodka had strengthened my liver. With rubbery legs I reached the entrance to their building and stopped, pretending to admire the view of the city and the Golden Horn Bay. For some reason, I was nervous as I climbed the stairs up to their apartment. I had not been able to advise them of my pending return and the anticipation of our emotional reunion had my heart pounding. I knocked and stepped back so that they would be able to identify me through the eyehole. Mama's shriek was not diminished in force by emanating from behind two steel doors. After a jangle of keys and the sliding of deadbolts, I was swallowed up in a massive hug. Papa smiled from ear to ear and even Timofey looked pleased to see me.

We promptly gathered around the kitchen table as I unpacked an assortment of smuggled cans of sweet potatoes, peanut butter, and a plethora of spices unavailable in Russia. We spent the entire day catching up and Mama must have walked ten miles between the kitchen and living room in an effort to make up for all of the lost meals. Plate after plate of my favorites, including smoked fish, borscht, caviar, freshly baked brown bread, Russian dumplings filled with cabbage, meat, and potatoes, and other delicacies came out in massive portions, filling the apartment with delicious aromas that brought back the feeling of being a part of the family.

Rumor has it that Russians are the kings of bread-making. Many things have changed in recent years, primarily due to the scarcity of ingredients, but fresh baked Russian bread is indeed in a class by itself. The bakeries supply several kinds of bread, from baguettes to brick-sized loaves. For the average Russian, no meal is complete without a loaf of bread. Since the bakeries do such a fine job, not many Russians bake their own. The one issue I have with Russian bread is that due to a lack of preservatives, it doesn't keep well. After two or three days, the brick-shaped loaves will actually become bricks. For Russians it would be rare for a loaf of bread to last more than a day or two, although if it does they will cut it into small cubes and bake it in the oven. The older Russians feel if they have these cubes, they will be prepared for anything, even prison, which is appropriate considering their name for these croutons is *sucharee* and the term for going to prison is *Soushet sucharee*, as in to prepare your bread for prison. I was told that during the Stalin years, every house had bags of *sucharee* just in case.

Russia has many other traditions and superstitions around bread that include serving bread in specific situations. One in particular comes into play when there will be a meeting between new business partners. When a delegation meets their Russian counterparts, the hosting company will have a woman dressed in a peasant outfit walk toward them with a large round loaf of bread, covered in a towel. She will open the towel to reveal the bread, and on top of the bread there will be a small bowl of salt. The guests should pull off a piece of bread (no knives allowed) and put a pinch of salt on it. This symbolizes that the guests are welcome and that they will be shown hospitality while in the care of their hosts. It is also customary to sniff a piece of fresh bread after downing a shot of vodka, although after trying this several times, I still can't swear to its effectiveness in reducing the burn.

Another tradition takes place during weddings. After the bride and groom leave *Zachs*, which is equivalent to the clerk's office in a courthouse where the betrothed register and record their union, the couple's parents present the newlyweds with a large round loaf of bread. First the groom and then the bride takes a bite. No hands are allowed. The one taking the larger bite will be the ruler of the home. The leftover bread is then divided and distributed to the guests.

When moving to a new house or apartment, it is customary to prepare the dough for the bread in the old house and then take it to the new home to bake. There are countless other Russian superstitions, but my favorite is devoted to an elf-like man (*Doma Voy*) who lives in homes and is responsible for any lost or missing items like keys, eyeglasses, and wallets. To get your items back you must whisper "Play, play, but give it back" and then leave a small glass of vodka or wine and a piece of bread in a corner.

My friend Tanya told me that when she was ten years old and in the Young Pioneers' Camp, she stayed in a dorm with several other girls. They left some bread and juice for the invisible elf and in the morning found that it was gone. Several nights in a row they left the bread and juice, and on the third morning there was a note saying: Thanks for the bread, but how about a piece of cake? Several of the boys were then heard giggling in the background. I believe that this tradition was started by a clever grandfather fond of a little "nip" before bed!

The following morning Papa gave me a ride back to Artyom and helped me unload several flowerpots full of herbs and vegetables to augment my window garden. I had packed an assortment of seeds for the family and Vitaly when I returned from D.C., hoping that they would prosper here despite the shorter growing season.

Returning to Artyom was exciting since I would have the opportunity to visit my friends as well as Vitaly. Again I was nervous, since there had not been an opportunity to say goodbye to Vitaly and the rumor mill was as well greased and functioning as those in the larger cities. I wanted to pick up foods and beverages for dinner since I anticipated a long evening. I wanted to bring a feast to Vitaly's house: we had never had the opportunity to celebrate the New Year together as planned. I stopped at several kiosks, smiling eagerly at the clerks who welcomed me back and at the passersby who stopped me to chat and question me as to my disappearance. When I finally started on the long walk up the hill and through the village I was weighed down by two kilos of "*Bush Nogi*" and plenty of accessories to go along with them. Also squeezed into my travel bag were a few weathered carrots and potatoes, a loaf of bread, and a bottle of Stoli vodka purchased directly from the nearby vodka distillery. I had forgotten how bare the store shelves were and taken aback by the stark differences between my life in America and the one I was establishing in Artyom. During my two months away, the effects of a downward-spiraling economy had further reduced the amount of food available for purchase. If not for the bounty from people's dachas, the local diet would consist almost entirely of potatoes, cabbage, and rice.

My pace quickened as the paved roads turned to muddy dirt tracks. I passed crop-less fields, some still pockmarked by islands of soot-colored snow, and then went up along the steep dirt road crisscrossed with streams of muddy water. My heart raced as Vitaly's roof appeared over the tree line and again, my lack of conditioning was evident as I was out of breath when I reached the gate. I knocked on his door, looking at the window, waiting for him to push the curtains aside. After a few seconds his face peered out and instantly lit up. "Hello, stranger!" he said. He came to the door and we embraced like a father and son. He squeezed me with all his might then pulled me back to look again before another hug. Our relationship had given him something to get excited about as he dealt with the loneliness of waiting for the day that his son would be freed from prison. I told him how terrible I felt about not saying goodbye and he expressed his sorrow that I had been "beaten by hoodlums" and how he had been worried that I would not return.

Vitaly took the grocery bags while I removed my jacket and boots. I heard him pouring water into the teapot as I took a seat at the kitchen table. He told me that after ten days had passed without hearing from me, he had stopped by the business center and Tanya had filled him in. Over a cup of tea, I told a watered-down version of the events. He was outraged, blaming Yeltsin's government for all of the corruption and crime, while shaking his head and repeating the word *kashmere,* meaning "nightmare": a frequent expression of older Russians. He was concerned that foreigners were affected by the violence that permeates Russian society: it was a further indication to him of Russia's loss of standing as a world power. Despite his understanding that this could have happened to me in any large city in the world, it embarrassed him. He brought two shot glasses to the table as I finished my story and then filled each to the rim with vodka. We clinked glasses, nodded to each other, and threw down the first of many shots.

I could tell that he was anxious to see what gifts I had brought and to keep the anticipation high, I kept my backpack closed so that I could hand him one gift at a time. He fidgeted like a child on Christmas morning. The first gift was a bottle of Southern Comfort. He treated it as if it were a bottle of fine Bordeaux, gingerly sniffing the golden liquid to partake of the bouquet. He poured us both a tiny amount so that he could save the rest for a special occasion. After a satisfied grin and headshake, he licked his lips. After I had given him all of the gifts, I told him that I had saved the best for last. I told him about my telephone conversation with his brother, and handed him the envelope with the money. His brother had made it clear he couldn't afford to sponsor Vitaly in Canada, since both his wife and daughter were suffering from long-term illnesses, but he did want to keep in touch. Concern about Vitaly's intentions had been the reason for the initial delay in his response to Vitaly's previous letter. It is unimaginable to me to fathom being separated from my family for so long and then to not be able to visit them because of politics. I told Vitaly word for word what had transpired between his brother and me, and then handed him the letter. He spent more than an hour reading and re-reading the five pages while I set about putting some dinner on the table.

FEBRUARY 18, 1995

I raced through my work routine with a fervor that had been missing prior to my departure. My clients are Russian entrepreneurs, most harboring grandiose get-rich-quick ideas with little thought as to the costs and effort involved. One client wanted to set up a factory to make boullion cubes out of road kill, which would have been funny had he not been serious. Despite the impracticality of some of the ideas, the greatest barrier to success was the key fact that I was unable to provide any financing personally or through the Peace Corps. Russian banks charged only slightly less exorbitant interest rates than the mafia, so getting financed was a major impediment to any start-up. Even at the high interest rates, which can exceed 50 percent, the banks are selective since few Russians have collateral or a credit history. This leaves the mafia as the only option for those convinced that they have a good idea. Even if one is successfully able to surmount the financial hurdles, getting your business up and running is difficult: the Russian bureaucracy is overwhelming. In Artyom, the mayor required that all new business applications be run past him before a license is approved. If an idea struck him as interesting, it would not be out of the realm of possibility for him to reject the application and then set up the same business via one of his associates. I was frustrated and felt that the whole system violated the loyalty I owed my clients. I was indebted to the mayor not only for my position within the city administration, but also for my apartment and the social opportunities that came with being part of the "in crowd." Nonetheless it was hard to stomach: the weight of seeing how disappointed my clients were when a license application was rejected, and then almost immediately resurrected by someone else. Eventually I began to send clients with solid business plans to the business centers in Vladivostok run by my Peace Corps colleagues or to other agencies, such as the Eurasia Foundation.

I also got back to working with the local teachers to expand my reach within the community. There are few English teachers due to the higher salaries English speakers can earn as translators for the trading and energy companies that were opening up daily in Vladivostok and other port cities across Russia. This led to many of the Peace Corps-sponsoring entities in Russian trying to encourage the business volunteers to also teach an English-language class to fill the gap. Sensing the change and our resistance to teaching, the Peace Corps administration determined that the next group of trainees would consist primarily of English teachers. Even without teaching English, I spend a considerable amount of time with local students through my involvement with the Junior Achievement program as well as regularly visiting local schools to talk about life in America. The Russian version of Junior Achievement is different in that Russian students have no basic business understanding, making it imperative to start with very basic concepts before building up to more advanced topics like competition and marketing. These kids had none of the early awareness of business that Westerners have simply from growing up around capitalism". Anna Gregorovna wants me to establish a business curriculum for a new business enterprise course that could be taught by Tanya or Yelena (my tutor) to help prepare the students for the challenges awaiting them in this new capitalist way of life.

FEBRUARY 28, 1995

It seems like there is a Russian holiday every week as the country, in a bit of national schizophrenia, has brought back Eastern Orthodox religious celebrations from the pre-Stalin days in addition to continuing to celebrate the Communist holidays. The "Men's Day" celebration, which originated as a way to honor veterans of World War II, has morphed into a celebration honoring anyone possessing a penis. I hadn't paid much attention to the pre-holiday commotion, figuring that I would spend the day relaxing with a good book, but the mayor invited me to a party he was hosting at his house. Being seen with the mayor was great for my ego and I ate it up despite knowing that I had done nothing to deserve the increase in stature. In particular, the rush I got being part of this group was the same that many of the local women felt in cozying up to me as I made them feel important as well. On the day of the party I spent an hour shining my shoes so that they sparkled like diamonds, which was no easy feat considering that these were my only pair of shoes and had been sloshing through the muddy streets of Artyom for half a year. Finally I put on my suit and tie and strutted down to the parking lot with all the swagger I could muster. I knew I was being ridiculous, but part of the experience was the ability to reinvent oneself, or in my case, live in an alternate reality that would undoubtedly come crashing down once I returned to America. Why not live it up?

Once I reached the local Miner's Union building and then found the banquet hall, one of the mayor's guys ushered me past hundreds of senior citizens dressed in their military garb, who were lined up waiting to get in. I was led to the head table and immediately felt out of place, worrying that my presence among these medaled pensioners might cause some resentment. But everyone greeted me with a friendly smile. The event opened with an awards ceremony with Valentina Constantinova, our local Duma representative, as the emcee. The first award, a large shiny plaque that she held up for all to see, was presented to the mayor. Feigning surprise, he stood to a roaring ovation and then, as if on cue, pulled a piece of paper from his breast pocket and began to read his acceptance speech. I wasn't sure what the award was for, but his face beamed with pride. He returned to our table with the crowd chanting "President, President," hoping to encourage him to run against President Yeltsin in the next election.

I was scanning the audience for familiar faces when I heard the word *"Americanyets,"* which translated to my being their American. I focused on the remainder of the announcement and, lo and behold, I was the next recipient. I had been daydreaming and had no idea why I was receiving an award. I was unaware of anything that I might have done to deserve any type of recognition, which further hindered me in trying to come up with something to say. Several hundred Russian veterans rose to their feet applauding as I made my way to the podium. I was flattered and wanted to show the proper amount of appreciation, but at the same time, nervous that my language abilities would prevent me from seeming grateful. When all else fails, thank the awarder! I thanked everyone for their hospitality and told them that it was truly an honor to be here among so many brave and honorable soldiers who had defeated the Nazis. I told them how important it was that American and Russia take the time to learn about each other so that our two great countries would not just be allies, but friends. Everyone stood and applauded and I returned to my seat, my sweaty shirt stuck to my back. My award was a book written by a Communist writer who had, at different points in his career, been a supporter of the Soviet Union and then later jailed as a freethinker. Nobody was sure whether his work should be recognized now that, with the new openness that permeated society, he was coming back into circulation. Russians regard books with great respect and authors like Pushkin and Tolstoy were treated as heroes. I smiled and shook hands, thanking everyone before returning to my seat and taking a big swig of vodka. The ceremony ended with coffee, pastries, and a few glasses of cognac that were surreptitiously passed around by the mayor's staff. I was preparing to return home to take a nap to sleep off the afternoon booze when the women I worked with ushered me into a nearby office and presented me with a big cake and a dozen Russian tchotchkes. It was customary for the women in your life to present you with gifts on Men's Day, but I had not expected to be a recipient, since I am a foreigner. Again, I would be lying if I said that I didn't love being the center of so much attention. Getting recognition without achieving either leads you to feel guilty or to lie to yourself and believe that you actually deserve the accolades.

Later that night, after finally grabbing a few hours of sleep, I was picked up by Uri the architect and brought to another party at a house belonging to another one of the mayor's business partners. Thirty people were already digging into their dinners when we arrived, but this didn't stop all heads from turning toward us as we entered. The table was covered with food and more alcohol that should be legal for a single meal. I recognized many of the men from prior parties and spent ten minutes walking around and shaking hands. I was shown a seat between two beautiful women and immediately handed a glass of vodka. The toasting was well underway, but by no means had I escaped the onslaught. One man stood up and made a toast in my honor, congratulating me on my speech earlier in the day. While I was clicking glasses with everyone within reach, one of the women placed a plate stacked high with salads, kielbasa, and pickled fish in front of me. Her name was Lyudmila and she told me between mouthfuls that she was 35 years old, had two children, was divorced, and worked at a bank. After I worked my way through dinner and several more shots of vodka, she asked me to dance. By the end of the second song we were dancing close and I realized that she must have liked me because she stuck her tongue half way down my throat. When the song ended, she told me that she had to get home and slipped me her telephone number. These parties have a way of getting louder and more hedonistic as the vodka consumption increases. The mayor's buddies own several brothels, nightclubs, and other assorted places of ill repute, so it was not unusual to have a parade of scantily dressed women arrive later in the evening once the wives and girlfriends had been escorted home. The rest of the night, like many that had preceded it, ended in a drunken haze followed by a brutal hangover the next morning.

On Monday I called Lyudmila and invited her to my apartment for dinner, half expecting her to have no idea as to who was calling. Instead, she sounded excited and asked for my address. I had trouble focusing on my work and left work early to shop for food and to clean my apartment. We had confirmed 7 p.m. and I was ready by 6:30, waiting on the couch. By 8:30 I assumed that she had blown me off, so I opened a bottle of vodka and sat on the couch listening to music, pretending that I wasn't disappointed. After several glasses of vodka, I realized that I didn't want to sit around feeling sorry for myself, so figured I would put on my boots and head out to visit Vitaly. As I reached for the door, she knocked on the other side. I welcomed her in and awkwardly kissed her on the cheek, taking her hand and leading her inside. Her hands were sweaty, which made me realize that she too must be nervous. I offered her a glass of vodka, more to help myself relax than anything else, since I didn't know how to act or what to say. In Artyom the beverage options are severely limited, so your choices consist of vodka, Champagne, cognac, or tea. We toasted our new friendship. She immediately refilled both glasses and we drank another shot, toasting to our good health. We remained standing in my tiny kitchen slamming shot after shot until our nervousness and inhibitions were beaten into submission. I asked her if she was ready for dinner and she replied that she wasn't hungry while stepping out of her skirt.

As we were naked and grasping at each other like teenagers, I suavely pulled a condom from my hidden stash under the sofa and began to tear open the package. Without warning, she knocked it out of my hand and gave me a shocked look that indicated that I had apparently misjudged the situation. "Do you think I am a dirty whore?" she asked. Stumbling over my tongue, I quickly responded in the negative. "I am not a whore and you don't need to worry about using one of those with me." I stammered out that I was only worried about getting her pregnant and she smiled and said that I didn't need to worry about that, since she had protection. I didn't have a bed, so we were confined to my scratchy sofa. The material was rough enough that it shredded your skin with minimal effort, so a blanket on the floor became the venue of choice. Immediately after finishing, she stood up and got dressed, explaining that she had to get home to put her two daughters to bed. She asked if she could stop by the same time tomorrow and I readily agreed.

I awoke the next morning with a big smile. I felt manly waking up with the smell of sex still in the air and only a marginal headache. This in itself would have kept me in a good mood, but I was to be further blessed, since the local laundromat was supposed to re-open today and I was precariously close to running out of clean underwear. I packed up my dirty laundry and whistled while walking the several blocks to the laundromat. Instead of elation, tears came to my eyes when I read the sign saying that the laundry would remain closed for another two weeks due to problems with the remodeling. The soles of my shoes scuffed the pavement as I dragged my sorry ass and my dirty clothes back home.

Once back at the apartment I dumped my clothes in the tub, poured in a cup of powdered detergent and then filled the tub with water. Due to the energy shortage, there was no electricity, meaning no lights, and thus I couldn't see that the water coming out of the faucet was a rusty brown color. I gave my clothes little thought as they soaked in the tub and it wasn't until the power returned that I returned to the tub to let out the soapy water and almost dropped to my knees when I saw a tub full of swamp water. I drained the tub and all of my clothes had taken on the same rusty hue. I spent the next eight hours squeezing brown juice from my clothes and then refilling the tub with clean water and detergent in a tortuous effort to get them clean enough so that I would be able to wear them again. My arms were cramping from the effort and I was feeling extremely sorry for myself when I heard a knock at the door. I had forgotten about Lyudmila and was embarrassed when I opened the door and she got a glimpse of my dingy clothes hanging from every curtain rod and chair in the apartment. At first she just stared, unsure of what to say, and then she burst out laughing as I told her how I had spent my day.

Most nights I ate dinner at other people's homes or invited friends over to my apartment; I preferred company to stewing in my own thoughts or the occasional dig down into a pit of homesickness. What I was craving most, though, was a more serious connection with a woman. After seeing Lyudmila a few times, I realized that although I was quite pleased to be getting laid on a regular basis, I wanted someone who had the freedom to spend the night and the next morning, or even to travel with me. The first step in my pursuit of a girlfriend was to find a good wingman, and who better than my partner in crime? Feeling that I owed Gary for all of his hospitality in Vladivostok, I invited him to spend the weekend with me in Artyom in the hope that we might meet some women. Unfortunately, with Uri out of town and no party invitations coming in, I might not have a place to bring him. There were no bars or restaurants outside of Won Mil Yon's place.

On the following Saturday, I had a leisurely morning before walking down to the train station to meet Gary. I was early, so I perched on top of a small hill overlooking the platform to get a good view of the arriving passengers. The sky was pure blue without a speck of cloud and with the sun's bright glare, it felt more like a late spring day than the end of February. When the train pulled into the Artyom station, I looked from face to face, searching for Gary's heavy jacket and goofy grin, but he was nowhere to be seen. It was out of character for him to be late, so I walked down to the platform and stared up into the windows as the train began to move. There inside the train peering out at me was Gary. In the millisecond that we stared at each other, there was enough time for a smile and a shrug in recognition that this was just another day in paradise. I pointed at a bench along the tracks as a way to let him know that I would be waiting for him, and the train picked up speed and disappeared into the tree line. The train's last stop was the depot two miles away, so he could either wait for the train to switch directions or walk back along the tracks. Either way I had at least an hour to wait, so I bought a bag of squid-flavored potato chips and sat down on the bench. The largest trading partners with the Russian Far East are South Korea, China, and Japan, so when it comes to buying flavored products like potato chips, the options are quite different from the Barbeque, Sour Cream, or Salt and Vinegar varieties back home. I am an adventurous eater and not easily dissuaded from trying something new, but it is hard to decipher exactly what flavor you are buying when the packaging is in Chinese characters. Sometimes you can guess by the pictures, but with flavors like squid, dried shrimp, and seaweed, it is often a crapshoot and you end up with a heavily salted fishy-tasting product.

I heard Gary's voice before I saw him—he had walked back along the tracks. Gary had not had the opportunity to visit Artyom, so I wanted to make the most of his visit and show off the character of my city. Once we dropped off his bag at the apartment, I grabbed the largest container that could hold liquid, which happened to be a plastic mop bucket, and then we walked down four flights of stairs, crossed the street, and stopped at a small cart that sold local beer. A rotund, Falstaffian man stood beside a wooden beer keg filling up various-size containers and charging proportionately. He combed his fingers through his beard in long methodical strokes with one hand while pumping the keg's tap with the other, all the while joking with each customer long enough to garner a smile. For customers arriving without a container, there was a chipped ceramic mug chained to the counter that he would shake upside down before filling it up to the rim. With such high rates of tuberculosis, flu, and other easily spreadable viruses, one would have to be quite desperate or drunk to from this petri dish of a mug. When it was our turn, the man didn't express any surprise as I handed over the mop bucket and he filled it while speaking non-stop in an incomprehensible mumble. When the bucket was topped, he chuckled while handing it over and asking for the rubles.

We returned to my apartment, careful to keep the beer from sloshing out of the bucket while walking up the stairs. Once back in my kitchen we used a ladle to fill and refill our glasses. Russian beers sold in the market or out of these types of kiosks don't have any preservatives, so the shelf life is limited to a few days before the taste sours. The beer is also quite strong, at 9–12 percent alcohol, so it doesn't take much before you start feeling the impact. When the ladle began to scrape the bottom of the bucket, we realized that it would probably be a good time to take a break and explore the town. I dug my Frisbee out of the closet and the two of us stumbled giddily outside to the small courtyard behind my apartment.

The concept of a Frisbee was as foreign to my Russian neighbors as squid-flavored potato chips were to me. The local population had never seen a Frisbee on television, much less in person, and within minutes we were surrounded by incredulous children and adults. I invited them to join us and soon a dozen kids were learning how to catch and throw. They giggled as the Frisbee flew off in unintended directions, crashing into apartment windows and nearby shrubbery. An hour with the kids proved to be more than enough exercise, so we made our departure promising to return the following day. Ideally we would work our way through a few bars in the hope that we would find a few women, but that was not an option in Artyom. So we were limited to buying more booze and getting drunk playing backgammon back in my apartment.

In the morning I walked Gary back to the station and made sure he got on the right train before returning to my apartment. I was a little hung over and was looking forward to a quiet afternoon, but before I could get up the stairs to my apartment I was accosted by three of the women who lived in my building. They were pointing at me and screaming and I stepped back, desperately trying to figure out what I had done wrong. Finally one of the women held up a piece of a broken plate pantomiming a throwing motion and it all clicked. Their children, following our tutorial, had returned to their own homes and substituted the family tableware in imitation of tossing a Frisbee. These mothers wanted to see my Frisbee to understand the fuss, as well as to ask me to promise to share the Frisbee with their children to prevent a repeat of the morning's destruction. I tried unsuccessfully not to laugh, which started a contagious ripple among the three of them. I showed them the Frisbee and soon they were as enthralled as their children had been, albeit playing with slightly less gusto. I think I have an idea for the next business proposal!

MARCH 2, 1995

Today was a national day of mourning for Vladislav Listev, the most popular television commentator in Russia. He was assassinated last night in Moscow and rumors circulated that the hit was organized by either someone within Yeltsin's government or the mafia, who were upset that Listev had cut them out of deals involving advertising contracts. Listev was a strong adversary to the President and often focused his reports on political corruption within Yeltsin's administration. Violence has become so much a part of daily life that reports of murder and extortion seldom elicited more than a short-term reaction, but when Listev—a stalwart of integrity—was killed, it made the average Russian think about the extent of the excessive lawlessness and ruthlessness within their society. All of the television stations stopped programming for the day in protest of the violence against journalists, showing only a photo of Listev and an announcement that he had been killed. Eventually Yeltsin held a press conference in which he promised to bring those responsible to justice. He portrayed the everyday Russian citizen as the victim and showed great sympathy, despite the fact that his family had often been the subject of the inquiries. Everybody at the office was teary-eyed and spoke admiringly of Listev, and used the occasion to bring out the vodka and cognac hidden in their desks.

MARCH 3, 1995

Apparently the local mafia had little concern for the overwhelming desire to end the bloodshed, as a huge bomb exploded in Vladivostok this morning, blowing up one of the biggest buildings in the downtown business area.

Rumor has it that it was an assassination attempt on the governor, but others think it was the governor's attempt to gain sympathy for himself despite his running the regional mafia group. This was the tenth bombing in the downtown area in the past four months and forced the US consulate to act; it could no longer ignore the danger. They immediately issued a warning that all Americans in the Vladivostok region should exercise extreme caution. Not to be left out, several prominent Russian businessmen held impromptu press conferences speaking out against the extortion and violence that cowed the business environment and prevented honest people from succeeding.

Meanwhile, the war in Chechnya is becoming more of a local issue and not a very popular one, contrary to how it is portrayed in the local papers. The mandatory conscription of eighteen-year-old Russian boys to fight an unpopular war has energized Russian mothers to the point where they are staging demonstrations in the city center and actively encouraging their sons to hide from the recruiters. The young conscripts are poorly trained, badly treated, and sent to the front lines where they become easy targets for the seasoned Chechen rebels who have been battling for years. University students are exempt from the draft, which benefits the wealthy children, since their families are the only ones able to afford the tuition at the once-free universities.

Lyudmila continues to stop by once or twice a week on her way home from work for a booty call before heading back to her apartment to cook dinner and put her daughters to bed. I don't mind the visits, but I end up feeling lonelier afterwards and pine for an actual girlfriend. I haven't met her children and have yet to be invited to her apartment or to any parties with her friends. I am appreciative for the regular sex and don't want to seem needy by pushing her to spend more time together. I decided that I would make a greater effort to increase my social network, so have taken up tennis at the city's sports club. Sasha, the coach, sometimes asks me to play with his students and although I am not great, I play well enough to keep up a volley and get a good sweat. Today I was introduced to Tatiana, the top-seeded player on the women's team. She is seventeen and quite cute, but far too young to pursue without my feeling sleazy. There are relatively fewer first names here in comparison to the US, so keeping track of all of the Natasha's, Julia's, Tatiana's and Anna's can get confusing. The first time we played, she was so nervous that she couldn't hit the ball over the net and I easily beat her. This infuriated Coach Sasha, since he wanted to show off her talents. The tennis court is actually a basketball court with a net strung across the midcourt line. The rackets are cheap Chinese replicas, and combined with the lack of access to new balls, the game can be quite challenging—every few serves the ball will simply not bounce back up.

MARCH 11, 1995

Stories of violence in Artyom, Vladivostok, and the rest of the Russian Far East had seemed exciting to me at first, as if I was watching a Western or gang movie. Even after smelling the acrid post-explosion smoke, or feeling the jolt when hearing the sound of emergency sirens, I would experience an adrenaline rush, wanting to run out and find out what had happened, following the crowds to the accident site, and straining to rubberneck like the rest of the people. I would have a new story to tell as a consequence, and somehow this made me feel alive and part of the excitement. This glamorization and sense of invincibility came to an end when my friend and her husband were brutally murdered in a horror-movie manner. Vera (who is one of the four women who managed the hotel in Artyom) and her husband were stabbed more than forty times while still in their bed, in a typical mafia-style statement attack. When Vera worked the night shift, she would invite me to join her for dinner, tea, or just to watch television, since she sensed my loneliness. Her husband often stopped by, bringing Champagne and chocolates, and he too was incredibly generous and hospitable. They casually tutored me with my Russian language and enjoyed looking at my photo albums. On holidays, they always stopped by to make sure that I wasn't going to be alone. Vera's husband was the director of New

Business Registrations for the city administration, which enabled him to decide which business licenses were approved. He was close to the mayor and part of the entourage that ran the city. I was nervous; I spent quite a bit of time with the mayor and his friends and I didn't want to get caught up in any turf wars. I was afraid in Artyom for the first time. I considered whether my status as a foreigner would help keep me safe, despite the obvious shortcomings of this concept—evidenced by my getting my ass kicked in Vladivostok. On the other hand, the Russian mafia realized the importance of foreign aid to the current Russian government and understood that anything that they did that would impede the flow of foreign investment would not be well received. I have taken to sleeping with a kitchen knife under my pillow and I leave a chair buttressed up against the door to ease my nerves further. The mayor, Uri, and even Anatoli have all been on edge since the murder, often fidgeting and constantly scanning their surroundings when we head out of the building or leave one of their homes. The multiple mafia groups remind me almost of American political parties; there are so many here who crave the power and prestige of running one of the groups. Most of these groups are comprised of former KGB operatives who lost their jobs when the economy tanked and the government could no longer support their salaries. People quietly speculated as to how the mayor would respond to the murders, but none did so without first checking to see if anyone else was listening.

I stopped by Uri's office the day after the funeral and he was in a somber mood. He lifted up his pant leg to show me a gun in an ankle holster and then opened his jacket to show me another. It was just like the movies, but scarier since I felt involved and at risk due to my association with the actors. There was talk of retaliatory hits, but I did my best to stay out of these discussions. The paranoia was contagious and I felt exposed as well, despite not really feeling like I was in any way a target. It was under this heightened stress that I returned to my apartment after work that day to meet Lyudmila. We had gotten into a routine that involved a few shots of vodka, casual conversation, and then the removal of our clothing. We were relaxing on the couch when a sudden crash against my door broke the post-coital well-being. This was followed by a male voice screaming out her name. She trembled and in that second, I realized how stupid I had been not to see that she had been lying to me about being a single mother. Everything came together at once: the post-work visits and the secrecy of our relationship. How could I be so naïve?

With an angry husband at my door, I held my finger up to my lips for her to be quiet while the kicking and screaming continued. I couldn't understand what he was saying, but the intent was clear. I pulled on a pair of shorts and grabbed the knife from under my mattress. I was already on edge from Vera's murder, and my back and shoulders tensed up in a mixture of fear and anger: fear that I might have to fight this guy and anger that Lyudmila had put me in this position. We remained silent until the screaming stopped and then we sat in silence for what seemed like another hour before even whispering to each other. I would now have to watch my back because this guy knew who I was, and where I lived, and he was obviously not pleased that I had been sleeping with his wife. I had no idea of what he looked like. But for the most part, I sympathized with him. Lyudmila poured two glasses of vodka and tried to calm me down as I paced back and forth agonizing over my limited options. I told her that we were done and that I didn't want to see her again. When she finally left, I began to feel a bit guilty, knowing that she was likely to suffer a worse fate. There seemed to be an acceptance of domestic violence in Russia, or at least of the authorities' willingness to turn a blind eye to it, which gave very little recourse to the victims. With the limited housing, many couples were forced to live together even after divorcing, since there was nowhere else to go. Add in the rampant alcoholism and the machismo of Russian men, and the statistics were a disaster.

I barely slept that night, imagining getting attacked, and as soon as the sun rose I got ready to head to the office, eager to tell Uri everything and to ask for his help. I was one loud noise away from complete panic and had tucked a kitchen knife into a magazine to carry on my way into the office.

After reaching his office, I closed the door behind me and dropped into a large leather chair with an audible sigh and a shake of my head. After I recounted my experience, Uri laughed and told me not to worry. He knew her husband and would let him know that Lyudmila had lied about being married. He'd warn the husband to keep his distance. He then pulled out a bottle of Cognac from his desk and poured two tall glasses, toasting to our health and survival. I closed my eyes, imagining how this situation would seem to my buddies back home as I sat drinking booze at eight in the morning with my mafia friend after begging for his protection.

March 8 is "International Women's Day." This is the counter to the Men's Day two weeks ago and is taken quite seriously in Russia. As with the Men's Day celebration, anyone with the appropriate plumbing expects to be treated with adoration and above all to receive gifts from the men in their lives. Mama made it clear that all she wanted was for me to spend the holiday with her, and considering the debacle with Lyudmila, I was eager to get out of town. All state offices and schools will close at noon on March 7 and are closed all day March 8, so it was not particularly surprising when the mayor sent me a note advising that there would be a party for the entire city administration on the seventh. I was a little flustered at the thought of having to run out and buy gifts for the thirty women with whom I worked; all of them had given me little gifts for Men's Day and I didn't want to hurt anyone's feelings. There are no shopping malls or discount outlets, so my only option was to visit the outdoor markets and hope for something to be available. It took all of ten minutes to walk around all of the stalls and realize that the only option was to buy them all flowers. I must have looked ridiculous walking down Main Street with thirty rose bouquets, but it was worth the thorns and rubles as all the recipients seemed pleased. The party started with the traditional speeches by the mayor and other staff members, the playing of an accordion (a Russian party staple), and the passing around of several bottles of Russian Champagne. After the party, I rushed to my apartment to grab my bags in the hope of catching the next train. Fortunately I glanced in the mirror as I was running out and caught my reflection. I resembled Bozo the Clown, having been plastered with an assortment of rainbow-colored lipstick from the thirty Russian women who had thanked me for the flowers. Once on the train, my breathing returned to normal and I began making a list in my head of all of the groceries that I would need to bring to the family.

I was incredibly happy to be back with the family and felt safe for the first time in days. This relaxed state, combined with a belly full of delicacies and Papa's generous pouring, kept me smiling and at ease. I kept my stories to myself for fear that Mama wouldn't let me return to Artyom, plus I was embarrassed about the debacle with Lyudmila. Mama cooked up the usual array of Russian specialties and had taken the initiative of inviting several of my Peace Corps colleagues to join us, as well as the family's close friends including a woman who had appointed herself as my Russian godmother. I didn't mind having another person to look after me, especially when she presented me with a pair of home-sewn woolen socks. They weren't exactly symmetrical nor did they fit the standard sock shape, but they were warm and given with love. The weekend surprise—there is always a surprise in Russia—was that March 15 was the official end of winter and as such, men are expected to shave off their winter beards. I was proud of my beard and expressed some misgivings about shaving, but when Gary consented, I had little choice but to follow. Irrespective of appearance, I was hesitant to comply due to the limited amount of running water, much less hot water, in Artyom, which made shaving time consuming. Besides, now more time would have to be spent on my hair, for when you have a beard it is much easier to get by with a messy head.

Instead of returning to Artyom on Monday morning, I stopped at the Peace Corps office in the hope of meeting Thomas Pickering, the new American ambassador visiting from Moscow. Mr. Pickering had a long career in the Foreign Service that included ambassadorships to the United Nations, India, Israel, El Salvador, Nigeria, and Jordan. Unfortunately he canceled at the last minute when a Russian/Chinese skirmish looked to be taking place only a hundred miles west of Vladivostok. Thousands of

Chinese troops had gathered along the border, which led to an equal show of force from the Russians. There have been countless border disputes over the past century, but this was the first since my arrival. The argument involved a land deal along the border that had been brokered between Beijing and Moscow. Moscow wanted the hard currency and Beijing wanted access to the raw materials like coal that were abundant in the area. The local Russian authorities also feared that the Chinese would use the land to build a connecting link to their existing railroad system, which would then give the Chinese a transit infrastructure that would compete directly with Russia's Tran-Siberian railroad. Since this is currently the only direct route from the Pacific Ocean to Europe, the Russians have a huge financial interest in maintaining the sole route to move goods in an East-West direction. Unfortunately the Russian transit system is so antiquated and poorly funded that it could never compete with a modern, highly financed Chinese system.

As if the border confrontation wasn't causing enough anxiety, several Russian armories along the border exploded, sending rockets shooting up in all directions. This caused both the Russian and Chinese militaries to stress out: both sides suspected an imminent attack by the other. The Russian arsenals have been depleted over the years by corrupt officers who sell everything from guns to grenade launchers to the mafia and the only way to cover up the theft is to set off an explosion to destroy all inventory records. Thank goodness calmer heads eventually prevailed and both sides backed down while the diplomats worked out a solution.

MARCH 12, 1995

March 13 is Vitaly's birthday, and with mine the next day, we planned a joint celebration. I was caught in a difficult balancing act between Vitaly and my host family: it seemed that no matter how I scheduled the party, somebody's feelings would get hurt. I ended up celebrating a day early with Vitaly, along with his friend Alex and Alex's son, as well as Eddie, Vitaly's old friend from China. Eddie, like Vitaly, had grown up as an exile in China having also been the son of a White Russian officer. They had grown up together in the Chinese city of Tianjin and had even attended the same school. They met again in Artyom by chance when Vitaly heard from Won Mil Yon that another old white man had come in to ask if they needed a translator. This piqued Vitaly's imagination, as he occasionally visited with the Chinese chef to practice his Chinese language skills. Vitaly got Eddie's address and took a bus out to visit him in his village. They now get together weekly to talk about the good old days over a bottle of cheap vodka—both are barely scraping by on their pensions.

I had spent a few afternoons with them and was amazed that after not seeing each other for half a century, they'd ended up in the same town. They had studied English at an American missionary school prior to World War II. When the war broke out and Japan had invaded Manchuria, they had both ended up seeking sanctuary with the US Marine Corps troops who, in addition to protecting them, taught them various ways to use the word *fuck*, among other off-color phrases. They would both speak English around me and try to impress me with their salty language, which led to "Mad Libs"-style conversations. With a Stolichnaya distillery nearby and vodka so cheap, there was never a shortage of bottles in my apartment, which made them prefer to meet in my apartment rather than at either of theirs, particularly since Eddie's wife wasn't pleased with the amount of their consumption. During these drop-in visits to my apartment, I often had to bite my tongue to stop from bursting out laughing when one of them would let loose with a string of obscenities that were entirely out of context. Eddie couldn't speak two sentences in English without saying *fuck* and I secretly nicknamed him Tony Montana after the Al Pacino character in the movie "Scarface."

I wanted to impress them by preparing authentic Chinese cuisine for the birthday meal. I had developed a decent relationship with Won Mil Yon, so it was easy to get him to give me some sesame oil, five-spice powder and other ingredients that were unavailable in the Russian kiosks. The meal was a success, except that I had forgotten that both Vitaly and Eddie had dentures that made chewing a difficult task. Due to the poor quality cuts of meat available and the fact that there is no refrigeration at the market, I was forced to cook everything well-done, making a tough piece of meat even harder to chew.

Throughout dinner their conversation centered on how difficult life had become since the government had transitioned from Communist to a democracy. The skyrocketing inflation rate had reduced their life savings to little more than a handful of worthless paper and now they were forced to sell family heirlooms in order to put food on the table. Eddie told me how the pensioners in his village relied on foraged mushrooms and berries from the forest to survive since they had already passed the point of skipping medication in order to put bread on the table. He complained bitterly, stating that before Perestroika both he and Vitaly could have lived comfortably. Now they lived like paupers with little dignity and for that reason, he yearned for a return to Communism. During a break in Eddie's *fuck*-strewn rants, Vitaly brought up that I had located his brother in Canada and that they were now able to correspond. This led to Eddie's asking for my help to find his long-lost relatives, which was a difficult proposition considering that he did not know where they had emigrated or whether they were still alive.

When both had stumbled out the door, I kicked off my shoes and sat down for a cup of tea and opened the local newspaper. If I hadn't already been walking around in fear due to the packs of rabid dogs, murderous street thugs, and jealous husbands, then the front page of the paper would surely have done the trick. There were two stories describing in detail how two Siberian tiger attacks within the city had occurred this week. The first involved people waiting for the bus and the second occurred at a nearby train station. Seven people have been attacked so far this year in Primorski Krai, my region. With so much of the tigers' natural habitat being destroyed by logging and the encroachment of people into their territory, it is not surprising that there are encounters between man and beast. Walking home from Vitaly's house at night now terrifies me, since his village borders a forested area and there are no street lights. The sun sets at 5:30, so by the time we finish dinner I practically run all the way home in the black night. Sometimes I hear dogs start barking and I wonder whether I am causing the commotion or whether there is something more sinister lurking in the shadows. By the time I reach my apartment, I am drenched in sweat and my heart is pounding a mile a minute. I have a recurring nightmare in which I am hiding under a parked car while a tiger circles, sporadically taking aim at me with an outstretched paw. The Siberian tiger is the largest cat in the world and they can get to 11 feet in length and weigh up to 700 pounds. As Eddie would say, you don't fuck with these guys!

MARCH 24, 1995

I returned to Vladivostok for my birthday, expecting to celebrate casually with the family and Gary, but the family had gone all out and arranged a surprise party for me. Mama had prepared all of my favorite Russian foods, including caviar and sea cucumber. The family presented me with an oil painting of a Russian landscape, which had been signed by the artist. Gary, Karl, and Charlie, as well as several of my Russian friends, attended. Karl played guitar while the rest of us sang a mixture of Russian ballads and Beatles songs. The Beatles were the only music familiar to both the Russians and Americans. Karl knew how to play "Yesterday," which led to multiple renditions, each successive one sounding better than the last thanks to a steady stream of vodka shots. I felt happy to have spent the night with close friends and this in turn helped to lessen the homesickness that often kicked in around holidays. This hit closer to home when Gary got a call the following morning telling him that his father was dying and that he was booked on a flight in the afternoon to return home. Papa and I drove him to the airport, offering our support. One of the most difficult aspects of being a Peace Corps volunteer is that you are so far from home. You feel disconnected from your family and in a time of crisis, it is frustrating that you can't help. There is limited phone availability, packages take up to three months to arrive, and there is only one flight out of Vladivostok each week.

MARCH 25, 1995

A client came to my office this morning asking me to help him obtain financing for a new business venture. He wanted to use computers to teach students math and science fundamentals, while simultaneously making them comfortable with the technology. He was organized, had a strong grasp of the business model and, above all, his enthusiasm was contagious. This was the type of client I had dreamed about and it pained me that I didn't have access to the financial resources necessary to help him. I did the next best thing, which was to arrange for the two of us to meet with representatives from the Eurasia Foundation and USAID in an effort to bring his idea to fruition.

MARCH 26, 1995

Ken had approached me earlier in the month to gauge my thoughts as to whether Artyom might be a good hosting city for the next group of Peace Corps trainees. I had a great relationship with the city administration, i.e. the mayor, and as Artyom was only a twenty-minute train or car ride from the Peace Corps headquarters, it did seem like a practical option. As such, Ken arrived the next morning and asked me to join him to discuss the idea with the mayor. There would be forty American volunteers with an average age of twenty-five. They, along with the support staff would be living in the city for three months before being assigned to their permanent positions. It would be a huge event for a city that had been closed to not only foreigners, but to most other Russians for the past forty years on account of the nearby nuclear submarine base. I was flattered to be included in the negotiations, since it was rare for a volunteer to get involved with the administrative aspects of the Peace Corps. Ken arrived with Helen, the woman who would be heading up the training program. She seemed like a straight shooter with a good sense of humor and, since Ken spoke highly of her, I knew we would get along. I was both excited and worried about Artyom hosting the next training. Being the only foreigner (outside of Won Mil Yon), I am the center of attention and get a special treatment from everyone from the kiosk workers to the local mafia. If I had to share the spotlight with forty other Americans, I would inevitably lose my position as the foreigner interviewed on the local television stations and newspapers as well as the almost nightly dinner invitations. During the meeting, the mayor referred to me as an integral part of the "city administration family" and expressed how happy he was that I had been selected to work in Artyom. I thanked him for his flowery commentary and praised him and the administration for their hospitality. Ken then got into the ass-kissing and told him that my situation was the model placement by which all future assignments would be judged. Despite the sense of overkill on everyone's behalf, I still felt pride that I had managed to come into a city and make a positive name for myself.

After the meeting, I took Ken to see the business center. I wanted some privacy to discuss what was happening with Vitaly: I suggested that it would be great public relations for the Peace Corps if we could somehow arrange to send him to Canada to meet his brother. Ken said it was a great idea; he would think about it and get back to me. Later that night, he called to say that he was willing to help and that he had already spoken with the Canadian consul general. I was so excited that I couldn't wait to tell Vitaly the good news. Raising money will be the main obstacle, but that was where Ken felt that he could help the most. He said that it would be great for the program to get publicity showing that business volunteers help in ways outside of business development. He mentioned calling the local *Newsweek* contact to write a human-interest story showing how Russia, Canada, and the United States cooperated on a humanitarian project. Vitaly was overjoyed with the news and if possible, even happier when I told him that it wouldn't cost him a ruble. He had been devastated by news that his bank had declared bankruptcy yesterday, driven by the bank president's disappearance with all of the bank's foreign reserves. This had been the bank account in which he kept his "Black Day" (or funeral) fund and now he worried that if he were to die, he would not receive a proper burial and would end up in a pauper's grave.

MARCH 27, 1995

I arrived an hour late in Solemka on the 8:35 *electrishka*, which was hard to believe considering that the ride from Artyom should only have taken fifteen minutes. I was the only foreigner on the train, although I felt that I now looked Russian enough to blend in with the locals. It had been a cold afternoon and I wore my Russian fur hat pushed down over my brow to keep my ears and as much of my face warm as possible. After living here for six months, my confidence riding public transportation was high and I no longer had to worry whether I had gotten on the wrong train. I was on my way to visit Anatoli, who had served as my interpreter at a conference earlier in the year (not to be confused with the mafia enforcer in Artyom). Over time we had become friends, and had met a few times for drinks in Vladivostok and occasionally in Artyom when he visited his son, who was living here with his ex-wife. He spoke English as well as any native speaker, which I assumed stemmed from KGB training although I never asked him directly. He never asked me if I was a spy either, but at least I had poor language skills to support my denial. His accent was flawless and his knowledge of New York City in particular was uncanny for someone who had never traveled outside of Russia.

Anatoli shared a house in the village with his grandmother, since she otherwise would be forced to live in one of the state facilities, which were woefully underfunded. His parents had died when he was a child and his two brothers had moved to Moscow immediately upon finishing at the local university, leaving him as the only caregiver available for her. Anatoli visited his son at least once a month, and when I was around, he would spend the night at my apartment, allowing me to catch up on the gossip and him to vent about his ex-wife's unfair treatment of him. We would also have a drink or two while playing backgammon to pass the time. He had invited me a dozen times to visit him in his village of Solemka and finally I was taking his offer.

He met me at the station on foot, apologizing for not having a car. It was a two-mile walk to his home and we chatted through our scarves as the wind forced cold air between every gap in our clothing. The street became darker the further we got from the station and the surroundings changed from a town to a village as the paved streets devolved to dirt roads and office buildings were similarly replaced by small cottages and kiosks. Barking dogs ran from one end of their fenced-in yards to the other, giving me cause to think that they could sense, or maybe even smell, my foreign-ness. Flickering candles lit up many of the windows since the increasing price of electricity had forced many villagers to revert to basics in an effort to save money for more important purchases. After twenty minutes, we approached a metal gate in front of a well-kept yard. No lights shone through the windows, leading Anatoli to mutter that his grandmother must have fallen asleep. The air carried an earthy vibe, much different than the coal dust and exhaust that permeated Artyom. I heard him groping for the light switch and seconds later, a rocking chair, bureau, and other rustic furniture appeared from the darkness. Photographs and religious icons hung on the walls and I felt that I was in a Pushkin novel. I had started to unpack the goodies from my bag when I noticed a seriousness to his voice as his repeated calls to his grandmother went unanswered. Then I heard him sigh loudly, followed by "Nyet, nyet, nyet!"

Imagining the worst, I walked to the doorway and saw him kneeling by the bed, his body silently shaking. I put my hand on his shoulder, squeezing gently because there were no words to convey my sadness for his loss. I backed out of the room, giving him some privacy, and sat at the table. He eventually returned, shaking his head slowly as we locked eyes. He thanked me and then, using the edge of the bread knife, he opened a bottle of cognac covered in Cyrillic writing, grabbed two shot glasses, and filled both to the rim. His hand shook as he passed a glass to me, then he toasted to his grandmother. I reached out to clink glasses and he pulled back, saying, "We never clink glasses when toasting a death."

We drank a few more shots in silence and then he began to weep. In America, the death of an older family member often leads to expressions of sympathy followed by a statement that the departed had lived a full life, had children and grandchildren, etc. Unfortunately, in Russian villages, this isn't the case: most people struggle from birth through death enduring hardships as part of their daily lives. I don't want to come across as condescending, but comparing theirs to my own sheltered life in America I feel great pity for my Russian friends as they struggle during this transitionary period between Communism and whatever comes next. Anatoli's grandmother, similar to the other village babushkas, had struggled to provide for her family and to instill the right morals in her grandchildren. She wasn't a complainer and took on her role with dignity. I relaxed as the last shot of cognac eased from a slow burn to a shallow warmth that spread from my throat to my chest. Once composed, Anatoli told me to stay put while he went next door for help. I sat at the table, feeling the effects of the cognac, and I sensed his grandmother's presence in the next room. My mind wandered to my own grandmother and I felt tears welling up. Anatoli returned with two of his grandmother's friends, who briefly shook my hand before solemnly walking toward the bedroom, aware of the significance of their task. Anatoli commented that they would prepare her for burial while he and I would go out to take care of the other arrangements. He poured two more shots of cognac for the women and carried them back to the bedroom. I heard one of them say, "*Die bog*" (as God wills).

Anatoli asked me to join him to run the necessary errands and I nodded in agreement. I followed a step behind him in silence as he trudged down the dirt road toward the town's center. I contemplated my own mortality and that of my family back home as we passed through the night, stopping at several homes to let the community know of his grandmother's passing. Eventually we entered a gate and walked down a slate path to a modest one-story cottage. A burly, bearded man opened the door before we had a chance to knock and took Anatoli into a bear hug while I kept to the side to allow them to discuss the business at hand. I caught snippets of the conversation, recognizing the word for *coffin* and little else. With the negotiations for the purchase of a casket complete, we were ushered inside and offered a seat and a few shots of vodka. As soon as we had swallowed the first shot, we returned the glasses to the table where they were promptly refilled. After the second shot, the man nodded for us to follow him through a door leading to the back of the building, where several coffins rested upright under the cover of a tattered awning. Anatoli selected one and then nodded toward me indicating that he needed my help. I was hesitant; death had always been something distant to me. I had always been sheltered from the reality of being close to the feel and smell of death. We have ambulances and morgues that pick up our dead; they remove the signs of struggle and pain and we are free to mourn with our family and friends. But this was as real as it could get and as much as I wanted to shy away from my responsibilities, I shuffled over and grabbed a handle. The three of us lifted the casket and side-stepped our way down the path to the gate and then out into the street. Within minutes my hands ached and I felt the pain spreading to my arms and shoulders. Eventually we reached Anatoli's house and carefully navigated our way through the front door and into the living room, where we laid the casket on the kitchen table, which had been cleared and set against the wall. I stepped back and accepted a shot of cognac from one of the babushkas before collapsing into a chair. My arms were numb and my head was spinning. The three of them began talking in Russian and I allowed the sounds to fade away and let my mind wander off to a far-off place.

I vaguely recall being led to a sofa and given a pillow and blanket and thinking how strange it felt laying down to sleep only steps away from the body. But eventually I fell asleep. I woke to the smell of coffee and the sounds of muffled whispers coming from the kitchen. Whether I imagined the whiff of decay, or merely had it ingrained in my consciousness, I was eager to step outside and suck in the fresh spring air. It would be a taxing morning, but I was relieved to be outside with a brisk chill to keep my nervous perspiration from showing on the back of my shirt. Anatoli explained that he had to notify the police and then find someone to lend him a truck so that he could transport the coffin to the cemetery. Once these arrangements had been completed, we stopped at the market, where Anatoli bought a case of Stolichnaya vodka to bribe the gravediggers to make sure that the gravesite would be ready for the funeral. He also explained how he would have to sleep over at the gravesite when the headstone was cemented in place to ensure that it would not get stolen.

The chill in the air remained a few days later, although the wind had died down by the time we got to the cemetery. The cemetery stretched off from both sides of the highway as far as the eye could see and we could see other families engaged in similar activities. Surrounded by a dozen friends and neighbors, Anatoli wrapped his arm around his son's shoulders and began his eulogy. There was no priest to preside over the ceremony: there was a shortage of Russian Orthodox priests due to the sixty-plus years of Communist rule that had forced believers into the shadows. Anatoli made a short speech and then two workers lowered the coffin into the grave using a set of ropes. Once the workers had stepped back and removed their gear, each guest took a turn to drop a shovel of dirt onto the casket before the workers filled in the grave. Several feet away a bench and chairs had been set up, stacked with baskets of food and vodka. It took several minutes before the mood lightened as the older women from the neighborhood regaled us with stories of his grandmother that included a great deal of pantomime and hand gestures to help me understand. Anatoli smiled as he listened to what must have been oft-repeated stories dating back to his childhood.

That night I lay in bed with the covers pulled tight to my chin. I tried to read, but gave up as my head swam with thoughts of my family and of how easy we have it back home. Tears slowly rolled down the side of my face as a heavy loneliness enveloped me, dragging me into a restless sleep.

MARCH 28, 1995

"You are invited to Oleg's and my anniversary party!" Tanya practically danced around the office as she described the plans, smiling from ear to ear. No matter how tired, hung over, or homesick I may have felt, I would cheer up whenever Tanya would bounce into the office each morning. I would immediately catch a bit of her enthusiasm and soon I too would be smiling. I gratefully accepted the invitation: it allowed me to experience a traditional family event and feel as if I had passed from being the American to being considered an actual friend.

I arrived in my nicest clothes, laden with chocolates and Champagne. It was a fun evening, with laughter, massive amounts of food, and more vodka toasts then I could count. By ten o'clock I was tired and quite inebriated and begged their forgiveness for needing to leave, since the party was still going strong. Nobody was in any shape to drive, so I stuck out my thumb to flag down a ride back to my apartment, which was only a few miles away. It was cold enough that attempting to walk and stumble my way home would have put me at risk of hypothermia. The danger of hitchhiking in Artyom was significantly less than in the larger cities and I wanted to get into bed as soon as possible, which helped make the decision to hitch a ride that much easier. I quickly got a ride, offered a few rubles to cover the cost of gas, and with minimal small talk promptly arrived in front of my building. As I fumbled with the keys I could hear the phone ringing. This was unusual since few Russians had a phone and even fewer called me due to the cost. "Hullo," I mumbled, nervously running through emergency situations that could explain the late-hour call. It was my friend Nicolai, who owned the photo shop on the first floor of my building. "Do you want to have a drink with me?" He had never called before, and although we were friendly it still took guts for a Russian to reach out to me. The cultural differences are the most pronounced in the early stages of any relationship and I didn't want to offend him by saying no. So I invited him up and put a pot of water on to boil so that I could drink a quick cup of instant coffee to balance out my exhaustion and drunkenness. I was surprised that he was working so late on a Friday night, but it made sense when he arrived arm in arm with his mistress. This was disconcerting to my American sensibilities, since it had been only last week that I had been introduced to his wife and family in passing. In this way, the Russians seem to have more in common with the French in accepting outside relationships. Some have tried to rationalize it as a result of the housing shortage, which forces unhappy couples to stay together because there is no option for one to move out. Whether that's true or not, as a foreigner I accepted the cultural norms. Who was I to judge anyone after my experience with Lyudmila?

I covered my surprise with what I hoped was an adequate poker face and invited them into the kitchen so that could slice some kielbasa and cheese to accompany the bottle of vodka they had brought along as a gift. I toasted to my guests, they toasted me, and then Nicolai and I toasted his mistress. It took us less than an hour to drain the bottle and I hoped that they would take the cue and say goodbye. It would be rude to tell someone that it was a bad time for a visit, so to save face for everyone it is customary in situations like this for the host to offer the guests a cup of tea filled to the brim. Guests will take the hint and leave upon finishing the tea. As a foreigner I had some leeway, and since I was significantly inebriated and too tired to make a pot of tea, I explained that I was ready to call it a night. Once I had turned out the lights and collapsed on top of the blanket on my couch, I thought about the night's experience and realized that I had spent the entire evening with Russian friends and had spoken entirely in Russian, at least while with Nicolai. I had crossed a line from feeling like an outsider to feeling like I belonged.

After suffering through three months of sleeping on the couch, I finally smartened up and bought a mattress from the Artyom furniture factory. It cost $35 and will thoroughly change my life: I will no longer have to fit my five-foot-eight frame on a five-foot-long couch. No more waking up with aches and pains and more importantly, a more appropriate setting for a date to spend the night.

MARCH 30, 1995

I had agreed to help Karl prepare for his birthday party, which in Russia means providing a meal and plenty of booze. Back home, folks my age typically provided chips and maybe a cheese plate to go along with the booze, but Karl wanted to combine the Russian style of a more complete meal with traditional American dishes as a way to share our culture. This was difficult due to the lack of supermarkets stocked with everything you could possibly need; we were forced to scavenge for whatever we could find in the street markets and kiosks. We ended up making nacho chips and a bean dip, which none of the Russians realized was more Mexican than American cuisine. The party was not without drama since Karl had invited three women from the university with whom he had a relationship, which created a level of tension that distressed him but thoroughly amused the rest of us. He was turning thirty-three, which seemed only slightly less than the combined ages of the three women. Several of our host families had been invited, including my own, which lead to his apartment being packed like a sardine can.

Inviting a large number of guests and having them all show up is dangerous: everyone feels obliged to make a heartfelt toast to the host as well as to a myriad of other causes when it comes their turn, which in turn leads to copious amounts of vodka consumed by one and all. With nothing non-alcoholic to drink, everyone quickly became intoxicated and one poor girl spent the better part of the evening with her head in the toilet. This was a problem due to Karl's toilet being broken and unable to flush ... and as he had only one toilet, the Conga line wrapped from the bathroom all the way through the apartment and out into the hallway. Demonstrating another big difference between our cultures, nobody thought much about the fact that Karl would be forced to use a plastic bag to defecate while waiting for the repairs, which could take weeks. This was still better than having to go outside to a frozen outhouse, which several of the volunteers endured at their homes. Whenever I started to complain about my accommodations, I would remember this and smile, realizing that I was indeed fortunate.

I returned to Artyom Monday morning and was met at my office door by a reporter from the local television station. He wanted to interview me for a program airing later in the day. During my first months in Artyom, I was flattered when interviewed by the local press, feeling proud that people actually cared about my opinions. Now the gloss had worn off and I was less impressed, realizing that I didn't have anything really important to share with the local community; besides, the viewers were primarily concerned with how my Russian-language abilities had progressed. But it was important to participate and accept these opportunities as a guest in their community. And with the rumors that more Americans would be coming to the city, there was an increase in attention to my presence. I would be asked how I liked Artyom, whether I thought Russian women was as pretty as American women, whether I liked Russian food, and finally, whether I would ever marry a Russian women. I would often bring Tanya along so that she could translate. She enjoys the attention and it makes the interviews easier and more fun when she translates, throwing in her own comments, often ridiculing the reporter. I understand most of the Russian, but having Tanya there gives me more time to formulate an answer and also protects me from eroding any semblance of credibility by exposing my lack of gravitas and shitty grammar.

I drank a cup of tea in the station's waiting room while Tanya fixed her hair and makeup for the millionth time. I was wearing a suit and tie and had polished my shoes in an effort to seem more professional. All of the fuss had made me a little nervous as I tried to imagine the questions and the reason for this last-minute request. Two minutes into the interview, I found out why they were so eager to have me on live television: Earlier in the day the Russian Interior Minister had issued a statement declaring that all American Peace Corps volunteers were spies. The reporter's first question was whether I was aware of the report and the second was whether I was indeed a spy. At first I thought he was joking and I laughed. Then I looked over at Tanya's shocked face before looking back to the reporter whose gleeful expression revealed that having caught me off-guard was a coup in itself. I realized the importance in responding in a serious manner since we had always been under a cloud of suspicion and I didn't want to do anything to perpetuate the inaccuracy. My response could have serious implications to not just my safety, but that of the other volunteers in the region. I calmly replied that I wasn't a spy and to my knowledge, none of the other Peace Corps volunteers were, and then went on to explain the reason for our volunteering and that we were here to improve understanding between our countries, not to do anything that could have a negative impact on the thawing of relations. Tanya was angry that he had sprung the question without giving any warning, but he had a job to do and I am sure that his listeners were interested in my answer. The reality is that the question wasn't that strange, due to the suspicion concerning why a "wealthy" American would give up the good life at home to struggle in Russia where daily outages of electricity and water were part of life. The rest of the questions were less confrontational and he ended the interview by asking whether I had found a Russian girlfriend yet. We shook hands after the interview and then Tanya tore into him for being unprofessional and an embarrassment to the country. I was a little saddened as my feelings of belonging had been dashed and, once again, I felt like an outsider in my community. Time for a drink!

After the interview I thanked Tanya and told her that I would not be returning to the office that day, since I had promised to visit Vitaly and wanted to stop at the market to pick up some food. I wanted to stock up his cabinets because the inflationary pressure on the ruble had increased sharply over the past few months, diverting more of his disposable income from food to medications and making me worry that he wasn't getting enough to eat. My Peace Corps stipend, of the ruble equivalent of $400, was way more than I could spend since I didn't have to pay rent like many of the other volunteers and I was invited to dinner several nights a week. I was in a mood to cook as well, missing my days in a working kitchen. Cooking has always been a good way to improve my outlook. I showed up with a shopping bag stuffed full of kielbasa, cucumbers, apple juice, potatoes, and even some oranges, which I had never before seen in Artyom. Oranges were luxury items well outside of Vitaly's budget and, for that matter, rare finds outside of the bigger cities. I was excited anticipating his reaction to seeing an orange, since I knew it would result in a story about his childhood in China. He would lean back in his chair, stroke his stubbly chin, and begin to describe the smells and sounds of the markets in Tianjin. I had deliberately brought a bottle of apple juice instead of vodka in an attempt to cut back on my drinking. It was getting hard for me not to drink, particularly since I felt that if I didn't I would no longer receive the dinner and party invitations. I was waking up hung over most mornings, and although this too was not uncommon in Russia, it had started taking a toll on me physically and mentally. I had little experience with alcoholism growing up, but had seen enough movies and heard enough horror stories that I realized I needed a bit of a lifestyle change. Unfortunately, no sooner had I arrived and unpacked my goodies when Vitaly's friend Alex arrived with a bottle of vodka tucked inside his jacket. Vitaly smiled at me when he saw the bottle, saying that it was a good thing that I wasn't drinking because now they wouldn't have to split it three ways. We had a leisurely dinner that seemed much more leisurely than usual because I was the only sober attendee. By the time my interview aired at 7 p.m., I was ready to head home. We crowded around Vitaly's black-and-white TV to watch the program and both men gave me a hard time as we waited for my segment to run. It was strange seeing myself on television, particularly since I was introduced as a local celebrity. They had teasers at the beginning of the show hour, showing still shots of me alone in front of my office and then alongside the mayor at one of the town's festivals prior to the ten-minute segment. My voice sounded strange, but otherwise I looked confident and relaxed. Vitaly and Alex drank a shot to my success while I took a big swallow of apple juice. "Are you a spy?" Alex asked, as if I would tell him the truth had I in fact been lying during the interview.

Alex dropped me off at my apartment at 8:30, and before I could collapse on my new mattress, I was disturbed by a loud knocking on the door. My neighbor Leonid yelled through the door that he needed a favor and asked if I could stop over in a few minutes. This was the first time that he had knocked since helping me get back into my apartment when I'd returned to Russia, so I had no choice really but to agree. After dressing, I knocked on his door only to find him sitting on the sofa with a shit-eating grin. His wife and daughter were away and he had his arm around his mistress, Lena. Ignoring my unease, he came right out and asked whether I would join them for a few drinks because his mistress's friend Irina had seen me on television and had wanted to meet me. I was annoyed that he was putting me in the position of being an accessory to his cheating but, again, I was in his debt. I agreed, hoping that Irina would at least be cute and single.

We climbed into his car and stopped off at a kiosk to pick up vodka and Champagne before heading to Lena's apartment, where Irina was waiting for us. I was tired and struggled to maintain a smile while shaking hands with my date. Irina was quite attractive, showing off a nice figure behind a sheepish smile. My annoyance quickly turned to anticipation and my energy returned. Leonid opened the bottles and we quickly toasted to new friends and old. So much for my being on the wagon! We sat around toasting until both bottles were finished. Leonid gave me a wink and said that he would go home later, and that I should walk Irina home to make sure she got back safely. We walked hand in hand and reached her apartment within a few minutes, whereupon she invited me in for a nightcap. This was one of the benefits of being a celebrity in a small town and I was only too eager to take advantage of my position.

MARCH 31, 1995

I have been spending as much time outdoors as I can, with the weather slowly looking more and more like spring. This in turn has strengthened my relationship with the neighborhood kids as I bring out my Frisbee and within minutes have a dozen children begging me to throw them the "plate." They are all less than ten years old and I can't help but smile when they yell "Reech" in unison whenever I approach, reminding me of the bar patrons yelling "Norm" on the TV show "Cheers." They have trouble understanding that I'm not fluent in Russian and speak so quickly and with local slang that at times I can only shrug my shoulders and hope that I didn't just agree to buy them all ice cream. Their parents have become friendlier as a result of our play times, which has led to more dinner invitations, which are conveyed by one of the kids knocking at my door. Sometimes I open the door and find a child holding out a jar of home-made jam or a plate of pastries, and now my refrigerator is packed full of unopened jars. The neighbors refer to me as "*Nash Americanyets*" or "Our American" and they have become my advocates in the market, looking over my shoulder when I order and giving the vendors stern looks to ensure that I am not being cheated.

Yesterday there was a general sigh of anguish when the city administration announced that the hot water will be shut off this week and that it won't be turned back on until November on due to the energy shortage. Hot water runs from a steam turbine in the center of town and is distributed via large above-ground water pipes. There are no individual hot-water heaters or boilers in the apartment buildings, and that means that when the city is in dire straits, all the residents share the pain. This doesn't apply to the mafia mansions on the outskirts of town, but for the common folks it is dispiriting. And it was a big disappointment because they had promised to keep the hot water running until July. I have adjusted to living without hot water, but I still felt as disappointed as the rest of the locals; I like hot shower to start the day and heating water in a bucket just doesn't feel the same.

My denial of being a spy created quite a stir in Artyom. Now strangers are approaching me in the street to tell me that they know I'm not a spy and that they are angry with the reporter for asking the question. I thank them for their support, not knowing what else to say. My increased celebrity status has led to an almost constant barrage of introductions and awkward conversations when I am in public. More people are taking the initiative to say hello and ask me questions, feeling emboldened by the recent publicity. I did love the attention at first, but now I occasionally stay home instead of running out to the kiosks because I dread the struggle to be constantly "on" and have conversations in Russian. I still think in English and need to translate everything in my head before speaking. Somehow when drinking, the flow of Russian becomes more natural—or maybe I no longer care about making grammatical or syntax errors.

APRIL 4, 1995

I was a little nervous about my second date with Irina, since our one and only meeting had taken place under a foggy, alcohol-induced haze. I didn't know much about her or her expectations, but since we had already seen each other naked, how anxious did I really need to be? I had suffered though enough awkward dinners where I waited until both my date and I were drunk enough to lose our inhibitions and hoped this wouldn't be the case again, as Irina speaks zero English and I had little recollection of whether we had anything in common. Our only phone conversation was short and included my inviting her to dinner and then giving her my address when she said yes.

Leading up to our 6 p.m. date, I cleaned my apartment, prepared a few snacks, and chilled a bottle of vodka. My nervousness was replaced by agitation as the time passed and it seemed that she had decided not to come. By 6:45 I was sitting alone, pissed off that she didn't have the courtesy to call to cancel. I was thinking of walking over to the Chinese restaurant when she knocked on the door. After an awkward moment of silence, she apologized for coming late. She told me that she wasn't hungry yet, so we went into the living room and sat on the couch. I put on some music and began the photo album routine. I opened a bottle of Champagne to lighten the mood while pointing out friends and family in the pictures. We made it through all three photo albums and the entire bottle of Champagne before she expressed an interest in eating.

I had seasoned a chicken with local herbs and placed it on a metal tray inside my oven to bake. I also made some macaroni and cheese to give her what I would call a traditional American-style dinner. I had learned that Russian women were often hesitant to eat in front of me, especially on the first date, so I wasn't expecting her to eat much. I have been told that it is rude to use the host's bathroom too, and as this was our first real date, we hadn't reached the appropriate comfort level for that yet. She was impressed that I could cook, as most Russian men tend to stay clear of the kitchen and only express an interest when grilling outside for a *shashlik* [picnic]. I was about to set the food on the table when there was a knock on the door. I heard Leonid's voice and opened the door to see that he and Tamara, his wife, had mysteriously decided to stop by in the middle of my date. I assumed that Irina had been nervous and had asked Leonid to drop by to help break the ice, which further explained why she had arrived so late and then made me wait even longer before serving the meal: she was waiting for Leonid. I had been warned that Russian women were cunning.

Leonid's wife Tamara held a tray of baked fish and a bottle of Champagne and seemed embarrassed that she had been suckered into their scheme. I smiled and played along, pretending that I had been expecting them. We ate and drank and I actually was having a fun evening. None of my guests spoke any English, so I was forced to concentrate intently on the conversation to not appear uninterested. I even managed to tell a few jokes in Russian, which they pretended to find amusing. Dinner lasted until 11:30, when Tamara and Leonid excused themselves and returned next door to their own apartment, leaving me alone with Irina. We moved back to the living room and embraced awkwardly, trying to get comfortable with each other. She told me outright that she wanted to take things slowly and that the other night was an aberration and not something that she "did." I was fine with that: I wanted a girlfriend more than an occasional tryst. Somehow my agreeing to take it slow must have signaled that I wasn't using her: it led to her subsequent request to spend the night and the removal of her clothing. She was a noisy lover, which made me laugh because I knew that every sound in my apartment was transmitted across the street to the administration building's basement to the amusement of some low-level FSB agent.

Once a month Irina takes the train to the Chinese border city of Sui Fen Hei, where she buys inexpensive clothing to resell at four times the price in Artyom. I like her entrepreneurial spirit and sense of humor and genuinely enjoy her company. Since our first dinner together at my apartment, we have been inseparable, spending every night together. This has led to my putting off dinners with Vitaly and visits to Vladivostok. I realized that I shouldn't blow everyone off because I was getting laid, so I invited myself over to the family's apartment in Vladivostok. It had been more than three weeks since I had last seen them and I felt guilty—guilty enough that I bought each of them a gift in addition to stocking their liquor supply with several bottles of Champagne for Mama and a bottle of cognac for Papa as well as a gallon of ice cream for Timofey. As usual, I was met at the door by an incredible aroma. Mama had baked a cake in honor of my visit, and Papa, not wanting to be outdone, presented me with a dozen bottles of Russian beer. I had mentioned that I was cutting back on my drinking and he understood this to mean that I would now drink beer instead of vodka. I didn't want to seem ungrateful, so I drank a few beers while he and Mama finished the Champagne. Tim ate several bowls of ice cream after dinner and then immediately returned to the sanctuary of his bedroom. For a skinny kid, he could pack away the food like nobody's business. I had found a box of cornmeal mix while perusing the local market and decided to surprise them with corn muffins for our breakfast. After dinner I mixed the contents of the box with an egg and some oil and then poured the batter into a muffin pan. I sat with Mama in the kitchen while they baked and unfortunately, they smelled so good that both Mama and Papa were unable to control themselves and pilfered half the batch before I could stop them.

The next afternoon I arranged to meet Karl at the Hare Krishna temple, which would sound strange as a meeting place for non-Krishnans were it not for their vegetarian restaurant, which was open to the public. They served flavorful, healthy food: a rare find in Vladivostok considering that the fruit-flavored vodka is thought of as a good source of vitamins. I also took advantage of their market, since they sold Indian spices like cardamom, turmeric, and curry. I cleaned out shelves by the armful, thinking that the spices would make great gifts for my fellow volunteers. After lunch I returned to Artyom, looking forward to spending the night with Irina. I enjoy the concept of having a girlfriend, but after spending a few days apart the infatuation had lessened. I caught myself looking at other women on the train, and even though I didn't act on these impulses, I felt incredibly guilty. That night when we were together she blurted out that she loved me. I was very uncomfortable. I didn't know how to respond and ended up smiling stupidly. She repeated it as if thinking that I hadn't understood and I had to do something to get the stupid look off my face, so I told her that I loved spending time with her and then gave her a quick kiss before taking a swig out of the vodka bottle.

Over the weekend Irina invited me to spend the night at her apartment so that I could meet her family, including her five-year-old son. She lives in a communal apartment building where there are private bedrooms on each floor with a shared living room, kitchen, and bathrooms. If this wasn't awkward enough, her mother and youngest brother live next to her on the same floor. Her son had been spending the nights with Grandma when Irina stayed at my place. I was not too eager to spend the night there as I dreaded the formality of being on display in front of her family and the other neighbors. Irina's bedroom is between her mother's and brother's bedrooms, which offered little privacy. When dinner was finished I thanked her mother and then followed Irina into her room. She had instructed her son to spend the night with Grandma, but with the walls so thin I could hear the television on either side of us, and suspected that the sound of our activities would be equally well heard.

As a foreigner I'm given a great deal of leeway in my behavior. I'm not held to the same standards as a Russian: all my strangeness is blamed on my being American. I'm also free from America's social constraints, which leaves me in a cultural limbo where I am only limited by my own constraints. I try not to offend my hosts; I remember to follow the Russian customs, such as taking off my shoes when entering an apartment, but sometimes it is easy to forget. Last week I committed the faux pas of whistling while inside a house, which will lead to bad luck for anyone who hears. I also had given an even number of flowers in a bouquet to Mama and was quickly told to take one flower out because an even number was only appropriate for funerals.

In the big picture nothing highlights our differences more than the financial situation. All around me, ordinary Russians have been watching their life savings crumble to nothing under the strain of hyperinflation, while we volunteers get our stipend of $400 each month in rubles, triple the amount the average working Russian earns in the same time period. I continually remind myself of the worry that stresses out my Russian friends and family as their prospects for the future get gloomier by the day. Under Communism, the social safety net ensured that everyone received free health care, a place to live, free education, and food subsidies if applicable. Now society had evolved into a free-for-all in which an "every man for himself" attitude reigned. Panic lies just below the surface as one bank shuts down almost as fast as the rumors pointing to the failure of the next one. The mafia and oligarchs are the only groups prospering under this chaos, establishing financial empires and building walls to protect their assets from those less fortunate.

Despite the myriad problems, I have hope for a better future for them. It isn't easy to get over seventy years of having a closed society. The pressure from the West to jump head-first into a free market system forced changes that might have been less disruptive had they been spaced over a longer time period. Living here during these times allows me to witness the transition and to witness capitalism in its infancy. You can't teach this in a classroom and it is hard to explain in my letters home. When I first arrived, there were no billboards or advertising of any kind, whether in newspapers or television. Now signs for Wrigley's Gum and Proctor & Gamble laundry products mark the back of public busses and newspapers have begun printing ridiculous advertisements for weight-loss elixirs and super vitamins. When working with clients, I find that many disagree with my recommendations to allocate resources for marketing, since they believe that only inferior products need to be pushed and that good products will be able to sell themselves. I have much to learn. It will not be an easy journey to economic stability. I think that in order for Russia to succeed, they will need to slow the evolution of their system or risk having the changes seem too extreme, leading them to end up back under an authoritarian-style government.

APRIL 15, 1995

I paced before my office window, watching the children across the street scamper around the kindergarten playground. They were cute, but annoying: yelling and screaming for absolutely no reason while running in circles like little drunk people. It wouldn't be that bad if I didn't hear them all day; it's making me pine for the cold winter days when they took their recess indoors. Ordinarily I would work through the noise, but today I was on edge because I was to meet with Anna Gregorovna to review my goals for the next three months and evaluate my progress to date. Missing six weeks while I was in the US had disrupted my original goals, leading to my having to reestablish my contacts at the schools and in turn, spend less time at the business center. The fact that my computer and printer were destroyed during my absence didn't help my productivity either. Prior to my departure I had built a steady clientele, but when I left without saying goodbye most of my clients didn't think that I was returning and took their business plans to other centers in Vladivostok.

Svetlana, a friend who is both a member of the English Club and a local English teacher, often came by my office to chat and browse through the English-language newspapers and magazines I had on hand. This afternoon she stopped by to ask me for a favor. "Please come to my Classical Dance class," she begged; they were desperately seeking men. It didn't take much once I heard that there were fifteen women and not a single man in the class. Despite my inherent clumsiness on the dance floor, I agreed to give it a shot and told her that I would attend the next class. I had managed to get through high school dances and nightclub experiences by consuming large quantities of alcohol and pretending I was John Travolta in "Saturday Night Fever," but I doubted this would be an option in this type of class.

Realizing I was late to meet with Anna, I ran down the hallway and up the stairs before stopping to catch my breath and knocking on her door. She immediately put me at ease with her broad smile and a welcoming wave toward the chair across from her desk. We discussed what I would focus on during my remaining time in-country as well as what resources I would need from the city administration. I felt comfortable agreeing to additional time with the schools as well as reestablishing a clientele at the business center. I also agreed to continue teaching a Junior Achievement class that I had started prior to my evacuation. I walked out of the meeting feeling invigorated and excited to meet the challenges ahead.

APRIL 16, 1995

Walking to the dance studio in fifty-degree weather kept me from sweating and allowed for what I imagined to be a suave entrance to meet my fellow dance students. A chorus line of spandex stretched from one side of the room to the other, each woman positioning herself in what I imagined as suggestive postures. As the only man, I puffed out my chest and strutted

like a rooster appraising his hens. Despite the strong start, I lost all sense
of machismo the second the music started and my obvious lack of rhythm
and confusion over "right" and "left" made it abundantly clear that I was
indeed a poseur. The instructor was yelling out instructions in Russian
over the sound of the boom box, causing me to confusedly step on toes
and bump into the women who were no longer smiling back at me. This
great idea had quickly become a nightmare, and at the end of the hour they
seemed grateful when I told them that I would not be returning for future
lessons. I knew I had embarrassed myself and hoped that it wouldn't reflect
negatively on Svetlana for inviting me.

Irina has started showing up at my apartment unannounced, as if she
is checking to make sure that I am not entertaining another woman. I told
her that I wanted her to call before showing up, and that I wanted to slow
things down so that I could spend time with Vitaly and my other friends.
She was hurt and told me that she would no longer visit my apartment,
saying that I would have to come to her if I wanted to be together. She was
upset with me, but also with life in general. Her business had been doing so
well that she had caught the attention of the local mafia, who advised that
she would now have to increase her protection payment to a whopping 35
percent, up from the 15 percent she had been paying. I wasn't sure if she
was telling me so that I could interfere on her behalf with the mayor or
whether she was looking for sympathy after feeling that I was losing interest in our relationship. I didn't promise anything, but I did make a mental
note to speak to the mayor.

APRIL 25, 1995

Every six months, all of the volunteers are brought to a central location for
"In-Service" training, which is a way for the staff to update us on program
changes and for the medical team to shoot us up with a new round of vaccinations. During our free time, we can bounce ideas off of each other as
to how to be more successful in our business dealings. The training usually

concludes with our taking a language proficiency test to ensure that we aren't spending our tutoring money on vodka. Since this would be my first post-beating event with my fellow volunteers, I anticipated plenty of questions. I was equally interested in hearing the rumors that had circulated regarding the incident. I doubted that any would be as colorful as the truth, since Gary and I had sworn to keep the details private. Gary had not yet returned from his father's funeral, so once again, I would be responsible for telling our story.

We were staying at a resort called the *Sanatoria Soyuz*, a Russian-Japanese joint venture that resembled a Red Roof Inn in both quality and décor. Although these in-service training seminars were intended to provide us with tools so that we could be more efficient in our jobs, each of us had such a unique job that there weren't many opportunities to pick up tips to help us in our day-to-day jobs. Several of the volunteers were without jobs altogether, because the program was new enough in Russia that our local hosts often didn't know how to take advantage of our skill sets. These volunteers were bored and wanted to work: it was depressing hanging around the Peace Corps offices trying to maintain some sort of routine and sense of purpose. We were now down to eleven volunteers from our original eighteen, and many of our gatherings quickly break down to bitch sessions that spoil my celebratory mood. But I felt fortunate after hearing everyone else's complaints. I enjoy my role in Artyom and the social standing I receive via my relationship with the mayor, and I like my life. As the only volunteer in my city, I had been forced to develop a network of Russian friends in order to survive. In the cities or towns that had more volunteers, the volunteers tended to spend a significant amount of time together and lost out on the possibility of forging closer ties within their communities.

Before dinner I needed a break from the group, and decided to stop at the hotel bar for a drink. I ended up sitting next to another American, which was unusual since almost every foreigner in this part of Russia stayed at the Vlad Motor Inn, including the consular staff and the Alaskan Airline crews, due to the high level of security and creature comforts of a Western menu. My new friend, Bob, had been hired to install an industrial oven at a future grocery store that would be situated on the Vladivostok city limits. The concept of a supermarket was new and the investors, both Russian and American, hoped that this Walmart-type concept would catch on and lead to a chain of stores across the country. The concept was of working with local farmers to sell their produce directly to a single entity (the supermarket), which would then offer the goods to the public. Quality control would be enforced, creating a more efficient system for the customer, while creating economies of scale in order to lower prices. The grocery included a bakery, smokehouse, and butcher shop. The only problem that the American partners had failed to plan for was that any success they had in streamlining the process would end up cutting out the middlemen, who in this case were the mafia. The mafia wasn't pleased and they demanded protection money. The American investors refused to pay any bribes or protection money, which led to the mafia hijacking several of the trucks and blowing up construction equipment that was being used in the building. So far nobody had been hurt, but in my opinion that would just be a matter of time.

Bob's job installing the ovens for the bakery required that he test the equipment prior to full turnover to ensure that it was working properly. This was a problem since his job skills did not include any baking expertise. Since he couldn't bake, and none of the Russian bakers spoke English or had any familiarity with these types of units, nor did they understand the conversions between the American measurements in ounces and Fahrenheit temperatures, he was in a difficult position. I was in a unique position as the only person within a thousand miles who had experience baking, had worked with American ovens, and spoke both languages. I offered to help on the condition that I be permitted to bake something to bring back to the training, since I knew I would need a good enough compensation to persuade the Peace Corps staff to allow me to miss part of the training. He agreed and I easily convinced the Peace Corps staff to excuse me for the following morning's sessions.

That night after dinner we had time to socialize, which meant split-ting up into cliques and getting drunk. Tales of romantic interludes and our cultural faux pas kept us laughing as we commiserated over glasses of vodka. I exchanged a few winks with Karl when hearing others talk about their misadventures, knowing that neither of us wanted to share our own stories of misconduct. We were sitting in the lounge when Caroline brought out a bag of popcorn kernels sent by a thoughtful family member back home. Popcorn, like peanut butter, was one of the things you never realized how much you missed until you didn't have it. Based on my ability to charm Russian kitchen staff, the group sent me to beg the hotel's kitchen staff for the use their stove. I accepted the assignment and valiantly strode off full of vodka-induced bravado to speak with the chef. I was armed with two bottles of Champagne and the biggest smile I could muster.

I was met with incredulous stares from the staff the second I passed through the swinging kitchen doors. The crew was in the midst of tiding up from the dinner service and, as I soon realized, they seldom had hotel guests visit the kitchen. They weren't sure if I was there to complain. I introduced myself as an American chef and told them how impressed I had been with the dinner. I inquired whether they could show me their setup. Their curiosity about me outweighed any reluctance and I was led around one of the cleanest kitchens I have ever seen. The staff of eight, all women, seemed to enjoy the attention, particularly when I pulled the Champagne from my bag. We proceeded to open both bottles and toasted to our com-bined good health and to their hospitality. Before I had the chance to down the second glass of Champagne, a bottle of vodka appeared. Shots of vodka were poured and chased down by more Champagne and the buzz of conversation rose up to match the buzz I was feeling from the alcohol. I suddenly remembered the purpose of my visit and pulled out the bag of popcorn kernels, asking if I could borrow a pot and some oil. They had never had the opportunity to make popcorn and eagerly pulled out a large stock pot and some oil. Within minutes the stockpot began to sing as the kernels exploded, filling the kitchen with an intoxicating aroma. I waited for the popping to subside, then scooped out several bowls, added a pinch of salt and handed them out. They started out taking one piece at a time, but soon were grabbing handfuls. I realized that I had to save what was left for my fellow volunteers, so I handed the staff what remained of the bag of kernels and headed back out downstairs.

I tried to look sober when delivering the popcorn, exaggerating the sacrifices I had to make to complete my mission. At first my fellow volunteers were perturbed by the delay, but the sweet smell warmed their hearts and I was soon forgiven. When the last of the popcorn—including the unpopped kernels—had been eaten, I went back to the kitchen to return the stockpot. I brought my camera, wanting to have a record of the experience. As soon as the kitchen staff saw me with a camera, they ran to the back office to remove their hair restraints and apply thick coats of bright red lipstick. I lined them up for a photo and watched as they sucked in their guts and pursed their lips. While I took turns posing with each individually, the others jumped into action throwing pots on the range and chopping garlic, onions, and myriad other ingredients. They explained that they wanted me to try some real Russian delicacies as a way to show off for me.

A table was set with plates and more Champagne and vodka. I watched in anticipation as they put out platters piled high with king crab, smoked salmon, and assorted pastries and torts. I felt like a king and couldn't stop smiling as my glass was refreshed and additional servings of delicious food graced my plate. The head chef, a large woman who I was able to identify by the giant mole on her forehead, pushed a plate before me and demanded that I taste their specialty dish before spoiling my palette with the rest of the food. This was *trepong* or sea cucumber as it's known in the West. My prior experience with these turd-like slugs had been with Papa when preparing for Timofey's birthday party, when we had eaten them raw on the boat. They didn't look appetizing by any means, but the second the food hit my lips I had fallen in love: not just a passing infatuation, but deep-down, true, heartfelt love. When cooked, the texture was similar to calamari and the taste an incredible blend of flavors that sent quivers of pleasure into my stomach. The night ended with me begging to leave since I had to get to my room and get some sleep. I didn't want to end up sleeping with any of these women, and I didn't want to be any more hung over than I was already likely to be. My drunken dance down the stairs and along the hallway would have been amusing had I not been thinking about how bad I would feel in the morning.

RECIPE FOR SEA CUCUMBER *SOYOOZ*, COURTESY OF THE *SOYOOZ* KITCHEN STAFF

Sea cucumbers are expensive and hard to find in the US, but if you happen to find yourself near the coast in northern California or Oregon, you may find yourself in luck. This recipe calls for fresh or frozen sea cucumbers, but they are also available dried. If you use the dried sea cucumbers, soak overnight and save the liquid.

Ingredients:

10 sea cucumbers

6 cloves garlic, minced

1 large onion, diced

1 cup grated carrot

¼ cup tomato paste

1 tablespoon soy sauce

1 teaspoon hot pepper flakes

1 tablespoon chopped fresh parsley

1 tablespoon basil

⅓ cup sliced scallion

½ cup red wine

½ cup bouillon

Vegetable oil

2 tablespoons flour

½ cup sliced tomato

Optional: 1 cup cooked thinly sliced pork or chicken

Clean the cucumbers by slicing them open lengthwise and running the insides under cold water. Scrape as much of the refuse out as possible. Put the cleaned cucumbers in a pot covered with water and bring to a boil. Let simmer for 1 ½ hours. The consistency of the meat should be firm, yet not too elastic. Rinse under cold water and remove any tendons that are on the inside; these will be whitish in color. Chop the cucumbers into small strips, and then into squares. In the meantime, heat a large frying pan over medium heat and put in enough oil to sauté the onions, garlic, and carrots. When the carrots are soft, add the sea cucumbers, the tomatoes, tomato paste, and the flour. Stir until the flour is dissolved and add the herbs. Stir for two minutes and then add wine and bouillon. Bring to a boil and then simmer for twenty minutes or until the cucumbers are very tender, not chewy. You may have to add more bouillon or water so that the mixture doesn't burn. If you add pork or chicken, do so after you add the wine and bouillon. Some people also like to add cooked white or pinto beans to this dish, but I think it detracts from the flavor.

APRIL 26, 1995

I awoke slightly hung over and still in my clothes. I looked at the clock and realized that I had less than ten minutes to shower before I was to meet Bob. I cursed myself for drinking too much and jumped into the shower. When I got outside Bob was already waiting with the driver. He looked relieved. We drove to the grocery and the driver, like all other Russian drivers, was out of his mind once he got behind the wheel and seemed to hit every pothole as he zigged and zagged his way through traffic. When we finally pulled into the parking lot, we were met by a stoic-looking Russian wearing an ill-fitting suit. He introduced himself as the manager on the Russian side of the joint venture. He seemed relieved that I was able to speak Russian and even more so when he learned that I knew how to operate the ovens. Now all I had to do was actually deliver on my promises!

Once inside, we got a quick tour and I was introduced to the head baker. I translated for Bob, and soon a game plan was established. It took a few moments to get familiar with all of the equipment and to line up the ingredients, which consisted primarily of yeast, flour, lots of butter, and some sugar, along with the bowls, trays, and various utensils that would be needed. While Bob checked to make sure everything was hooked up properly, I activated the yeast and after ten minutes added the other ingredients. It was a little stressful having the Russian baker looking over my shoulder, particularly as I was working without a recipe and straining to recall the measurements to make enough dough for a few dozen croissants. I put the Russian baker and even the manager to work, rolling out the dough and running out to find me some chocolate to stuff inside them. The oven worked perfectly and everyone, including me, was pleased with the outcome. Within minutes of the trays coming out of the oven, word spread and so many workers began showing up for a sample that I had trouble securing enough croissants to bring back to the hotel. Bob was so relieved that everything had worked out that he felt guilty that I couldn't take any money for my efforts. He offered to treat me at the bar later that evening.

Despite the croissants, the overall mood of my fellow volunteers had been tempered by a slew of rumors indicating that our business program was to be shut down. Ken held an impromptu meeting to discuss both the rumors and his thoughts on how best to deal with the future. At times the arguments got intense, with some volunteers complaining bitterly about being given teaching assignments instead of the business opportunities that had been promised, while others didn't have a job at all. I felt bad for Ken and was embarrassed at how petty we seemed, which may have been easy for me since I had a job I enjoyed. We had been reminded from Day One that being a pioneer volunteer in Russia would require both patience and flexibility. Despite the warnings, our idealistic nature had led us to ignore the potential for problems and focus only on the promise of successful working relationships. We were here to change the world and were willing to sacrifice our creature comforts, but not exactly ready to feel the impotency of being idle and non-contributing. What bothered me most about my fellow volunteers was the lack of motivation those without jobs showed in trying to find a solution. They could have been hitting the streets and meeting with people within their communities to find a job to invigorate themselves, instead of sitting back and complaining about the boredom.

After the meeting I was so disgusted with the group's treatment of Ken that I shrugged off the offer to hang out in one of the conference rooms with the other volunteers and instead went to the hotel bar in the hope of meeting Bob to claim my gift of free drinks. Bob was indeed at the bar and already well into his celebratory infusion of Russian vodka. He jumped up and hugged me as though we were long-lost friends and then refused to allow me to pay for anything, making sure that I ordered only top-shelf imported liquor. I told him about my life as a Peace Corps volunteer serving in Russia while quaffing as much Johnny Walker Black as I could get down. Eventually the conversation turned to my passion for food and cooking, and Bob asked why I didn't incorporate this into my work here in Russia. A light went on as I recalled my obligation to complete a secondary project. I hadn't decided on one yet: why not write a Russian cookbook? My audience would be my fellow volunteers and the Peace Corps staff as well as any American expat living in the region. I would provide insight on how to prepare Russian specialty dishes to recreate when back in America, as well as how to prepare American favorites using local ingredients. I quickly realized that I could also include the history and tradition of each dish as well as anecdotes from my fellow volunteers describing their adventures cooking in Russia.

MAY 1, 1995

With Easter being the holiest of the Russian Orthodox holidays, my host family made it clear that I was expected to spend Easter with them in Vladivostok. Gary was also invited, since they now referred to him as their second American son. I don't know if they were trying to make me jealous with their attention to Gary, or whether Papa pushed the issue to ensure that he would have a drinking buddy in case I was still on the wagon. It had been several weeks since my last visit, so in an effort to maximize my time with both friends and family, I left a day early to visit with Gary alone.

There is not much of a nightlife in Vladivostok, at least of the type that would keep us safe and out of the local FSB offices. This evening though, lady fortune had rewarded us: the local Gorky Theater was putting on a performance that was partly burlesque cabaret and part satire of the Russian government. The show had been highly promoted within the expat community, primarily emphasizing the scantily clad "ballerinas" that made up the cast. We weren't too excited to fork over $20 for a ticket and hoped to negotiate a discount considering our status as humanitarian aid workers.

Our karma must have been in prime form, for we arrived at the ticket booth at the same time as a visiting American Rotary Club. With a quick exchange of winks, Gary and I slipped among the crowd and were ushered in alongside them without having to pay a cent. Once inside we took a seat at a back table in an effort to keep a low profile. A waitress appeared and we ordered drinks while congratulating ourselves on being so clever. We were on our second drink when the lights dimmed and the sound of Russian folk music drifted from the speakers. The curtains parted and several dancers appeared on stage, fully dressed in typical ballerina attire. After thirty minutes without a hint of nudity, there was an announcement that the actual cabaret part of the show would follow a brief intermission. Excited that we hadn't been sold a false bill of goods, we signaled for another round. We were in the midst of frivolous conversation when the US vice consul general approached our table with as smug a look as I had ever seen. We had dealt with her during our "mugging" incident and gotten off on the wrong foot. She treated the Peace Corps volunteers as secondary citizens in comparison to the American business expats and other consular staff, constantly proffering condescending remarks at our expense. Skipping all pleasantries, she asked if we had snuck into the show. I exclaimed how rude we found her suspicions. She was only a few years our senior, but the difference in our roles couldn't have been larger out here in the Russian Far East. She stomped off muttering under her breath when we falsely bragged that we were dating two of the ballerinas and had received complimentary tickets. From our first days in Russia, the consulate staff had treated us as though they were older siblings forced to babysit the younger children when the folks went out on the town. The show was uneventful, although, without a doubt, more exciting than if we had stayed put in the dorms.

After a good night's sleep and a modest breakfast of coffee and hard-boiled eggs, we made our way to my family's apartment. Mama had prepared an incredible spread for Easter lunch and since there was no tradition of going to church, the celebration consisted primarily of sharing this big meal. The meal started out with more hard-boiled eggs and some black bread. This was promptly followed by platters of pastries, salads, and potato dishes along with a bottle of quality Georgian cognac that Papa seemed especially excited to share. It was an enjoyable and relaxing afternoon; I had to loosen my belt twice to accommodate my food intake. Mama couldn't quite understand that Gary was a vegetarian and would place heaps of chicken or pork onto his plate, which he would then push off onto my plate the second she turned her back. The afternoon ended with Mama preparing care packages to send home with us prior to Papa dropping me off at the train station.

MAY 2, 1995

Two unfamiliar men walked into my office this morning and proceeded straight to the big map of the United States that hung near the entrance—not a glimpse in my direction. Most Russians were hesitant to enter and looked almost sheepish when they explained the reason for their visit. These two ignored me completely and stood staring at the map while mumbling to each other. After a few minutes, I joined them as they sounded out "Philadelphia," "St. Louis," and a host of other cities. I cleared my throat and they turned as if finally noticing that they were not alone in the room. "How much would a house cost in Kentucky?" one asked. "$150,000" I responded, having no real basis of knowledge, but wanting to sound confident. After several more questions concerning real estate prices, they left without thanking me or responding to my questions as to the purpose of their visit.

A few minutes later, Uri poked his head around the door and with a mischievous grin, asked if I would like to join him for dinner this evening. Knowing that any night out with Uri was bound to be exciting, I agreed, forgoing my plan of sitting home alone with a pot of ramen noodles. I met him at his car in the parking lot at 5 p.m. and we promptly drove to the mafia enforcer Anatoli's mansion. No sooner had we exchanged greetings and hung up our coats when I was put to work translating the instructions for a newly purchased bread-making machine. Anatoli had recently returned from a shopping trip to Japan and had picked up several appliances that were unavailable on the Russian market. These types of goods were a signature of the nouveau riche and often were positioned around people's homes as if they were paintings or sculptures instead of kitchen appliances. I translated the instructions while Anatoli's wife scribbled down my every word, and in return, I was led to Anatoli's private den and offered a stale Cuban cigar that crumbled when I twirled it around in my fingers. Alongside one wall of his office was a glass showcase exhibiting more than a dozen firearms including everything from assault weapons to revolvers. He unlocked the doors to the case and handed me one of the revolvers, which had supposedly come from a German World War II soldier. As if fearing that I was not yet fully impressed, he put his foot up onto a chair and pulled up his pant leg to show off a more modern handgun that was secured in his ankle holster. Anatoli had been a mid-level KGB officer. When the Soviet Union disintegrated, he had hitched his cart to the mayor and now served as his head of security. There were many "organizations" throughout the Russian Far East run by former KGB officers, but none were strong enough to consolidate power, which lead to frequent power struggles complete with assassinations, car bombings, and kidnappings. In addition to his work for the mayor, Anatoli bragged about his brothels, nightclubs, and various "trading companies." In his mind, he had taken what the country offered and was a survivor—he felt no qualms about how he lived his life as long as he was able to feed and shelter his family. When I first started attending his parties, I was amazed at how many beautiful women hung all over us as if they had a fetish for fat, balding middle-aged men. I had no idea that they had little choice and were surviving just like Anatoli and the other party attendees. I would often shake my head in amazement the morning after a party, trying to understand how I had hooked up with such a hottie with so little effort. It wasn't until later that I realized what was happening; there were never any wives or girlfriends present and the women were employees from the mafia brothels.

After the gun show we walked across the street to the mayor's house. It was the mayor's birthday and I felt honored to have been included on the guest list—even more so when I realized that I was one of only three guests. Was I now "Consiglieri Reech"? Maybe they thought that I was a spy and figured that if they got me liquored up I would divulge some vital information, or maybe they saw me as a harmless good-natured guy whom they enjoyed getting drunk. Either way, I sat toe-to-toe with them drinking vodka like it was, well, vodka. We drank out of shot glasses shaped like cowboy boots and feasted on an array of delicacies prepared by the mayor's wife. At times I was lost in a vodka-induced haze and unable to follow the gist of conversation, daydreaming about scenes of Ray Liotta in "Goodfellas." I tried to look tough, pretending that the vodka didn't burn on the way down and that the alcohol had little effect on me, which was clearly not the case when I stood up to use the restroom and knocked over two chairs before crashing into the wall. How do these Russian guys drink so much and maintain an appearance of sobriety?

I awoke the next morning with another major-league hang over, fully dressed, with the imprint of the sofa cushion embedded in my cheek. I chased two Advils down with a mug of leftover coffee and then braved an ice-cold shower before jumping on a bus to one of the outlying villages to teach my first Junior Achievement class. The lecture was on "Competition, Monopolies, and Intellectual Property Protection." I had practiced my speech in front of the mirror a dozen times and had tried to prepare for questions the students might ask. Capitalism was in its infancy and none of the students had any of the foreknowledge that American kids would have at this age. I was still a bit of a novelty, as the American, which likely contributed to the interest in the class—and although prepared for business questions, I doubted that any of the questions they actually asked would be related to my lecture.

Yelena, who served as my Russian-language tutor, was also the teacher assigned to work with me on this project. She flashed a huge smile when I walked into the teachers' lounge and introduced me to the other teachers as her American friend before ushering me out into the hallway for a quick tour of the school. I hadn't realized how important this was for her, not just because she had initiated the Junior Achievement program, but because my presence elevated her profile within the school.

When we reached her classroom I saw that it was decorated in a similar manner to my office, with tourist posters and world maps adorning the walls. Yelena chatted uneasily as the high school juniors and seniors took their seats. Judged solely by their actions, they could have been students in any American city. The boys sat in the back looking uninterested while the girls crowded into the first three rows, all staring up. Yelena introduced me and the students clapped. I said "Hello," then moved in front of the teacher's desk and asked a few questions in Russian to break the ice. They seemed shocked that I could speak Russian and I made sure to thank Yelena for tutoring me in the language. Once the tension had eased, I began speaking in English with Yelena translating.

As I finished my prepared speech I asked if anyone had a question. This led to all of the students simultaneously lowering their heads, eyes focused on their desks or the back of the head of the kid in front of them. I told them that if nobody spoke up, I would randomly pick the person who looked most interested in hiding. Yelena gave a prodding stare at a student and her hand shot up. She asked me if I was married. My first reaction was to laugh, assuming that this was a joke, but when nobody else laughed I responded. "No, I'm not." This opened up the deluge of questions and a dozen more hands shot up, each question pertaining to whether I found Russian girls attractive, whether I would consider marrying someone from

Artyom, and what I thought of the Russian people. One of the students asked me why I was still single at twenty-seven. This answer required a little finesse as I tried to explain the cultural differences between our countries as well as how the average age for marriage in America differed by the part of the country in which one lived.

I was disappointed that not a single question had anything to do with my lecture, but then again, for most of these kids, I was the first American they had ever met. Without access to an independent television news program, they learned all that they knew from Hollywood soap operas like "Santa Barbara," which were dubbed in Russian and shown on the weekends. Part of being a Peace Corps volunteer was to build bridges with our host country and I was fortunate to be in a position to discuss my version of American culture to the next generation of Russian leaders. I answered their questions honestly without straying too far into Russian or American politics. During the question-and-answer time, I bypassed Yelena's translation, speaking slowly in my best Russian in an effort to better connect with the students. In concluding, I made the mistake of inviting any of the students to drop by my office if they wanted to practice their English or chat about America. As soon as I mentioned it, I envisioned daily visits from the teenaged girls who continued to stare up at me.

When I arrived home, still on a high from the Junior Achievement class, I found a note from my neighbor Tatiana (Leonid's wife) wedged into the crack of my door. She had invited me to join her in a big "celebration" this evening. I was nervous about getting too close to this pair of my neighbors, since I had witnessed his dalliances with his mistress and on the occasions when she would cross paths with me in the hallways, she was overly touchy-feely, letting her hand linger a little too long on my arm. Against my better judgement, I wrote a big "DA" on the note and slid it under her door. That night I dressed in a clean shirt and slacks with my shiny black shoes and knocked on the door, a bottle of Champagne tucked under each arm. Tatiana opened the door, gave me a big hug, and then whispered that she had a friend that she wanted me to meet. "Great,"

I replied since almost every one of my Russian friends felt compelled to play matchmaker as if I was a helpless soul unable to meet anyone on my own. Three couples and a single woman were sitting around the kitchen table, drinks in hand, when Tatiana walked me in. We shook hands and then I was shown to the only empty seat. Vera, my blind date, seemed a little nervous and talked so quickly that I had no idea what she was saying. I just kept nodding my head and drinking the occasional shot of vodka as toasts were made. I felt like I was being auctioned off as Tatiana boasted of my cooking prowess and how I loved Russians and Russian food. I felt like I was with my grandmother in the lobby of her apartment building, listening to her brag about me to the other retirees.

The night ended with Vera joining me for a nightcap in my apartment. I was drunk and a bit sheepish as I didn't want to put forth any more effort understanding her staccato of Russian. She had been chatting all evening and I was lucky if I captured 10 percent of what she said. This didn't seem to be a problem since she had little interest in continuing our discussions. I woke at 6 a.m. with a wicked hang over and half of my ass hanging over the side of the mattress. With my tongue stuck to the roof of my mouth and a painful haze enveloping my head, I made my way to the bathroom, threw a pot of water on the range to boil for tea, and tried to figure out a plan to get her out of my apartment. I needed more sleep and the thought of having to carry on a conversation was daunting. I decided to shower quickly, which was the only option considering the lack of hot water, and then pretend that I had to go to the office. This proved successful: we left together ten minutes later and then I walked back to my apartment and immediately got back in bed.

MAY 7, 1995

The fiftieth anniversary of the end of WWII is this week and all of Artyom is going nuts in preparation for the parades and parties. For the past month, veteran's committees have been cleaning the streets, painting government buildings, and polishing the Lenin statues that still stand guard outside those government buildings as a beacon of Russia's past military strength. Valentina invited me to a celebration sponsored by the city administration to which more than a thousand guests were expected. On the day of the event, I joined Valentina and the mayor at the head table along with the admiral of Russia's pacific fleet. I had a short speech memorized just in case I was asked to make a toast. This was smart planning: I watched nervously as everyone else at the table took a turn at the podium to address the crowd. It felt inappropriate to address these Russian veterans during such a solemn ceremony when I was just a twenty-seven-year-old American whose closest connection to serving in the military was dining next to a poster of Colonel Sanders at a Kentucky Fried Chicken. At the same time, the whole thing fed my ego and by the time I thought I was up for my speech, I felt as though I deserved to be included. As the speeches dragged on and the toasts continued, my head got foggy and the sweat starting rolling down my face. Fortunately, out of either pity or some other reason, the ceremony concluded without my having to address the audience. I was greatly relieved and smiled as they continued to fill my glass with Stolichnaya amid toasts to the greatness of the Soviet troops. When dinner was served, each person at the table made a short toast to fallen comrades or lost family members. When my turn arose, I recited the speech that I had prepared and everyone seemed quite impressed. When the dishes were finally cleared, the mayor and Valentina left to make the rounds shaking hands and acting political, leaving me like a lone scarecrow in an empty field. I realized that nobody was paying any attention to me, so I silently walked toward the exit left feeling tired, drunk, and far from home. I wanted to return to my apartment, listen to my own music, and look at my photo albums. Homesickness was pressing down hard and I yearned for the voice of a friend or a smile from a family member.

I'd changed into a T-shirt and jeans and put on a pot of water to make tea when my self-pity was interrupted by a soft knock at the door. I looked out through the peephole and didn't see anyone. I asked who was there and instead of an answer, another knock followed. I was wary of opening the door to strangers, but my curiosity got the best of me. With a flashlight gripped tightly in my right hand, I slowly opened the door with my left. In a flurry of action, a small white kitten flew into my apartment as the shadow of a small boy disappeared down the stairwell. I could have kicked myself for acting so foolishly. I had been warned to watch out for this exact thing, since there were few, if any, Russian veterinarians. In Russia, neutering or spaying a pet is considered cruel, so every spring thousands of puppies and kittens are born to families who don't want them. Parents tell their children that if they can't find a home for them, they will have no choice but to drown them in the bathtub. This, of course, doesn't sound cruel to them! The children often resort to the famous "knock and run" trick to prey on the kindness of idiots like myself.

I got down on my hands and knees to inspect my tiny guest and, since the boy was long gone, I knew that I was stuck with this kitten. I couldn't possibly throw it back outside and leave it to a fate unknown. I didn't want a pet, but since I was feeling down and this little kitten cheered me up, I decided to hold on to it for a while. How hard could it be to find it a home? I thought of Vitaly, but he already had a cat that he constantly complained about. Irina had just gotten a puppy for her son, but she was soft and I suspected she wouldn't be able to say no once she saw it. I took the red bow off of a bottle of jam and tied it loosely around the kitten's neck before sticking it into an empty shoebox. I ran down the stairs and into the street, where I flagged down a taxi to take me to her apartment. Once outside her apartment, I checked to make sure the bow was still around the kitten's neck and then knocked on the door, hoping that her son would be home. It worked out perfectly: Irina fawned over the kitten. Within an hour the kitten was curled up next to the puppy, both soundly asleep. Irina's son hovered over them, his serious five-year-old face looking concerned as he struggled to come up with the perfect name. He chose "Mooka," the Russian word for flour. That night when I reached my own apartment, I saw several children playing in the parking lot. I asked them what they had eaten for dinner and then told them that I had eaten a very delicious kitten, rubbing my stomach for added drama. I hoped that word would spread that the American ate cats and that this would prevent any future "knock and run" encounters.

MAY 8, 1995

The United States Agency for International Development (USAID) hired an American consultant to set up small-business incubators in Vladivostok. This was an innovative approach that had worked well in other countries, and I hoped it would catch on here. I looked forward to meeting the consultant, since several of my clients were in a good position to benefit from the contacts and potential funding offered by USAID. It has been frustrating working with really bright entrepreneurs and developing business plans and then having to sit idle while we searched for financing. I spoke to the consultant and agreed to meet him at his hotel, which happened to be Vladivostok's most expensive—it catered primarily to foreign businessmen, mafia elites, and high-end hookers. In the two weeks that the consultant had been in town, he had earned a reputation among the other volunteers as a good contact. This may have had as much to do with his expense account and eagerness for company than with his ability to help our clients.

Unfortunately, he had also earned a reputation as a big partier, which was evident when he showed up sloppy drunk for our meeting with a scantily clad lady on his arm. "You must be Rich?" he slurred. I nodded, surprised that he would care so little about me that he would show up drunk for a lunch meeting. He asked if I minded his "friend" joining us as he maneuvered us toward the bar. Ten minutes into our meeting his hand slid up the woman's thigh and under her skirt, making both the woman and me a bit uncomfortable. I excused myself, gathered my briefcase, walked out of the restaurant, and then stood in the lobby trying to understand what had transpired. I was insulted and angry that I had prepared for a serious meeting with a US government representative and had been treated in an abhorrent manner. It seemed even more of an abuse when I thought of how much US Treasury money he was spending without making even a pretense of trying to help us.

With the weather warming above zero and signs of spring in the air, most Russians begin to get antsy to return to their dachas to start clearing the dirt and planting the gardens that would sustain them during the fall and winter. My host family was caught up in the excitement too, and called me to say that they would pick me up Saturday morning and that I should be ready to get my delicate little American hands dirty. Back home in New Jersey I would have been scanning the sports pages for updates on the Mets spring-training games, but here I was chatting about the amount of rain and snow we got over the winter and whether the conditions were appropriate for seeding the garden. Papa, Gary, and Timofey picked me up with the goal of my returning with them to Vladivostok at the end of the day. Papa appreciated our assistance, despite our lack of any formal farmhand experience. Fortunately, skill wasn't much of an issue since we spent the entire morning clearing old roots and twigs before digging six-inch trenches to plant potato, carrot, squash, and zucchini seeds. Our delicate American hands were soon covered with blisters while Papa, unfazed by the effort, seemed happy to be spending his day sweating while accomplishing real work. By noon I had built up quite an appetite. As the person in charge of our meals, I walked to the side of the dacha to build a fire in a small pit dug into the earth. Over an open fire, I grilled prawn and conch kebabs, which we ate with a salad and some rice that Mama had packed up to sustain us through our efforts. Papa pulled out a bottle of his homemade wine, which we passed from hand to blistered hand. It was sour, tasted like Robitussin cough medicine, and went down like water. Our pace slowed significantly after the meal and was nearing a standstill when Papa gave the sign to pack it up. Gary and I collapsed under the shade of an apple tree while Papa gathered kindling for the *banya*. This wasn't the fancy, marble-lined banya that the Mayor had in his house, but a traditional country *banya* that consisted of a small wooden frame, a bench or two inside along with a heating box and chimney. When smoke began to pour from the chimney and the coals glowed in anticipation of our arrival, Papa stripped down to his tighty whitey underwear and beckoned us to follow. There wasn't enough room for more than two at a time, so Gary and I took turns so that Papa could serve as the *banya* master, waving a birch branch over the steam and then whacking us on the back and shoulders to beat the heat into us before dousing us with buckets of ice-cold rainwater from a rooftop tank. Supposedly the toxins in your body are removed via this process, but I had serious doubts.

When we finally got back to Gary's apartment, aching and blistered, we collapsed around his kitchen table with *kolodnya piva* (cold beer) and acknowledged just how much of a pussy we each were for being this beat-up after only a few hours of work. Before we could finish the first beer, one of the other Americans in Gary's building burst into the room to fill us in on the latest gossip. Three of our American colleagues had been arrested by the Russian border police on charges of espionage. Both of the local television stations reported that they had been caught filming video along the North Korean border. The rumor mill provided us with the additional information that they had taken a weekend road trip to the town of Khasan, which sits along the section of Russia that borders both North Korea and China. They took along a video camera to document their exploits, which included heavy drinking as well as their pissing on the border fence, and a few minutes of skinny dipping, which I doubt they would have done had they known the extent of the pollution. The Russians were constantly on guard of an attack from their Asian neighbors in this strategically sensitive area, since the land contained large quantities of raw minerals. The Russian side was sparsely populated while both the Korean and Chinese sides were bustling with activity and heavily populated. China was aggressively seeking deals for access to the Russian coal and oil reserves, and the North Koreans were all but starving and would emigrate at the first opportunity. With the confusion between Moscow and the outlying regional governments, no deals were possible due to the large number of hands that would have to be greased. The three Americans were unprepared for the welcoming party when they were surrounded by a dozen heavily armed Russian border guards who were still on edge following an incident the day before that led to a death in their group. Apparently, frog hunting on the Russian side of the border is much better than on the Chinese side, so a gang of Chinese poachers snuck across the border to harvest the amphibians, and they ran into a small Russian patrol. A shoot-out followed and one of the Russians had been killed. When I first heard about this I found it too strange to believe. I could only imagine how I would explain this to my friends back home: that I had to be on guard against roving gangs of dangerous frog poachers, Siberian tigers, and the occasional pack of feral dogs.

The story got better as we garnered additional information. Supposedly the Americans were stopped by the border guards on their way into the area and told to leave immediately. They were warned that that the guards were under orders to shoot anyone approaching the border without proper authority. The Americans left the area and ended up in a local bar, which must have affected their map-reading abilities because when they got back on the road they re-entered the border zone. After having a bit of fun, they ran into the same border patrol and were taken into custody, interrogated, and labeled as spies in a statement that was released to the international press. Eventually the American consulate intervened and the volunteers were released, but not before the news had spread throughout the region. The Peace Corps was already under heavy suspicion of working for the CIA, so this did little to improve our relationships with the Russian government or press. One of the Americans was immediately deported, while the other two will remain under house arrest. Having dealt with the Russian police and FSB, I did not envy these guys in any way. In our case, we had denied everything and it was our word against the mafia's. For these guys, their stupidity in filming themselves had removed all doubt as to their actions.

MAY 26, 1995

Each Peace Corps volunteer is given four weeks of vacation time, with a push to stick within their region. Visits home are highly discouraged, but with international telephone service spotty and the mail service even less reliable, many of us were homesick and thought constantly about a few weeks of rest and relaxation back in the States. The Peace Corps push for local travel was two-fold in nature: to allow us to add to our experience by seeing more of our host country and to limit the possibility of losing volunteers who would decide to stay home. My six weeks in Washington, D.C. had satisfied my homesickness for the most part, and I was eager to see more of Russia. With international transportation as unreliable as the phone service, it made sense to focus on the easily accessed St. Petersburg and Moscow, eight time zones to the east and farther away from Vladivostok than California. My buddy Ted agreed to meet me in St. Petersburg. There we could stay with a friend of my host family's daughter Ira before eventually taking a train to Moscow to see the sights.

With my travel plans complete, I spent time daydreaming of the great meals I would soon be eating. Artyom still has just the one restaurant, and the few in Vladivostok have similar menus, leading to meal fatigue. In the absence of supermarkets, your home-cooked meals are limited to whatever you can scavenge in the local outdoor markets or kiosks. These aren't great options and after a long winter, I am tired of potatoes, rice, and pasta: I yearn for a plate of osso buco and polenta. Even more disturbing to my pursuit of a better meal was a story on the local television reporting that a man had been arrested in Vladivostok for selling human flesh advertised as beef. He admitted that he had stolen the "meat" from the morgue and tried to sell it to make ends meet, since he was out of work and hungry. These stories would be humorous if they were less prevalent. My co-workers in the city administration building were so embarrassed by the story that they quickly shifted the blame to the central government, insinuating that if not for such dire conditions, people wouldn't be forced to commit such atrocities. I wouldn't blame people for stealing a cow or chicken to feed their families, but I just couldn't get past the idea of raiding the morgue.

MAY 27, 1995

After twenty hours of travel, including stopovers in the cities of Irkutsk and Novosibirsk, I landed in St. Petersburg. Air travel in Russia is an adventure, especially when flying on Aeroflot. The planes seem to be held together with duct tape and the service is more akin to that in a cheap Mexican bodega than what you expect from an airline. My in-flight meal consisted of a roasted chicken leg served in a plastic sandwich baggie. The beverage choice was water and it was served in a chipped coffee mug that looked like it hadn't been washed in years. These poor food options were still superior and significantly more attractive than what was available during my stopovers. These airports are ill-prepared to service incoming planes and provide little in the way of amenities or facilities. Planes frequently are stranded after landing due to a lack of oil to refuel, leaving passengers to sleep in unheated terminals for days until a supply can be negotiated.

Fortunately my flight proved uneventful and I arrived on time with all of my bags intact. I made my way to the pick-up area to meet Arkady, the ex-father-in-law of Timofey's sister Ira. Having never met him or even seen a photograph, my only guide was to look for an old man with white hair carrying a newspaper. When I walked out to the waiting area, there were a hundred men fitting that very description. With no chance of identifying him, I stood patiently trying to stand out from the pack of tourists rushing to and fro, in the hope that my being the only foreigner would set me apart. My plan worked. Barely five minutes passed before a man approached and offered his hand. "Reech?" he asked shyly. "Arkady," I responded. There was an immediate sense of kindness about him that put me at ease, as if we were old acquaintances instead of strangers. I told him all about my life in Vladivostok with the family during the 45-minute drive to his apartment in downtown St. Petersburg. He was patient with my Russian-language ability and responded slowly so that I didn't have to ask him to repeat every sentence as I often was forced to do when introduced to new accents. St. Petersburg was distant from Artyom and considered part of Europe as opposed to the Far East. People here were more cosmopolitan and spoke quickly, reminding me of the differences between Iowa and New York City. It was apparent that he lived alone, with visitors infrequent: his apartment was extremely cluttered. Every inch of wall space was filled with photographs and paintings and likewise, every inch of table, counter, or bench space was stacked with books, magazines, and assorted knick-knacks.

I sat at the table looking through his photo albums while he busied himself in the kitchen. He mentioned that he had not had a visitor in several months and he had never had a foreigner, much less an American, in his apartment. The smell and sound of sizzling garlic, onions, and peppers made my mouth water. I could barely sit still waiting for him to return, and when he did, I was not disappointed. Platters of kielbasa, smoked fish, and caviar covered the table. While I feared that the table would collapse under the weight of all of the food, he returned with a dusty bottle of Georgian cognac. "I have been saving this for a special occasion!" he said, his smile reminding me of Papa.

Arkady's bulbous nose and rosy cheeks gave away his penchant for drinking and his warm character and charm made me want to listen to his stories all night. We toasted to each other and then to the health of our families and friends before setting into the feast. After a few more drinks I realized that he looked strikingly similar to Boris Yeltsin, although this might have had more to do with my consumption of cognac than it did anything else. He was an animated speaker and the more we drank, the louder he got, as if he wanted to make sure that I understood every word. He was a retired history professor and his stories kept me spellbound despite the jet lag. We discussed the cold war from the American and Russia vantage points as well as his personal account of surviving the nine-hundred-day siege of Leningrad. I wanted to stay awake and hear more, but the eight-hour time difference combined with the enormous amount of food and drink proved too much. I raised the white flag and took refuge on his sofa under a pile of blankets.

The next morning I woke to the smell of freshly brewed coffee, a treat that I had been missing for quite some time. I splashed water on my face, brushed my teeth, and then spent the next hour eating a tremendous breakfast with my new friend. Our plan for the day was to meet up with Ira, my host sister, and then visit the Hermitage Museum. We gingerly walked to the train station, with Arkady pointing out each landmark, until we turned the corner into the Hermitage courtyard. Ira came running toward us, her face aglow. As with Arkady, I felt an instant kinship and it must have been mutual because we hugged like we were actually related. After a few minutes exchanging pleasantries, we sat on a nearby bench so that she could show me photographs of her children. After this we spent hours walking through the Hermitage Museum before heading out along the Neve River, down cobblestone streets and through open-air markets. It seemed that every twenty feet we would pass another intricately carved statue or fountain. The city was one of the most awe-inspiring places I had visited. At 3:30 Ira had to catch a train back home to meet her two children and Arkady and I left for the airport to pick up my friend Ted.

From behind a security fence, we watched Ted come into view dragging a large duffle bag past the customs' checkpoint and through the security gate. Seeing him was like getting a shot of adrenaline: the months of being away from all that represented home hit me like a punch to the gut. I introduced him to Arkady, translating between English and Russian before grabbing his bag and leading the way to the line of taxis. With Ted and Arkady unable to understand each other, it was difficult to have any meaningful conversation and we ended up listening to Arkady's description of what we were passing until we reached his apartment. In the spirit of Russian hospitality, Arkady left us to chat while he prepared another feast complete with two more bottles of cognac. It was difficult for me to translate everything Arkady said into English and then immediately translate Ted's response back into Russian, especially after finishing the first bottle. Our meal lasted well over four hours in typical Russian fashion, which pushed Ted's stamina to the breaking point since he had flown out directly after working a double shift as a surgical resident in New York. By the end of the meal he was sound asleep at the table with his head resting on his arms.

We spent three days in St. Petersburg, touring the city and catching up on each other's lives. I introduced him to the patience necessary when encountering Russian customer service as we spent a great deal of time waiting for restaurant and bar servers to acknowledge us, much less take our order. The lack of service became so infuriating that we ended up eating at Pizza Hut and McDonalds instead of at the finer Russian restaurants. I was amazed at how modern St. Petersburg seemed in comparison to the Russian Far East. In addition to fast food restaurants, the city featured stores that accepted credit cards, which was still far from reality in Artyom. The buildings here were beautiful, with exquisite attention to detail in their style and decoration. This was an awe-inspring city, and it was understandable why the residents showed such pride. When Peter the Great had assumed power, he wanted to create a city that would rival those in Europe—Paris, Vienna, and Prague—and he set millions of engineers, architects, and construction workers out to build this beautiful city.

On our final day in St. Petersburg we visited Ira and her children. Her apartment was two hours north of St. Petersburg and located in a private area reserved for Russian aerospace employees and their families. It was rare to have foreign visitors, especially Americans, within the compound. We were the first Americans that Ira's friends and neighbors had met, making us the center of attention and subject to countless questions about our lives in America. It was a status symbol to have foreign guests, and now that Russia had opened its doors to the West, or at least was attempting to do so, Ira was keen to show us off. She had invited a dozen "close" friends over for dinner and I volunteered to lend a hand in the kitchen while Ted played with her children, aged six and ten. They had trouble understanding that he didn't speak Russian, repeatedly explaining the rules to their games and then getting frustrated when he didn't play correctly. The dinner was another Russian feast lasting several hours and incorporating dozens of toasts. Translating was tiresome and at some point I took a break. A few minutes later I turned to find Ted asleep again in his chair at the table. I know it must have been painful to sit through a five-hour meal while still dealing with the jet lag and I promised that this would be the last time he would have to sit through a Russian family meal.

We left for Moscow the following evening on the overnight train and arrived at the Yaroslavsky Terminal in Moscow at 7 a.m. The weather in Moscow was a dismal 50 degrees and rainy, leaving us damp and shivering. The terminal is the starting place for the Trans-Siberian railroad, the world's longest train line with its endpoint across the country in Vladivostok 9,288 kilometers away. I was familiar with the station in Vladivostok, a replica of the one in Moscow since both were renovated by the same Italian contractor. The building here was immense and so crowded that the flow of people propelled us toward the street. Russia is not a tourist-friendly location and as such, there was no information or tourist desk; we staggered from place to place trying to get our bearings. We needed a hotel and decided that the best way would be to leave our bags in a locker at the station and then set off on foot. I had a map of Moscow indicating where the hotels were and we designed a course that would take us past the Kremlin, Lenin's tomb, and St. Basil's Cathedral while allowing us to stop at hotels along the way.

We stopped at eight hotels and at each we were rudely advised by a receptionist that there weren't any rooms available. Sometimes they would keep us waiting ten minutes before acknowledging our presence and then with a condescending sneer we were asked what we wanted. I felt like yelling, "It is a fucking hotel, what do you think we want?" On the eighth attempt I was exasperated, as I knew that there was no way all of these hotels could be at 100 percent occupancy. I confronted the receptionist and begged her to tell us why we couldn't get a room. Sympathy must have overruled her contempt because she actually responded and advised that the only way a foreigner can secure a hotel room was to go through the

Russian governmental tourist agency called Intourist. The Intourist agent would get a commission, as would the hotel receptionist. We followed the directions to the nearest Intourist agency and booked a room in the hotel we had just left, paying a $30 service fee to be split between the agency and the receptionist. I didn't mind the additional cost as much as the hassle and lack of communication. If I had been traveling to a foreign country I would have done my research ahead of time to better understand the customs and procedures, but since I had been living in Russia for over a year, it never occurred to me that I would not have the street smarts necessary to get basic services.

When we returned to the hotel with our Intourist receipt, the receptionist took a look at our passports and visas and shook her head at us. What could be wrong now? I asked gruffly. She said that Ted's visa was missing the accommodation stamps identifying where he had spent the night while in St. Petersburg, and without these she couldn't stamp it for his stay here without getting herself in trouble. Prior to being issued a visa to enter Russia you had to provide the name and address of every hotel where you would be staying. If you plan to stay with a Russian national, you were required to obtain the government's approval in writing prior to doing so. This relic of the Cold War had led Ted to make reservations at one of the expensive international hotels in St. Petersburg since he had no way of reaching me to get Arkady's information and then apply for approval. It was much easier to just make a reservation and then cancel it after getting his visa issues, which was what he had done. The hotel receptionist played hardball until I offered to pay her a $30 "correction fee" to provide the stamps for the missing dates. Ted and I were both pissed at our own naïveté and the general sense of having to "pay to play" but knew that our complaining would do little to change the situation.

Now that we had a room, our only objective was to return to the train station to retrieve our bags. The light sprinkling of rain had now turned into a full downpour, forcing us to run from one covered door to the next. When we got to the train station, soaking wet, we pushed our way through to the luggage storage area and retrieved our bags. Not wanting to brave the weather again just yet, we huddled under the cover of the terminal and drank a few bottles of Russian beer. Russian beer at 10 percent alcohol content hits pretty quickly, so we drank slowly, enjoying the people-watching. Babushkas were viscously waving to prospective customers in an effort to sell their stock of vegetables, sunflower seeds, and loaves of bread. Gypsy children braved nasty glances as they scampered among the commuters holding out their small palms in the hope of a few coins.

Taking advantage of a break in the weather, we made it back to the hotel and dropped off our bags. It had been an inauspicious start to our Moscow adventures, made worse by Ted's inability to communicate and the difficulty that we faced getting even the simplest of tasks accomplished. I too was tired: tired of translating and tired of feeling that I had to defend Russia and its inadequate infrastructure. We left the hotel in search of a restaurant, second-guessing our decision to leave the beauty of St. Petersburg. It was at this moment that we passed a travel agency boasting posters in their windows of white sandy beaches, palm trees, and a glistening sea. The contrast with the glum visuals before us led to an instant decision to step inside. We bought two round-trip tickets to Cyprus, one of the only sunny locations that didn't require an additional visa, and miraculously our smiles returned. Ted had a single-entry visa to Russia and we asked whether this would pose a problem, since he had to return to Moscow to catch his return flight to the United States. The agent assured us that since our flight from Cyprus was on the same date as his flight back to the United States, he would automatically receive a transit visa from the Aeroflot office in Cyprus.

After eating dinner at an overpriced bistro, we walked through Red Square and the Kremlin grounds looking at a history that we had only witnessed via Cold War movies. We tried to get into a nightclub but were turned away by the mafia thugs guarding the door, leading us to return to the hotel for a good night's sleep. In the morning we took a taxi to the airport and flew to Cyprus, where we were greeted by friendly people and the white powdery beaches that we had seen in the travel agency window. For six days and nights we listened to live music, ate fantastic Mediterranean food, and relaxed under the sun. It really felt like a vacation. When it came time to leave, we checked in with the Aeroflot agent to get Ted his transit visa. They assured us that he didn't need one since his connecting flight to the United States was out of the same airport.

Five days in Cyprus was just what the doctor had ordered. Total sunshine, a raucous nightlife, and inexpensive and friendly restaurants and bars. The time had sped by and it was almost painful having to return to Moscow. In hindsight, Ted should have changed his flight and bypassed Russia: we immediately ran into trouble upon arrival. The Russian immigration officers refused to allow Ted to pass though immigration because his visa specified a single entry and within seconds guards led him away, without giving us the opportunity to explain that he only needed a transit visa since he had a ticket departing later in the day. I was left holding both of our bags and was afraid that once we were separated, I wouldn't be able to find him. I ran after them, only to be held back by another set of guards. I explained that I wanted to give him his bags, but they refused even to listen to me and I was ushered back to the waiting area. I watched them lead him to a secure area. We made eye contact and could only shrug our shoulders as we waited to see what would transpire. The Russians were waiting for somebody with authority to show up and after a few minutes, the guards went back to their business. I saw an opportunity when none of them were paying attention and hoisted his bag onto my shoulders and then tossed it several feet in the air to clear the barrier. Ted grabbed his bag and then pretended to be at ease waiting for the guards to return. A few seconds later a guard approached me and walked me toward the arrival gate, giving me only a second to wink at Ted before leaving him behind. I had no idea what to do in case Ted needed assistance, but none of the security guards would provide me with any information as to his status.

By 7 p.m. the final international flight had departed and the airport was closing. I hoped that he had made his flight, but I had no way to know. The doors were locking around me and the lights were turning off section by section. I ran to the information desk to see when the next flight was leaving for Vladivostok and the woman just shook her head, telling me that the only flights to Vladivostok went through Moscow's domestic airport. Her rudeness and sarcasm gave her reason to smile while inside I fantasized about wrapping my hands around her throat. I had been highly stressed and waiting around the airport for an entire day and all I wanted was a little compassion. Her smirk sent me over the edge and I snapped, swearing at her with my best Russian slang. I knew the words were bad, but didn't really know exactly what they meant . . . but apparently it served its purpose as her face turned a bright shade of red and she began to shake. Deciding that it was best that I leave the area immediately, I walked outside the doors dragging my duffel bag. There was no public transportation between the two airports after 5 p.m., so my only option was to take a taxi. The asking fee was US $150, but I talked one into driving me for $80 considering the late hour. An hour and a half later we pulled up to Domodedovo Airport. I was exhausted and just wanted to get on a plane and fall asleep back in Vladivostok. I went straight to the information desk and found out that there was a flight to Vladivostok leaving in an hour. The bad news was that they didn't accept credit cards or US currency. The worse news was that domestic airports don't have currency exchanges so I had no way of getting Russian rubles. Tears formed in the corner of my eyes and I collapsed on a bench, my head in my hands, struggling to make sense of the idiocy of the past twelve hours. I barely had enough money for a bus to downtown Moscow and would then have to find a hotel that accepted credit cards— those consisted of the upscale hotels catering to foreign businessmen and they charged upwards of five hundred dollars per night, which far exceeded my Peace Corps monthly stipend.

It was pitch dark when the bus entered Moscow's central bus depot. I looked around for a friendly face, since I had no idea where to go. Several vagrants approached, but I gave them such a viscous look that they quickly backed off. I walked out into the street and aimed for the tallest building I could see, assuming that this would be in the downtown business area. I stopped at a few run-down hotels along the way, but none accepted credit cards or could even recommend one that did, leaving me to drag my sorry ass farther down the street. The bus driver had given me the address of the Aeroflot hotel, which he thought accepted credit cards. Eventually I found the address, but to add insult to injury, a sign advised that the hotel was closed for repairs. If it weren't for bad luck, I'd have no luck at all! I walked another two miles, swearing non-stop, until I reached the Radisson Hotel Rossiya. I realized that I did not look like a typical foreign guest as I dragged by duffel behind me. The clerk politely advised that the lowest-priced room was $350 per night. I tried to reason, explaining that I was in Russia as part of a humanitarian aid program, and I offered to pay him fifty dollars to let me sleep in a chair in the lobby until daybreak. Unable to get any sympathy and thoroughly exhausted, I desperately needed to find a place to lie down and close my eyes. I continued to several of the other high-end hotels, all yielding the same result. Out of desperation, I succumbed to my aching feet and snuck in between a row of bushes alongside a hotel and, with my back against the wall and hidden by the shrubbery, I pulled my sleeping bag out of my backpack, covered myself, and drifted off to sleep.

Splat, splat, splat. I woke to drops of water hitting my face. I was disoriented and had no idea where I was or what was happening. The rain had returned and I was exposed. I looked up for a covered area and when I saw none, I knew I had to move elsewhere. I rolled up the sleeping bag and returned it to my backpack, pushing my body against the wall in an effort to stay out of the rain. It was coming down hard and at an angle that didn't allow me any protection. I pushed through the shrubbery and walked back toward the hotel entrance, not exactly sure what to do. The hotel guard didn't want to let me in, but my practice swearing in Russian and pained countenance prevailed and he stepped back far enough to let me pass inside. It was after midnight and I was wet, cold, and close to losing my sanity. My hair was plastered over my brow, my clothes were dirty and stuck against my skin, and I just didn't care. The same manager who had earlier told me that there was nothing available under $350 per night gave me a look of disdain that only fueled my anger. He must have realized that I wasn't going to leave, so he told me to sit down while he made a few calls. Ten minutes later he told me that he would pay for a taxi out of his own money to take me to a nearby hotel that charged seventy dollars per night and accepted credit cards.

It was 3 a.m. when I opened the door to my hotel room. There was no running water, no phone, and the cockroaches ran for cover as soon as I flicked on the lights, but I wasn't complaining: it was dry and there was a bed.

For the second time in six hours I woke up without knowing where I was and had to look around to piece the night together. I went into the bathroom and the dry hissing sound of air was the only thing to come out of the pipes when I turned on the spigot. The face looking back at me from the mirror was almost unrecognizable. Without any water to wash, I doubled up on deodorant and did the best that I could with my hair. I was hoping that I would not come across as homeless, since I needed to find a travel agent that would be open on a Sunday as well as one that accepted credit cards. I had slept for eight hours and felt refreshed in body if not in spirit as I strolled through Moscow under a bright blue sky. I was actually smiling by the time I walked the narrow cobblestone streets near the older part of the city, keeping my eyes open for a travel agency. My luck had turned: within minutes I passed a store with a Citibank Visa sticker displayed in the window next to a series of photos of Paris, London, and an idyllic beach scene. The travel agent was cordial and sold me a ticket on a new airline that serviced the Far East called Orient Air. There was a flight leaving later in the afternoon and all I needed was to get back to the airport. My spirits soared and I whistled while walking back to the hotel, stopping only for cup of coffee and an Egg McMuffin. When I returned to the hotel I was pleasantly surprised to see that the water problems had been fixed and that I would get to take a shower. The water, despite being ice-cold, felt great as two days of dirt and grime washed down the drain. The only drag on my mind was wondering what had happened to Ted. I hoped that he had fared better than I had and had made it back to the US.

JUNE 6, 1995

The two weeks of vacation had recharged my batteries. I resumed my work routine with renewed passion, arriving early in the morning to see clients before spending a few hours working on my cookbook or meeting with students. The warm weather had brought Artyom out of hibernation. Temperatures soared to the mid-50s and buds began to appear on the trees. Even the old babushkas offered an occasional smile when I passed, forgoing their typical scowl. On the second morning after my return, a man arrived at my office carrying a weathered briefcase. His clothes labeled him as one of the local mine workers. He had a gleam in his eyes signaling a brain spinning with ideas, and I could sense a vibrancy about him that set him apart from the majority of my clients, who generally wanted to sit down and drink a cup of tea before getting started. He couldn't wait to tell me about his idea of opening a battery manufacturing plant in Artyom. At that time, all of the batteries available in the Russian Far East were imported from other countries. He explained how the raw materials were purchased from Russian mines by neighboring countries, which would manufacture the batteries and sell the finished product back to Russians. "Why can't we manufacture them locally and do away with the middlemen?" If he could secure financing, then it would be easy to put his plan in motion. He had identified the steps that he needed to get the project moving forward and his enthusiasm proved contagious. We spent close to five hours compiling checklists and agreed to meet the following Monday, since I was heading to Vladivostok for the weekend. I agreed to stop in at the other business centers to obtain contact information for organizations that might be willing to provide funding. I had hoped for this type of project, instead of spending my time translating the appliance instructions for the wives of the local mafia.

JUNE 7, 1995

I traveled to Vladivostok to visit with Gary and my host family, excited to share my stories about Cyprus with Gary and my time with Ira and Arkady with the family. I got off the train and walked to Gary's apartment to find him gallantly engaged in conversation with a newly arrived American woman who had rented a room across the hall from him in the dorm while trying to find a suitable apartment in the city. Maggie worked for a non-profit group based in San Diego and had come to Vladivostok, San Diego's sister city, to promote educational exchanges between Russian and American students. New to Russia, she talked non-stop about everything she had seen in the streets as well as her goals to promote the project in Russia. She definitely enjoyed talking more than listening, and I hoped that she would calibrate her expectations prior to jumping in head-first to set the world on fire. As we had learned during our first few weeks here, it is time well spent to understand the Russians and their system prior to advising them on how they should change.

On her first day Maggie had rescued a puppy from the garbage dumpster outside the dorms and had taken it back to her room, given it a bath, and fed it some mystery meat that she purchased from a kiosk. She was actively trying to find it a home. But unlike in America, there is a general antipathy toward feral cats and dogs here due to the incredible number of them that roam the cities. When the economy crashed, families had to choose between being able to feed their families or their pets, and the dogs and cats lost out and ended up fending for themselves. There are so many strays that the police conduct a culling every six months in which they warn pet owners that they will be setting out poisoned meat and then circle back the next morning to collect the dead animals. In America people would be rightly furious, but here in the Russian Far East, roving packs of dogs have attacked children and even been responsible for the killing and eating of drunken homeless people in their will to survive. It is not completely one-sided; I have also come across bloody dogs that had been killed and cooked over makeshift barbeques by the homeless as they too struggle to survive. Dog eat dog, dog eat man, man eat dog!

Anyway, over several glasses of vodka I explained all of this to Maggie, which helped her to understand why she was having so much trouble finding a home for the puppy. At midnight she returned to her room across the hall and Gary went to sleep, leaving me alone and agitated on the sofa. I was always a bit nervous sleeping on Gary's sofa since there were so many rodents that I feared being nipped at or worse during my sleep. I was tossing and turning on the sofa imagining the pitter-patter of mice when the shrill cries from the puppy across the hall brought me to my senses. I couldn't block it out, despite covering my head with a pillow and blanket. Finally at 2 a.m. I marched outside into the hallway in my boxer shorts and began to pound on her door. "What the fuck are you doing to that dog?" I screamed.

An equally shrill Maggie replied, "He's crying because I won't let him sleep with me." "Hand him to me," I snapped back. The door opened up wide enough so that she could hand me the puppy, then she slammed it in my face along with a curt "Fuck you." I returned to the couch with the puppy resting on my chest and was a moment away from sleep when the whimpering returned. I turned on the light and watched the puppy licking at its paw. I separated the pads to see if there was a cut or scratch, and the ungrateful little bastard chomped down on my hand. Already in a bad mood, I was sent over the edge and I tossed the puppy head-first into the hallway. I rinsed the bite marks and then shoved cotton in my ears to drown out the puppy cries and eventually fell asleep.

I woke to the smell of coffee and saw Gary pouring two steaming mugs. "Did you hear that fucking dog all night?" I asked and then proceeded to tell him what had happened. He laughed and asked where the dog was now. "I threw him in the hallway," I replied as I opened the door expecting to see the puppy sleeping outside the door. Instead, my heart skipped: the puppy was lying on its side, its little chest heaving while a puddle of white foam gathered around its mouth. "Gary, you've got to see this!" I said, gulping.

Gary took one look and then began beating on Maggie's door. She stuck her head around the door, looking about as happy to see us as we were to see her. "Look what you brought into my fucking apartment!" he yelled. Her eyes focused on the puppy and she stepped forward, kneeling, but not before I grabbed her wrist. "I'm not a doctor, but foaming dogs aren't something you want to touch." After saying this, I looked down at the red puffy skin on my hand and muttered something that would not have made my mother proud. "I—I'm sorry! OK?" she stammered, returning to her dorm room and, again, slamming the door. I took a sip of coffee and then walked down to the office to borrow their phone to call the Peace Corps nurse. I had to hold the phone away from my ear as her laughter echoed inside my head. "You must really love me considering how much time you spend in my office!" She further advised that I not let anyone near the dog until she showed up with the local Russian doctor who had been assigned to care for injured Peace Corps volunteers and consular staff. Unfortunately, he and I had also become close buddies over the past few months.

Sarah, one of the Peace Corps nurses, and Dr. Luzhinski arrived an hour later. And after taking one look at the puppy, donned plastic gloves and carefully slid the puppy into a shoebox, telling us that they would have it tested and get back shortly. Sarah told me to be available. An hour later she phoned and told me to come to her office to begin my rabies shots. Gary, initially finding the situation funny, was no longer laughing: he too had to get the shots since the puppy had licked his face. On a positive note, while at the Peace Corps medical office I checked my mail and was pleased to find a letter from Vitaly's brother that contained the invitation letter that would pave the way for Vitaly getting a Canadian tourist visa. I couldn't wait to tell him the good news.

On Sunday morning, Papa drove me to Artyom, since he wanted to check the dacha along the way to make sure that none of the neighbors had stolen their vegetables. I would have joined him, but I was impatient to deliver the letter to Vitaly. When I got to Vitaly's house, I wanted to make small talk for a few minutes before giving him the letter, but I couldn't do it and I immediately handed him the envelope. Within minutes of opening the letter, tears rolled down his cheeks while he fixated on the photographs of family members he had not laid eyes on for more than fifty years. He pointed out his brothers, father, and sister, all separated from him in 1947. He hugged me repeatedly and then brought out a bottle of vodka. Anger came to replace his nostalgia and after a few shots he began to curse the Communists for stealing his life and separating him from his family. It was one of those times when I realized just how much I took for granted having grown up in America. I couldn't wait to call my family and tell them how much I loved them.

JUNE 8, 1995

After many hours sitting in front of my computer and putting all of my brainpower into remembering recipes, I have finished writing my cookbook. I am hopeful that the Peace Corps office will help to get it published and am both excited and anxious to have my peers get a crack at reviewing it. Having a food-centric personality, I jumped into this effort with a great deal of passion, but the fear of rejection and criticism weighs heavily on me. In most of the countries where the Peace Corps operates, there is a volunteer or staff member who puts together a cookbook of local recipes that gets handed down from one group to the next and reprinted. Since Russia is a new country for the Peace Corps, no current cookbook existed. With shopping difficult at best here, I had included shopping tricks as well as recipes, so that the reader could find ingredient substitutions to prepare dishes both American and Russian. I had provided the history and traditions associated with each recipe, so the volunteers could bring the book home with them and it would help them share their experiences with their friends and families in America. While investigating the Russian recipes, I had interacted with many Russian cooks, of both the professional and home variety, who proudly provided their own family recipes and often invited me into their kitchens to watch them prepare and eventually eat the fruits of their labor. I found that cooking and eating was a way for me to connect with my hosts, providing us a way to share our passions and build off of our similarities. Everyone loves a smiling chef! The volunteers would now be able to prepare bagels, nacho chips, and pizza for their Russian guests.

My "research" for the book consisted primarily of dining with Russian friends who were quite eager to help me assemble recipes that highlighted local traditions. Unfortunately for the health-conscious, Russian cuisine showed little concern for the nutritional value of a meal. The concept of cholesterol or fat content was seldom mentioned for two reasons: many of my Russian friends had suffered through food shortages and the idea of having sustenance outweighed the notion of eating healthy; also, the poor transportation infrastructure in Russia made it difficult if not impossible for the government to promote a healthy diet because they had no way of getting fresh fruit and vegetables to the people outside of the growing areas. The result is a life expectancy that mimics that of sub-Saharan Africa, with men averaging a lifespan of fifty-seven. This is attributed to a combination of unhealthy diets, alcoholism, and poor access to quality medical care.

JUNE 13, 1995

The mayor called me to his office to tell me that his administration had agreed to host the new group of Peace Corps trainees in Artyom as long as I am part of the process. "Reech, you know us and I believe you will act in a manner that will prevent problems." I wasn't sure whether he was complimenting me on having established a strong relationship with the city or was warning me to make sure there weren't any problems. Either way, I knew that Ken and the Peace Corps would be pleased with the decision and I quickly called to advise them. The process of bringing the group to Artyom would include interviewing prospective host families, finding housing for Peace Corps staff, and locating classroom space.

I enjoyed my new role: it provided me with a feeling that I was important and there were deliverables that I could look back on to judge the success of my efforts. The satisfaction of contributing was often absent in my day-to-day activities as a volunteer and this new sense of value was invigorating. My relationship with the Peace Corps had also changed with these efforts as I spent considerable time coordinating with the Peace Corps staff. The increase in visits to Artyom also helped me because I was able to share rides with them and I didn't have to take the local train twice a week to get my rabies shots. The downside to spending so much time away from the office was Anna Gregorovna's concern that I was neglecting my duties at the business center. I explained that my clients often heard about the business center via word of mouth and that my increased visibility with the community would only be accentuated by my visits and discussions with potential host families. I don't think she bought it, but since the mayor had signed off on the process and requested that I be part of it, she didn't have much leverage to push back.

The flurry of activity is mind-blowing. We will need approximately forty-five host families, which will require us to interview close to a hundred to make sure that we have an adequate number of qualified families from which to choose. We also needed to find enough Russian-language instructors, which was difficult because this would be a three month position only, and most qualified teachers were already employed and hesitant to quit a full-time permanent job for a short-term gig. In addition, there was a considerable amount of political wrangling necessary to secure classroom space and housing for the Peace Corps training staff. When I think about sharing Artyom with another forty-five Americans, I have mixed emotions—I will miss being the sole American and center of attention.

The host family interviews are quite time-consuming since we received over a hundred applicants. We have to meet with each family to discuss what would be required of them and what they could expect from the trainee as well to determine if the living conditions would be acceptable. Of equal importance was to identify any particular skills, hobbies, or interests of the host family to help us in the pairing process, so that we could match the family with a trainee who has similar interests. Each visit required at least an hour, with some taking an entire evening because they included dinner invitations. Our goal is to weed out the families who were primarily interested in the weekly stipend for hosting a trainee. Some nights I would finish an interview that included a huge dinner and drinks and then head off to another interview and dinner. The families assumed that my recommendation was critical and I did little to sway them from that opinion. The Peace Corps administration wanted and actually needed my help, but at the same time I felt that this was primarily their game and I was just a volunteer helping them out. Although I understood this, I couldn't help but feel some ownership, a craving to have my contributions acknowledged and appreciated.

JUNE 14, 1995

Tiffany, a volunteer living two hours north in the city of Ussurisk, had invited Gary and me to visit her, since she was feeling a little homesick. It took all of two seconds to accept the invitation: the bond between the remaining members of our group was strong. There were a few volunteers who I would not spend time with were we back in the States, but while here in Russia we had much in common and could relate to each other's frustrations with being a foreigner. We could vent to each other, as well, without sounding like spoiled brats. I admired Tiffany and enjoyed spending time with her. She had been a Peace Corps volunteer in Africa prior to signing up for a second posting in Russia. She worked as an agribusiness consultant in a rural area and had been frustrated by the rampant sexism that interfered with her ability to get the job done and minimized her credibility. Russian men, especially those living in the smaller cities, resented taking advice from any woman, much less a qualified, confident American woman who knew her shit. Twenty minutes after confirming my visit, she called back to say that she hoped that I wouldn't be angry that she had volunteered my cooking skills to support a colleague who owned a restaurant in town. Supposedly this was Ussurisk's only upscale restaurant and when the manager heard that an American chef was visiting, she insisted that I teach her staff some American dishes. I was excited by the idea of cooking in a professional kitchen and, despite not knowing anything else about the situation, I gladly agreed.

On Friday, Gary came to Artyom and together we boarded the train to Ussurisk. One beer turned into two and then three and so on, so that by the end of the two-hour trip we were feeling pretty good. Tiffany met us at the station and we continued drinking at her apartment while sharing gossip, news, and updates on our respective experiences. The next morning, Tiffany dropped me off at the restaurant while she and Gary met some of her friends who had invited us to join them for a *shashlik* the following day. A *shashlik* is similar to an American barbeque, as far as I could tell, except that instead of drinking beer and eating hamburgers and hot dogs, you guzzle warm vodka and eat grilled pork kabobs that had been marinated in yogurt.

In hindsight, Gary and Tiffany would have preferred switching positions with me: they were both vegetarians, and while I spent the day prepping in the kitchen and meeting my new assistants, they helped slaughter a pig for our cookout. I imagined them holding in their gag reflexes while watching the pig corralled, killed, and butchered.

Meanwhile, back at the restaurant, I couldn't be happier. Tiffany's friend Tamara, who managed the restaurant, was a stunning, single twenty-eight-year-old woman who treated me like a superstar chef. I'm not sure what Tiffany had told her, but I wasn't going to dispel her of the opinion. She had sent out a note to her regular diners offering a special dinner prepared by the American chef and told me I had free rein in the kitchen. Thirty people had RSVP'd, so it would take some serious prep time to ensure that I didn't disappoint them. I spent a few minutes designing a menu with Tamara to identify what ingredients she would need to pick up to complement what was already in the kitchen refrigerators. She assigned three young women to assist me, but unfortunately they were so nervous that they were of little help. When I showed them what I wanted and asked them to continue, they stared back at me as if I had two heads. After several hours, we had prepped the portions and all the *mis en place* and I was ready to discuss how I wanted the plates to be presented. I drew diagrams for each course identifying everything from the position of the primary element to the garnish, but all I got in return were blank expressions.

I'd created a five-course menu that allowed me to show off without straying too far from that to which the Russian palate was accustomed. Russians are not the most adventurous eaters and if I put out anything too far outside of their comfort zone, they would likely smile and push it aside. As such, I took traditional Russian dishes and enhanced them with a slight French twist. The first course consisted of two types of handmade ravioli, the first stuffed with crabmeat and scallions and the second stuffed with spinach and cheese. These would resemble the popular Russian *pelmenyi*, which were typically ravioli stuffed with potato, cabbage, and ground meat. The second course consisted of small portions of filet mignon served with freshly grated horseradish and potatoes gratin. Again, this wasn't too different from what you might find in a Russian restaurant, although Russians tend to prefer their meat prepared well-done, which I couldn't possibly do and still consider myself a professional. The third course was a cream of wild mushroom soup. The Russian Far East has such an abundance of delicious mushrooms that I wanted a dish that would bring out the richness of the flavors of these local mushrooms while adding a burst of color by adding sautéed fiddlehead ferns and a roasted red pepper coulis. Most Russian soups are variations of borscht, so I hoped that they would be open to trying something new. The fourth course was a pan-seared local salmon filet accompanied with a cucumber and dill salad. The final course was a result of Tamara delivering two beautiful pork tenderloins from one of the guest's farms. Despite already having a beef course on the menu, there was no way that I couldn't use the meat without offending the customer and Tamara both. I had already prepped the other courses, so in the end there would be a lot of overfed guests. I coated the tenderloins with a garlic and herb crust and served them alongside roasted zucchini, squash, and onions. Russians are accustomed to long, multi-course meals, so having several entrees wasn't as unusual as it might seem.

At the start of the dinner, I stepped into the dining room and smiled while Tamara introduced me. Staring at thirty hungry guests was a bit intimidating and I began to second-guess my menu. Fortunately, once I got back to the kitchen and we started slamming pots and plating food, instinct took over and my only thought was to make sure that each plate looked perfect prior to going out the door. I assumed that the guests were pleased as I tried to watch the plates came back to the kitchen to be washed, looking to see what had not been eaten. Surprisingly almost every plate came back with little more than a sheen of grease. I was not responsible for the desserts, so once the final pork dish had been served I helped clean up and relaxed with a cold beer or two. It was a fun but challenging exercise for me, since it had been a while since I had cooked in a real kitchen. While the coffee and pastries were being served, Gary and Tiffany returned and the three of us joined the guests for a glass of cognac and a toast to a successful meal. I had refused payment for my efforts, so the owner presented me with a crystal bottle of cognac in appreciation of the effort. I felt a connection to Tamara and would have liked to explore the possibilities—seeing whether the feelings were mutual—but she had work to do and Gary, Tiffany, and I had a bottle of cognac to drink!

With the beer and cognac kicking in, the three of us excused ourselves for the walk back to Tiffany's apartment. I was still pretty buzzed when we arrived at her apartment so was nonplussed when she asked me to look in the sink. Earlier in the day, when I heard that Tiffany and Gary would be helping to kill a pig, I had jokingly said that it was a shame that I would miss it since I would have loved to cook the head. I don't know why I said it or why I thought that it would impress them, but apparently Tiffany had mentioned this to her friends and they'd brought the head to Tiffany's house as a surprise for me. So here I was at midnight staring face-to-face with an enormous 50-pound pig head. Gary and Tiffany were rolling on the kitchen floor, clutching their stomachs, with tears running down their cheeks as I paced back and forth with the pig's eyes following me with every step.

I have never even thought about cooking a pig's head, much less eaten one. The only idea I could come up with was to marinate the tongue and then later grill it on the barbeque. The only drawback was the pig's lack of cooperation. Rigor mortis had set in and I couldn't pry the jaws apart to cut out the tongue. I tried to hack through the jaw with Tiffany's butcher knife to no avail and then, in desperation, Gary and I carried the head to the balcony and dropped it three stories down to the pavement below with the hope of breaking the jawbone. We had to repeat this several times before the head finally split open. Between our screaming and the sound of the head splatting against the pavement, we scared the hell out of the neighbors, who must have thought we were tossing people off the balcony. I eventually cut out the tongue and marinated it in a mixture of olive oil, garlic, and a smattering of every spice in Tiffany's kitchen. My stomach and face hurt from laughing so hard and, since we had now finished the bottle of cognac given to me by Tamara, it was time to hit the sack.

The next morning we packed up the tongue and stumbled down the steps into the fresh air and sunshine where Tiffany's friends waited in their truck. Her friends were stocky Russian farmers with imposing physiques and ruddy complexions. They were excited to have three foreigners ride along and promptly took off at an alarming pace that did little to settle my stomach. The ride took us into the agricultural heartland of the region as pavement gave way to dirt roads, leaving a cloud of dust in our wake as we passed blossoming fields of wheat and corn. We finally came to a stop at the end of a dirt road where a wooden shack stood out starkly among a forest of birch and oak. There were no creature comforts here. No indoor kitchen and nothing but a beat-up outhouse as far as bathrooms were concerned. Nature and all of its beauty has a place, but after a hard night of drinking and with the look of another one in the making, I would have appreciated an air-conditioned room with a hot-water shower and accompanying Western-style commode. We took a seat on benches outside the shack while our hosts unloaded the truck. I didn't know whether to feel insulted that we weren't asked to help due to our being scrawny in comparison, or if it was just because we were guests. We swatted at mosquitoes and watched as Tiffany's friends unloaded plastic bins full of salads, the pork *shashlik* that had been marinating in yogurt and onions overnight, and several loaves of fresh bread that left the air smelling wonderful. Then out came the crate of vodka bottles! It was nine in the morning, but it may as well have been nine at night the way they began to drink. Oleg, the more talkative of our hosts, ripped the cap off the first bottle and tossed it into the trash, a signal that we were to finish the bottle as a tribute to our new friendship. Tiffany, Gary, and I were still hung over, but it would have been rude to turn them down. We took turns toasting until Oleg jokingly turned the bottle upside down and pretended to squeeze the last few drops into his glass. It was now 9:30 in the morning.

An earthy springtime smell mixed well with our vodka-induced bliss as the sun strengthened and began to warm us. Memories of baseball season flashed before me and after a quick word to Gary, I began to fashion a baseball bat from a tree branch while he made a ball by wrapping twine around a core of crumpled newspaper. It was hard not to laugh when noticing the Russians' puzzled expressions. Just as our preparations were coming to an end, two more pick-up trucks screeched to a halt in a cloud of dust and out stepped four women and two men, adding to the number of available players for our game. It wasn't exactly opening day at Wrigley, but it provided an opportunity for us to share a little Americana while also giving us a break from the steady stream of vodka that was being pushed by our hosts. The Russian men enjoyed playing, although they often forgot to run the bases after making contact with the ball, which resulting in our assessing them with penalty shots of vodka. This was our way of evening out the playing field, since they seemed intent on testing our drinking abilities. The Russian women ignored the rules of the game, focusing solely on trying to tackle Gary and me as we rounded the bases. They were big women and they flirted aggressively, refusing to accept our resistance as any indication of a lack of interest. They pinched our asses at every opportunity and followed this up with attempts at seductive smiles, which frightened me. Tiffany laughed hysterically at the cat-and-mouse theatrics, all the while egging the women on. The game ended when Gary hit the ball into the trees, where it got stuck high up in the branches. Another bottle of vodka, our fourth of the morning, was opened in celebration of Russia's first spring-training baseball game. We had worked up quite a sweat, which led to our being invited to swim in a nearby river. While Gary and I walked behind the shack to change into our bathing suits, the Russian women noisily snuck around the corner to spy on us. I cringed as the women glared at us with gyrating hips, running their tongues across their teeth.

After our swim, we returned to the picnic area where the coals for the barbeque now glowed red. Skewers of marinated pork, sliced peppers, and big chunks of sweet onion were gently laid across the makeshift grill as sunlight filtered through the birch leaves; the river gently gurgling nearby gave a sense of the mystical. I sat down with my back against a tree and felt completely relaxed, as if realizing for the first time how life should be. It didn't hurt that I was inundated with the wonderful aromas of the grilling meat and feeling quite mellow from countless shots of vodka. Out of the corner of my eye I noticed Gary slip off with one of the women. He was suffering from a combination of too much vodka and a touch of celibacy over the past few weeks. Despite his attempts to be discreet, word quickly spread, giving hope to the other Russian women, who now doubled their efforts for my affection. Assuming that the best way to avoid a difficult situation would be to pretend to be asleep, I closed my eyes and immediately heard the rustle of footsteps in the leaves. I let out a fake snore and then jumped as I felt a hand slide under my bathing suit and grab a hold of my johnson. A loud chorus of laughter erupted and instead of showing any sort of embarrassment, the woman leered over me as if I could have no reaction other than to swoon over her beauty and bend her over the nearest log.

JUNE 18, 1995

Since receiving the letter from Vitaly's brother Nicolai, I had renewed my efforts to complete the paperwork for his Canadian visa. I had also written a press release for Ken to use in his efforts to garner financial backing from his contacts at *Newsweek* and within the expat community. Vitaly told me that, regardless of the outcome, he was grateful for our assistance and that the excitement in and of itself was a boon to his mental health. Not all the attention was positive, though, as some of the Peace Corps staff in Washington D.C. was concerned that a *Newsweek* article would lead to widespread requests to other Peace Corps volunteers. I understood their concerns, but I wanted this so badly that I was willing to risk any negative reactions. This was a special case involving two brothers who hadn't seen each other in fifty years.

I headed out early Saturday morning to visit Vitaly, since I had promised to help him build an outdoor shower and *banya* beside his house. This would require a great deal of energy, as there aren't any Home Depots or Lowes here and everything from the lumber to the cement had to be either carried in or made from scratch. I was excited to do some physical work for a change, especially now that my gardening blisters had hardened into calluses. Vitaly greeted me in his work clothes and with a stern look of impatience as I made my way up the dirt road to his house. He stood with one hand on his hip and the other grasping a cup of tea, a big smirk upon his face. He explained that since I was young and strong, my job would be to carry the buckets of sand and pebbles from the outskirts of the village to his back yard, whereupon he would add them to the concrete mix and water to make cement. In addition to fetching the buckets of sand, an equal number of trips to the well to pump water and then carry it back followed. By noon, every part of my body was screaming in pain: my arms and back were one large ache and my hands continually cramped up in a frozen grip. The only thing that pushed me forward was the thought of how happy Vitaly would be, no longer having to walk three miles to the public bathhouse for his showers.

At noon we stopped for lunch, which consisted of a few slices of bread covered with thick slabs of butter along with some kielbasa, all washed down with a thermos of hot tea. I was so exhausted that I had to force myself to eat before drawing upon all my pride as a man to return to the task of carrying more buckets of sand and water. Vitaly pushed me hard so that we could finish by nightfall, giving the cement time to harden before we were to begin painting in the morning. We finished as the sun began to set. Covered in cement splatter, my shoulders slumped and a general sense of fatigue set in as I stared out from the top of the hill overlooking Artyom. I was surrounded by a small herd of goats that nibbled at the tufts of grass, oblivious to my presence. The sky darkened from a rich blue to a deep shade of purple. It was surreal being halfway around the world from my home, sore from hard work, but feeling wonderful for being able to help someone I had not even known a year earlier. A year ago I was lounging on Miami Beach, sipping tequila drinks in a beach chair and ogling bikini-clad women. As corny as it may sound, the old Peace Corps adage that serving as a volunteer will be "The toughest job you'll ever love" had come true for me.

Vitaly was all smiles when we washed the tools with the last bucket of water. We had built a complete shower system, with a storage tank and a heating system that was fed on coal. He could also pour water over heated rocks on top of the heating system to create a sauna environment. We were admiring our handiwork when a neighbor approached holding a puppy in his arms. He asked Vitaly if he wanted a watchdog, which made us both laugh considering how pitiful it looked. The puppy, a beagle/spaniel mix, immediately ran through the garden and defecated as if to mark his territory and let Vitaly know who was going to be calling the shots.

JUNE 21, 1995

On some days it feels great to relax in my own apartment in complete privacy. I can listen to my music and daydream. I don't have to focus on my translation or take concern over anyone else's feelings. Today was such a day. I spent the entire morning curled up on the sofa with a book in hand and BB King on the tape deck. Despite being the only person in my apartment, I knew that I would never be entirely alone with Big Brother listening to my every word, burp, and fart. At times this would be disturbing and I would do all that I could to offend my hosts by holding the stereo speakers up to the listening devices, but at others I was resigned to my situation and accepted that I was never really alone.

I went through two pots of coffee to go along with my bread and jam, but by late afternoon I was beginning to hunger for something a little more substantial. Without grocery stores, I had no choice but to walk toward the center of town to window-shop at each kiosk in the hopes of finding a can of tuna or salmon or a link of smoked sausage or kielbasa. I locked my door and headed down the dark stairwell, straining my eyes as much as listening, to ensure that I didn't step on anyone or anything asleep on the stairs. As I stepped out of the darkness on the ground floor I ran into the chest of Nicolai, who grasped me in a big hug as a smile the size of his body spread across his face. Before I could get a word out, he was telling me that today was a beautiful day and that he and I would meet me back at my apartment in thirty minutes for an early dinner and some vodka. He had kielbasa, cheese, and bread in his photo shop, so all I needed to do was to pick up the vodka. I cringed at losing my nice solitary evening, but culturally it would have been an insult to our friendship if I had declined his offer. We spent the night in my kitchen eating kielbasa and cheese sandwiches and drinking vodka, which turned out not to be so terrible. What made it even better was that Nicolai had an ulterior motive behind the invitation: he had a business idea that he wanted to run by me. His plan was to open a parking garage near the airport, since the only available parking lot was an open area controlled by the mafia. More often than not your car would be stolen when you returned from your flight. You would have to negotiate a fee to the mafia to get it back. I had known Nicolai for several months and this was the first time that he had trusted me enough to discuss his business plan. It was a big moment for me since I had so few real opportunities from a business perspective.

Within minutes of Nicolai's departure, I was into a deep sleep, dreaming of a big steak dinner, some fine wine, and a pretty lady, when loud knocking dragged me from my reverie. People stopping by without calling is common, since the majority of people don't have home phones and the only way to get in touch is to show up at someone's door. I tiptoed to the peephole to rule out Irina, and quickly recognized Vitaly's profile. I opened the door and he brushed past me to the kitchen without saying a word. He looked at the empty bottle of vodka in my garbage can, shook his head, and then proceeded to search my cabinets to see if I had another. He reeked of stale cigarettes and his agitated posture showed his despair. I put a pot of water on the stove for tea and then sat down across from him. Neither of us had yet said a word. He held his head in his hands and began to sob. I had never seen him this upset and was unsure how to react. I placed my hands on top of his and waited for him to recover. He wiped his eyes with his sleeve and cleared his throat, before explaining what had happened in a raspy, unsteady voice.

He had been out at Eddie's cottage and the two of them had been drinking and chatting about the old days in China. Eventually Eddie's wife had politely hinted to Vitaly that it was time to leave. He was drunk and tired, drifting off to sleep several times on the bus on the way back to Artyom. The two-mile walk up the hill to his house in the crisp evening air refreshed him a bit and he was daydreaming as he made the final approach. As he rounded the bend he noticed a stranger entering his yard. The man walked inside the gate and then disappeared inside the chicken coop. Vitaly had had several of his chickens stolen in the past two weeks and now was witnessing the thief in action. He slipped inside his back door and charged out with his shotgun as the man was backing out of the coop with a struggling chicken in his grasp. The man was a neighborhood thug and instead of cowering, he dared Vitaly to shoot him. Unfortunately—or maybe fortunately—the gun wasn't loaded and the younger man grabbed the gun and beat Vitaly with it while bragging how he was untouchable and that he would take anything he wanted, anytime he wanted, and that Vitaly couldn't do anything to stop him. Vitaly was left with a bloody nose and a bruised ego. As a pensioner, the eggs are a vital part of his survival. And as a proud citizen, this brazen attack and disregard for law and order was an affront to his sense of Russian society.

Vitaly was worried that the gun might be used in a crime that would then be blamed on him, so he walked to the police station to report the theft and assault. Instead of a sympathetic response from the police, the sergeant on duty ridiculed him, calling him an old drunk and advising him just to go back home and sleep it off. When Vitaly insisted on filing a report, he was told to take a seat and wait for an investigator to take his statement. After three hours without any acknowledgement or assistance, he walked out and went straight to my apartment. He had accumulated a limited number of close friends in Artyom over his eight years and was still considered an outsider by the other families in his village. He was frustrated by the "collapse of decency" that had come about with the rapid changes to the economy. "You are the only person I have left," he confided. Despite several cups of tea, we were now both thoroughly exhausted. I offered to let him spend the night at my apartment, but he was eager to get back home to check on his house. I offered to walk with him to make sure that he would be safe, but he shook his head and said that he would be fine. We hugged goodbye and then he walked out the door.

JULY 2, 1995

After being the recipient of so much neighborly care in the form of jam and other food-related gifts, I decided that it was time to repay the generosity of my neighbors by making brownies. Two boxes of brownie mix had mysteriously appeared in one of the kiosk windows and I almost had a coronary trying to get to the front of the line before someone else bought them. What my oven lacks in utility, it makes up for in character. The temperature fluctuates, regardless of the setting on the thermostat, and as such, the only way I could manage to keep a steady temperature was to layer the bottom and sides of the oven with bricks. Mixing together the ingredients and oiling a pan were easy enough, and soon both my apartment and the stairwell were filled with the foreign aroma of freshly baked brownies. I packaged up a dozen plates wrapped in aluminum foil for distribution to my neighbors and then proceeded to make the rounds. "American treats!" I exclaimed as I handed them out. The surprised looks bordered on confusion since it was unusual for a man to cook, much less cook something that smelled and tasted so good.

JULY 5, 1995

I received an invitation from the US consulate to celebrate Independence Day aboard the USS *Fife*, a US navy destroyer that was docked in Vladivostok's port. The *Fife* was a Spruance-class destroyer named for Admiral James Fife, Jr., a distinguished Submarine Force commander during World War II. Since this was the first time since the end of World War II that an American naval ship had docked at a Russian military port, the Russian press had been running stories non-stop leading up to the big ceremony on July 4th. This was disconcerting to the Russian navy: the comparisons between the "high-tech" American vessel and the run-down, rusty Russian ships docked alongside did little to boost morale among the Russian sailors. The more the Russian brass complained, the more the press reported on the rampant corruption of the Russian military, including the terrible abuse of cadets and the ill state of the Russian navy as a whole. The local politicians blamed Moscow for failing to provide the necessary financial support while Moscow claimed that the problems stemmed from local mismanagement, with the truth likely somewhere in between.

The majority of my Peace Corps colleagues also had received this invitation from the US consulate. We were all looking forward to the celebration.

I envisioned feasting on barbeque, downing bourbon, and hobnobbing with the "rich and famous" of the Russian Far East. On the morning of the third, I took the train to Vladivostok and immediately became aware of the American presence: hundreds of American sailors dressed in "Navy whites" flooded the central plaza. Their swagger was so different from the sulking figures of Russian sailors, which I attributed to their bravado at having been at sea for several weeks. I had come into town a day early to spend some time with Gary, but before I could get on a tram I ran into a trio of American sailors who seemed eager for excitement. I invited them to join me for a beer, offering to give a quick "lay of the land" before heading off to see Gary. Two of the three sailors were African American and the other was Hispanic. Russians have had few opportunities to see people of color outside of Hollywood movies, so they stared unapologetically as we passed. I explained the reason for the curiosity and soon my new friends were playing it up: smiling and agreeing to have their photographs taken with Russian bystanders who had come out to see the US *Fife*. At one point, several women ran up and handed them flowers and the sailors couldn't keep the smiles off their faces.

All three were nineteen years old and so they had two things on their mind: to get drunk and to get laid. I recalled the warnings that I had received as a new trainee in Vladivostok that the Russian women that I would meet in local bars were professionals, and that they too would be after only one thing—my money. I gave the sailors an abbreviated version of the warning and they listened about as much as I had, shrugging and advising me that they could take care of themselves. After stopping at a bar for a beer, we walked to the central bus stop to people-watch. I bought another round of Russian beer and within minutes two Russian sailors approached and invited us to their home for some food and vodka. I translated the invitation and the Americans accepted. Again I warned them: the Russians were accomplished drinkers and they would be doing their best to get the Americans shitfaced; I received the same look as when I warned them against the prostitutes.

We followed the Russians into one of the many concrete buildings, walked up a dimly lit flight of stairs and into one of the apartments. Our Russian host explained to his startled wife that they were having American guests. She disappeared into the kitchen while the six of us crowded around a small table in the living room. I sat in the middle to serve as both interpreter and toastmaster, relishing being the center of attention. Our host brought two bottles of Stolichnaya vodka to the table, along with six glasses. The Russians seemed a little nervous as they expressed appreciation that we had accepted their invitation and this led into the first toast by our host. Meanwhile, his wife brought out a plate of kielbasa and bread. I translated the toast and added in a few words explaining that this was a big deal to our hosts and that they shouldn't take it lightly. When I finished speaking, we clicked glasses and drained the vodka. The glasses were immediately refilled. I explained to my American friends that it would be appropriate for one of them to make a toast to our hosts, which I translated back into Russian, embellishing it with the words that I knew would have the most significance and ending with a hope that our two countries would lead the world together in peace and friendship. We drank, and then drank some more, and then drank even more. The two bottles turned into four and within hours all were empty. The comradery between the American and Russian sailors prevailed, with a great deal of laughter. With four bottles gone and everyone quite inebriated, neither side wanted to be the one to give in and call it a day. I took one for the team and apologized, saying that I had another commitment, secretly wanting to get the Americans back on their ship before anything bad could happen on my watch. They were young, drunk, and full of false bravado and testosterone, and I didn't want to be responsible for their conduct or well-being as they looked for trouble in a city not known for its hospitality to foreigners.

I hailed a rogue taxi to take us back to the port, but due to heavy traffic we were dropped off at one of the nearby hotels, which housed a late-night mafia disco. No sooner had we gotten out of the taxi when two of my new buddies began to wrestle, eventually crashing through the hotel's picture window. Luckily neither was injured, but the hotel security guards weren't as appreciative of that fact and forcibly grabbed them. These guys were mafia and would have liked nothing better than to add a couple of drunken Americans to their list of conquests. I quickly intervened, explaining that we would gladly compensate them for the damage to the window and for their own inconvenience. I didn't want the police to get involved and I sure as hell didn't want my name mentioned: we were only a few blocks away from the *Vladimir* nightclub where Gary and I had our big night. Fortunately we were in Vladivostok and not New York City: it only took twenty dollars to placate the guards. I immediately walked the sailors back to their shipmates and freed myself from any further responsibility.

The next morning Gary and I silently drank our coffee like an old married couple while leafing through old copies of *Newsweek*. I missed New Jersey's greasy diners, Sunday afternoon NFL games, and the ability to go out to a mall or restaurant to break up the monotony. In Vladivostok, the available leisure activities consisted only of an invite to someone's home for a meal and drinks or a stroll around the downtown area. We had been deluged with fifteen straight days of rain, leading to torrential rivers running down the streets and widespread flooding that also washed away our sense of joy. We needed activity, something to get rid of the angst that had built up these past two weeks. This frustration led to us braving the rain and heading outside to play some one on one baseball. We stole a piece of wood from a nearby construction site to make a bat and then resorted to our good friend "Mr. Duct Tape" to wrap up a wad of newspaper to serve as our ball.

We made our way to a grassy area near the university bus stop and I began to pitch to Gary, who stood stoically at the makeshift plate clutching the piece of wood in his hands, elbow cocked and a ferocious grimace upon his face. Ignoring the rain, I reverted to my ten-year-old backyard whiffle ball days, announcing the play-by-play action at the top of my lungs. "Pitching for the New York Mets, Tom "Terrific" Seaver. And batting for the Los Angeles Dodgers, the one and only Ron Cey." We soon had an audience: everyone waiting at the bus stop stared with incredulity as I continued my announcements while we ran the bases, dove in the mud, and screamed out in reckless, childlike enthusiasm. We were completely soaked, but it felt good. Eventually Gary hit a line drive over a nearby fence causing a temporary stoppage, but being resourceful Peace Corps volunteers we went to a nearby kiosk and purchased a dozen hard rolls to continue our game. The rolls crumbled quickly and did little to extend our game, but added to the incredulous looks we were receiving from the commuters.

At noon the sun had poked through the clouds and we left for the July 4th party aboard the USS *Fife*. Dressed in our sport coats and ties, we made our way to the port, showed our passports at several checkpoints, and then boarded the 7,800-ton, 563-foot destroyer. Despite the enormity of the ship and my high expectations, the food was disappointing. I had anticipated an extravagant party, not a keg party with hot dogs and baked beans. It was fun to hang out with the expats and consulate snobs while drinking free beer, but it would have been much better dining on smoked brisket and washing it down with a few Jack-and-Cokes. The Russian politicians received tours of the ship, while the rest of us listened to the band's patriotic music between spreading gossip about who was sleeping with whom and who was binge-drinking more than usual. By 5 o'clock the party was ending, so I walked to the train station and took the first train back to Artyom. It had been a challenging two days packed with a week's worth of alcohol and I was ready for a break, ready to get back to work.

JULY 8, 1995

As the date for the arrival of the new trainees creeps closer, I have had to spend almost every night eating dinner with the prospective host families to make sure we identify enough acceptable families. As a result, my clothes now fit like a sausage casing. Rumors have circulated that I can be bribed with food, which may be true: I am a good eater and can be easily swayed with a good bowl of borscht or plate of stuffed cabbage. I go to these dinners hoping to observe the family long enough to judge their adequacy in hosting a trainee, but end up spending most of my time answering questions about typical American behaviors and interests. Some of the families now regard me as a Pseudo-Russian as they ask me whether Americans would eat something that they have just served me and watched me eat. I take it as a compliment, but at the same time realize just how little they know about the world outside of Russia.

JULY 6, 1995

After almost two years of work, Uri had put the finishing touches on his new home and was throwing a house-warming party in grand style to celebrate. He had designed the house as a showcase of his architecture skills and the party was as much a business opportunity as it was a celebration of all of the hard work. Anatoli and several other mafia elites attended, as did several members of the city administration. The only women were Uri's daughter and his mistress, who seemed to be approximately the same age. In America, it would have seemed tacky for Uri to be seen openly with his mistress, but here it didn't seem to raise an eyebrow.

When the last course had been cleared from the table, my head was spinning. Throughout the meal, each guest had his own bottle of vodka as part of his table setting and the two women made sure that everyone's glass was full. My machismo was stronger than my common sense as I tried to hold my own and appear coherent. I tried to follow the conversation and jokes so that I would know when to laugh or nod, while deep down I prayed that the party would break up so that I could go home before I puked. Unfortunately, when the table had been cleared Uri invited the group to try out his *banya*. We walked down a short hallway and were ushered into a room where the warm air smelled of sassafras. A hot tub, constructed entirely out of black marble, rose from the floor reflecting the gold and glass light fixtures that hung from the ceiling. Along the walls were two shower stalls with gold-colored faucets and in the center was a cedar *banya* large enough to fit the ten of us. I opened the *banya* door and a wall of steam pushed back. Incredibly, there was a refrigerator inside that had been built into the wall, with a glass door showing a dozen bottles of Stolichnaya.

I turned back and saw the others, including the women, returning to the kitchen. Assuming that they had gone to change into bathing suits, I undressed down to my boxers anticipating that Uri's daughter and mistress would be joining us. I took a seat inside the *banya* on one of the benches and closed my eyes, focusing solely on the feeling of the hot, menthol air in my lungs. The silence shattered with the opening of the *banya* door. Eight loud, drunken men, all completely naked with protruding bellies, piled inside and in unison noticed my non-naked presence and began to laugh. I realized how ridiculous I must look sitting in my underwear and I laughed too, trying to explain, which only caused another outburst that echoed against the cedar walls. I took off my underwear and threw them outside. Turning back to face my fellow partiers, I realized that all eyes were on my penis. This is not usually a good sign unless you are hung like Ron Jeremy. An extremely uncomfortable conversation regarding circumcision followed and I was very relieved when Uri reached for a bottle of vodka and the conversation turned toward other issues.

JULY 12, 1995

Forty-five families were finally selected to serve as host families for the new trainees, which should put an end to my multi-dinner nights. I feel confident that those selected are engaging with the Peace Corps for the right reasons and that this will help in the acclimatization process for the trainees. Unfortunately, the families who were rejected blamed me for the decision and accused me of unfairly working against them. Many of these households came across as being desperate for the eight dollars a day and had few of the required conveniences (private bedroom, plumbing, etc.) and others just didn't come across as a good fit. When asked to explain why they weren't chosen, I found it difficult to tell someone that their homes were too dirty or that their living conditions didn't meet our standards.

The families that were selected were invited to a general information session to set their expectations. Mama and I were asked to attend by the Peace Corps staff since they referred to us as having the ideal host family/trainee relationship. Mama was a ham, telling stories and getting the entire audience to laugh at our initial mishaps. I spoke of the differences between American and Russian expectations and gave my opinions on how best to minimize any misunderstandings. I explained how difficult it had been for me to adjust to living with a family that didn't speak my language and how it felt to lose the independence and privacy I had been accustomed to while living in America. I further discussed how the cultural differences regarding privacy were significant and that it was not an insult when Americans would hide away to regroup. The trainee's lives had been upended and it was important for the host families to understand and not feel disrespected.

After the meeting I stopped to visit Nicole, a former Peace Corps volunteer who now worked as a trainer for the Peace Corps. She was scheduled to spend three to four months managing the environmental education program. She was from New York and shared my warped East Coast sense of humor. We'd spent many nights together walking through the city, discussing what we wanted out of life and drinking the occasional glass or two of vodka. I felt a sexual tension building but was hesitant to act upon it because we were working together and I wasn't sure whether the feelings were mutual. She will be in charge of twenty-five of the trainees and has thus been busy preparing lectures and setting up field trips with the hope that upon completion of the training the volunteers will be able to coordinate with other NGOs on environmental projects. This program seems a much better fit than the business program due to the rapid destruction of natural resources and a growing problem with air and water pollution here.

JULY 18, 1995

The new group of trainees finally arrived in Russia. After what seemed like months of planning, we were actually able to put faces to the names. I joined the training staff at the airport to welcome them, serving as the sole emissary from my group. With an average age of twenty-four, these trainees were significantly younger than our group, which had averaged out at forty-three. The age disparity was likely the reason for their higher level of energy upon arrival. We had busses ready to take them from the airport to one of the seaside resort hotels and the Peace Corps had graciously paid for my hotel room there so that I could answer questions regarding their upcoming homestays and life in Russia as a volunteer. The following morning they would begin their homestays, whereas we had been given a few days to acclimate at the dorms prior to moving in with our families. I brought a case of Russian beer as a welcoming gift. It was hard not to share in their excitement and nervousness. Again, I had mixed emotions as I envisioned all of these new American faces running around "my" town and of having to share the spotlight that had been mine alone for all these months.

The next morning started with a series of vaccinations and breakfast, followed by the first of many briefings. There was so much for them to absorb. At noon, there was a quick lunch and then the big event of meeting their host families for the first time. I was anxious to see how our match-making skills had played out: we had spent so much time and effort trying to match the trainees to the host families based on questionnaires that both parties had previously completed. As expected, the first few minutes were very awkward as the trainees repeated a series of memorized phrases and the Russian families strained to understand and communicate back. With both the families and trainees nervously trying to make a good impression, the volume rose considerably and everyone spoke at once. I helped translate, along with the rest of the Peace Corps' Russian staff, to ease the discomfort. I was remembering my awkward meeting with Mama and

Papa. After thirty minutes of chaperoned conversation, the host families were permitted to take their American home. I felt like a parent watching his child get on the school bus for the first time.

On the third day in-country, the Peace Corps held a welcoming party for the trainees and the members of the city administration who had been instrumental in helping cut through the red tape. Ken asked that I provide him with a list of local officials to ensure that no one was left out. I stretched the list a bit and invited those in the administration who had taken me under their wings, including Uri, who might not otherwise have been included in his position as town architect. It was important to have as much buy-in from the city as possible to ensure the success of the program, because the influx of so many foreigners was sure to create a few problems. It was a hot day, with temperatures in the 90s, which was unexpected and unwelcome since the ceremony took place inside a stuffy conference room. With only a few hot days like this each year, air conditioning was a rarity in the government-run facilities. Once eighty people crammed into the room, the temperature climbed even higher. This was such a big event for the city that nobody wanted to step outside and miss any of the action, especially with the local television station filming the entire event. My suit stuck to my back as I tried to smile to the cameras.

The mayor said a few words and then Ken followed with a few more, both intent on keeping their remarks short on account of the general discomfort and knowing that there was a cocktail party to follow. The next hour consisted of much handshaking and introductions as both the Peace Corps staff and the administration pulled at me to translate. As things wound down, the mayor nudged me to follow him outside to his car to invite me to an after-party at the beach. "Let's get rid of these jackets and have a little fun, Reech." I was tired from having stayed out late the previous night, but backing out wasn't an option: I wanted to maintain my strong relationship with him. So, for the sake of world peace, I toughed it out and slid into the car to drink with the big dogs! The cold sea breeze felt great as we stood along a cliff looking down at the surf. Bottles of vodka were passed from hand to hand: nobody had thought to bring glasses and apparently nobody cared. I didn't want to get drunk, so I initially resorted to the Ernest Hemingway trick of holding my tongue against the opening and pretending to drink whenever the bottle came my way. Eventually I took a few real swigs and when additional bottles appeared, I became a full participant. I enjoyed being part of the mayor's crowd. I liked the chauffeured drives and the access to parties and the feeling that I had few boundaries when out with them. Sometimes it felt manufactured, as if I was playing a part in a movie. The attention of the Russian women, the debauchery at the parties, and the overall feeling of being close to power proved addictive and as much as I tried to hold back, I allowed myself to be drawn into the whirlpool.

JULY 19, 1995

The welcoming party thrown by the Peace Corps training staff had been such a success that the city administration felt obliged to reciprocate. Tatiana, the finance minister for the *Primorski Krai* region, called me to her office the following afternoon to advise me that she was planning her birthday party and wanted the names of the Peace Corps staff so that she could send out invitations. The party was to take place at resort near the beach the following weekend. I jotted down the names and agreed to make sure that the invitations got into the right hands. When I called Ken later that afternoon he was pleased, noting how important it was to form close ties between the city administration and the Peace Corps.

There were only a few English speakers within the city administration and none had been invited to the party, which led to my serving as city's translator. This was awkward since there were several Russian Peace Corps staff who were bilingual and would easily catch my errors as I handled the introductions and emcee duties. But I felt proud of my increased sense of importance, relishing the opportunity to take center stage. The highlight was getting to make the second toast on behalf of the Peace Corps, thanking

Tatiana and group for their hospitality and enthusiasm in agreeing to have Artyom as the training city. I had made many such toasts in Russian at parties and events, but this was the first time that I got to show off in front of Ken and the Peace Corps staff. As the party was winding down, Tatiana took me aside and thanked me for my help before giving me a big hug. When I turned back to get into the car, I caught Ken's eye and smiled as he shook his head.

I went to the market early Sunday morning with the hope of buying a few chickens for Vitaly to replace the ones stolen by his neighbor. Although the thief was never officially arrested, the police had spoken to him and were able to retrieve the shotgun. Vitaly didn't feel any safer, but he had the insurance that the thief would be the first person investigated should anything further happen. Vitaly now kept his gun fully loaded and had invested in a lock for the coop.

When it comes to buying live chickens, there should be a pamphlet for beginners. I had no problem finding the livestock section of the market simply by sense of smell, but the task of actually selecting chickens proved more difficult. After a few inquiries to the vendors I was able to determine that the going rate was the equivalent of five dollars per chicken. I had to scream over the squawking to make myself heard and the obliging farmer grabbed two chickens by their feet and held them out upside down for my approval. Knowing little about chickens other than how to order off of a Popeye's or KFC menu, I had no idea whether I was being shown the Cadillac or the Pontiac version. I nodded in agreement and held open my shopping bag so that he could toss both birds inside. By the time I had walked twenty steps, talons were poking through the bottom of my bag. I made my way along the sidewalk toward the bus stop with the bag shaking and the chickens screaming at ear-piercing decibels. I jumped about like a lunatic trying to keep the bag and the talons away from my legs. Passersby laughed outright and there was nothing I could do or say to regain any semblance of respectability. I had gone from feeling like town big shot to the village idiot.

Eventually a bus stopped and I managed to find a seat without making eye contact with any of the other passengers. I battled the ferocious chickens for twenty minutes, until red with embarrassment; I tried squeezing the bag between my legs to force them into submission. My plan backfired and one of the chickens ripped through the bag and began running around the bus. I held the other between my arm and body like a football and began chasing the loose chicken, much to the amusement of my fellow passengers. Finally an older women reached out and grabbed the chicken by the neck and then by the talons, holding it upside down, whereupon it immediately stopped fighting and relaxed. She handed it back to me with a smile and the whole bus applauded. The bus eventually reached the stop outside of Vitaly's village and I carefully disembarked, holding both chickens upside down like a true professional. When I reached the gate, I set the chickens down and they both sprinted into the garden. I was exhausted, with my shirt, pants, and shoes covered with dirt and feathers. Vitaly was appreciative and insisted that we share the eggs. I knew how meager his pension was and how little he had to eat, but I felt I had to accept in order to protect his pride.

As we sat in his kitchen, I watched him pace around in a thick sweater. He heated his house via a coal oven, but the chimney had deteriorated over the years and he was losing as much heat as was circulating through his house. Again at the risk of offending his pride, I offered to pay to get the chimney repaired as winter was approaching. He nodded in agreement, although I saw that it pained him to accept my charity. After a cup of tea, we walked through the garden to gather berries and vegetables to supplement the caviar and sardines I had brought for our dinner. We ended up with boiled potatoes seasoned with fresh dill and a salad of fresh beets and scallions along with a loaf of bread. For dessert, we had bowls of raspberries, blackberries, and gooseberries. I had never given potatoes much thought, but after spending much of the past three months clearing soil, planting, weeding, watering, and building barriers to keep the puppy away from the plants, I was thrilled to reap the rewards of my labor. The potatoes were delicious, but I noticed a problem with his potato-planting philosophy. Vitaly planted potatoes harvested from the prior season to start the current year's crops. I watched as he would serve the larger potatoes for dinner and set aside the smaller ones to replant. Recalling my grade school biology class, I told him that by continuing to plant only the small potatoes, he was weakening the genetic makeup of future potato harvests. Vitaly listened to me, but shook his head and replied that Mendel used German peas and these were Russian potatoes, so the theory would never apply.

AUGUST 8, 1995

The Peace Corps has encouraged the volunteers from my group to visit the Artyom training site in an effort to foster closer ties between the two groups. Many of the trainees will eventually be assigned positions in the same cities and close ties would be for the sake of both safety and comfort: stronger relationships between volunteers help fight off homesickness and we can serve as emergency contacts for each other. When we had arrived in Vladivostok there had been so much animosity between the handful of remaining volunteers and the Peace Corps staff that few made any effort to meet us. I didn't blame the Peace Corps or the volunteers, because Russia was a difficult country in which to operate for the Peace Corps. There was no blueprint or history to reply upon to find appropriate jobs for the volunteers. Most of the staff's time was spent educating potential city administrations and universities to explain the Peace Corps mission. My group had the advantage of coming second and learning some lessons that improved the process, although the program still had quite a ways to go. This new group of trainees would have more possibilities than we had and the process would continue for successive groups. I had felt disheartened by Linda's lack of effort and I know many of my fellow volunteers felt similarly, which was why it didn't take much to get my group of volunteers to participate in the training of these new arrivals. Tiffany came out during their second week, combining this with a client visit. Her client owned a farm just outside of Artyom's city limits and since it was so close to my business center, she asked me to join her. The farm raised minks for clothing as well as a breed of deer that was unique to the Russian Far East and that grew antlers that supposedly were considered an aphrodisiac when ground up and infused in cognac.

I was thrilled to leave the city because the summer heat radiated from the pavement and formed a cloak of coal dust that made breathing difficult. Our driver took us along paved country roads that eventually turned to dirt as we passed thousands of small plots of farmland. After twenty or so miles, we came to a driveway flanked by a gate announcing the name of the ranch. Two men stood guard, although with their rifles resting against a nearby tree I doubt that they were too worried about our arrival. It seemed strange for a farm to have armed guards, but then again, this was Russia.

We slowly came to a stop outside a small barn, where a portly man with bright eyes rushed forward to shake our hands. The owner's name was Alexander and he looked as if he had just stepped off a tractor in his dirty overalls. He led us toward an open field that was filled with rows of cages raised up on small boxes that resembled milk crates. The smell was terrible. I couldn't look at Tiffany since I knew I would either throw up my breakfast or start laughing, neither of which would add to my credibility as a business consultant.

Each cage contained a single agitated mink that repeatedly lunged against the metal bars while snarling at us. I had grown up in a family that didn't favor fur clothing, but after two minutes walking between these cages my patience and compassion had waned. I had imagined them as cute and cuddly, resembling otters, while in reality they looked like oversized rats. Granted, being kept in tiny cages waiting to be slaughtered wasn't exactly humane treatment, so maybe I was being too hard on them. Alexander explained that the mink are "put down" by lethal injection to avoid damage to their fur, but by using poison they make the meat unsuitable for pet food processors. Alexander wanted us to help him find Western investors to provide capital to modernize his operations. This would ordinarily be a great project, but since he was unwilling to provide accurate financial information for fear that it would end up in the hands of the Russian tax collector, our abilities would be tested. Many Russian businesses had two sets of books: the first show reduced revenue to be provided for taxes purposes and the second showed inflated sales for use with investors.

After the tour we joined Alexander and his family for lunch. Fortunately my appetite proved resistant to the nauseating smell, since the table was packed full of plates containing an amazing assortment of seafood. Like many other Russian businessmen, Alexander used the barter system more often than currency, due to the high inflation. Few companies have access to capital, and when bartering there were no financial trails for the taxman to follow. Crab legs as thick as my wrist were served along with perfectly grilled halibut and an assortment of steamed shrimp, mussels, and scallops. For two hours we feasted and drank until I had to secretly loosen my belt.

Tiffany and I got dropped off at the training site to spend time with the trainees and we were pleasantly surprised to run into Chris Willis. He was in Vladivostok on business and had stopped by to meet the new trainees as well. It was unusual to have a single volunteer visit me, much less two at the same time. And since there wasn't much in the way of local entertainment, I invited them, as well as Nicole and Tim (one of the other Peace Corps trainers), to come with me to Vitaly's house for dinner. I hadn't checked with him, but knew that he would love the company, especially if the company included two women. We stopped to pick up vegetables, canned goods, and loaves of fresh bread before venturing toward the butcher's area. I decided on a bag of frozen "Bush legs" since the lack of refrigeration had left the fresh cuts of beef and pork speckled with flies. The last stop was the Stolichnaya distillery to pick up a few bottles of vodka. In Russia, there aren't any functioning government regulatory agencies to check on product safety, so when it came to vodka, we had been warned: many of the local products were distilled in discarded car radiators leading to high lead counts and occasionally lethal contaminants. Uri taught me to vigorously shake unopened bottles and then to hold them upside down to observe the size of the bubbles. If they were small and uniform in size, then the vodka was OK. Otherwise, not so much.

Vitaly is a loquacious person, so living alone meant that he pined for company. Having a house full of young foreigners who were enthralled with his stories was a gift in and of itself. Since he didn't have a telephone, I had no way of alerting him other than to yell out as we approached, which at least gave him time to tuck in his shirt. Our impromptu visit didn't upset him in the least, as I could attest from seeing his wide smile from a hundred feet away. Once introductions had been made, we deposited the groceries inside on his table. Vitaly was grinning so much that I worried that his cheeks might rip right off his face. Not wanting to waste our youthful energy, he handed baskets to the three men in our group to gather vegetables from the garden. With us out of the way Vitaly poured on the charm, leading Tiffany and Nicole to a shaded part of the yard where he served them tea and flirted unabashedly. He looked so happy that it made me realize just how much of an impact living alone must have had on his psyche.

During the meal Vitaly inquired about everyone's families, the type of work each did prior to joining the Peace Corps, and what they were doing in Russia. It always amazed the Russians that we voluntarily gave up our lives "of luxury" to serve as volunteers without pay and to live without our accustomed comforts. We finished eating just as the sun was setting, so we took our tea to the top of the hill and watched the horizon change colors. It was a beautiful way to end the evening and I was pleased that my friends were able to spend time with Vitaly. He had lived such a vibrant life in China prior to his moving to Russia, which had made his getting incarcerated immediately upon his entry to Russia that much more painful. After more than a decade in the gulag and then another thirty years forced to remain in the Siberian hinterlands, he was angry that so much of his life and opportunities had been stolen by the Soviet government. Having the chance to talk to us of the difficulties that he faced following World War II and his subsequent travails under Communist rule served as a form of therapy; he wasn't able to get the same type of reaction from other Russians since they too had suffered and were living the same type of hard life.

AUGUST 10, 1995

With the arrival of the new group of trainees, the feeling of being the center of the Peace Corps staff's attention has evaporated. Our whining was no longer tolerated; there were forty new trainees who had to be babied and cared for as they navigated the cultural differences and pitfalls of living with a new family in a foreign country. We had suddenly transformed into seasoned veterans whether we wanted to carry that mantle or not. Prior to the arrival of the new volunteers, we had the freedom of being able to show up at the Peace Corps offices unannounced and expect to meet and maybe even have lunch with Ken or the other staff. Now we had to make an appointment.

I felt torn between continuing with my day-to-day activities and wanting to help out with the trainees to maintain my sense of purpose. This led to Anna Gregorovna complaining that I wasn't spending enough time at the business center. I tried to explain that with the dacha season well underway my client volume had been dramatically reduced: everyone spent their free time tending to their gardens. There was always the possibility of trying to drum up additional business, but as the economy continued to slide the mafia became more aggressive in squeezing out payments. It seemed like every day there was another news story of a business being burned to the ground or an owner beaten up or killed. Rumors of the mayor's intrusions into my work had also been circulating and this further eroded my ability to entice entrepreneurs to confide in me.

It had been three weeks since my last visit to Vladivostok and I needed a release. It was also the one-year anniversary of our training in Seattle, so I jumped on a train to meet up with Gary. The two of us had developed a routine when I would visit that was based on having a meal and a few drinks following by the pursuit of some nightlife, albeit now with a reluctance to visit local mafia bars. While Gary rolled out dough to make pizza, I patiently went about my business hunting mice. The drawback of sleeping in his dorm was the presence of rodents. As soon as I turned out the lights at night I would hear scampering all around the sofa. If I flicked on the light, I would see beady-eyed mice jumping off the furniture to make a mad dash for the radiator where I couldn't catch them. Stories of other students having their fingers or toes nibbled while they slept scared the shit out of me and I became obsessed with killing them. Over time I had perfected my skills and it now became a game that I would play whenever visiting. I would bait a trap with peanut butter and then sit back with a beer to wait for one of them to inspect the prize. Typically, it would be only a few minutes before one of them would make a move. Two minutes passed before the first set of whiskers poked out, twitching eagerly from behind the metallic grid of the radiator. It crept closer and I felt my pulse quicken. I slowly sipped my beer, pretending not to notice the mouse creeping closer to the trap. He sniffed the peanut butter, then desire overtook caution and he stepped forward. BAM! The metal bar snapped shut. I pumped my fist, took a big swig, and then tossed both mouse and trap into the garbage. By the time the pizza was ready I had killed three mice and drained an equal number of beers.

AUGUST 12, 1995

The next morning I visited my host family. I got winded walking up the mountain toward their apartment, which made me realize that all of the meals in Artyom had taken their toll on both my waistline and my endurance. I decided to take a shortcut behind a row of apartment buildings, which I would normally have avoided because of a hooligan element at night … but during the day it seemed safe enough. I was trudging along one of the goat-paths that zig-zagged up the hill when I heard a deep growl that sent a shiver up my spine. Several deeper and more menacing growls followed. I froze, trying to get a bearing on where the sounds were coming from. I stepped forward cautiously, one foot in front of the other, my fists clenched. Thoughts of a tiger caused my sphincter to squeeze shut as complete and utter fear settled in. I reached down to grab a tree branch off the ground and continued moving forward, slowly scanning the bushes in front of me. I heard movement and caught sight of a tail, then the head of a dog, and then three more dogs emerged from the shrubbery and circled to my right. A German shepherd appeared in front of me, its ears pinned back. I waved the tree branch and shouted in the hope that my false show of strength would come through in my voice. The dogs backed up but kept their gaze upon me. I was so relieved that it wasn't a tiger that I relaxed a bit and kept moving forward while continuing to scream at the dogs, knowing that I only had a little farther to reach the road—I could hear cars passing. That was when I saw the hand. The fingers were grossly discolored and bent unnaturally. My eyes moved past the hand and along the arm where fractured splinters of bone poked through the skin. A sheet covered the torso and part of the face, but the Asian features were unmistakable. The dogs had torn chunks of flesh from the body and were growling to protect their meal.

I fought back the urge to run, worried that it might incite the dogs to chase me. I remained alert until I had passed the body and arrived at the street. My heart was beating furiously and I forced myself to take a deep breath. I entered the first apartment building I came to and pounded on every door until one opened. A woman, who turned out to be the superintendent, stepped out and demanded to know why I was making such a racket. I explained what I had seen and she shook her head and repeated the Russian word for nightmare. She was aware of the body. She had reported it to the police and they had let her know that the mafia had been extorting money from a group of illegal Chinese workers who lived in the building. An argument had taken place and one of the Chinese workers had been thrown off the balcony. The police had placed a sheet over the body and then contacted the Chinese consulate to deal with it, since there were no operating morgues in the city. The city's budget, much like those of the citizens, had run out of money and many civil servants were working with little to no pay. There was also so much animosity toward the Chinese, whether or not they were immigrants, that there was little incentive for anyone to go out of their way to help. It pained me to walk away, knowing that the body would continue to sit unprotected from the dogs, but I felt helpless in changing the situation.

AUGUST 14, 1995

I received an unexpected call from Holly. This surprised me because our relationship had been marginalized since the in-service training session in June. We hadn't argued, but her lack of empathy toward me and Gary following our mugging had been disappointing considering our prior closeness. Even more surprising than the fact of her call was that she asked if she could stay with me. She was flying out of Artyom and wanted to save on a hotel. Artyom had the only international airport in the area, so it was not uncommon for volunteers to ask to stay with me prior to their flights. After a second of indecision I said yes, hoping that we might resolve our issues. Artyom's only restaurant, the Chinese one next door, had limited vegetarian items that she could eat, so I ran out to the market to pick up wild mushrooms and an assortment of vegetables to serve along with lentils. To save time I put the lentils on the stove ahead of time to simmer, but unfortunately I forgot to turn off the stove when I left for the airport.

When Holly walked out of the terminal it seemed like we were back in Seattle. We both burst into smiles and I gave her a big hug and took her bags as we exited the airport and jumped into a taxi. We talked and laughed as if there had never been a rift. While walking up the stairs to my apartment, my mood quickly turned when I smelled smoke and immediately remembered the lentils. I ran up the remaining flights and opened the door, my heart beating wildly as heavy smoke poured into the stairwell. With my head down, I ran through the kitchen to pull the pot from the stove and then opened the balcony door to air out the apartment. The lentils were a charred mess, but fortunately they hadn't burst into flames and set anything on fire. The smoke detectors that ran along the ceiling throughout the apartment had apparently malfunctioned, adding further credence to my belief that they were actually listening devices. I stood atop one of the chairs and began ripping the wires from the devices. I followed the cords all the way to my closet where they were attached to a small black box.

I left the windows open and I took Holly next door to the Chinese restaurant since the lingering stench of smoke ruined any thoughts of dining in my apartment. Over a bottle of vodka, she told me about her life in Khaborovsk. She didn't mention a boyfriend and I didn't ask; I had no desire to bring up an uncomfortable memory. I remained quiet about my own social life, focusing on how my life had changed with the arrival of the trainees. The restaurant staff was used to seeing me come in with my mafia buddies and treated me accordingly, bringing out complimentary appetizers and a bottle of Champagne. We were pretty drunk by the time we returned to my apartment and I was wondering whether there would be a happy ending to the night when I noticed that all of the wires that I had ripped from the wall had been repaired. I had known theoretically that I was being watched and listened to by the local FSB, I'd even been warned occasionally by my mafia buddies, but actually seeing the prompt repair to the wires was disturbing.

AUGUST 15, 1995

Peter, the Peace Corps' newly hired business advisor, visited me in my office to discuss what I was working on and to ask whether he could provide any support. I explained how demand for my services had diminished once the word got out that I couldn't provide any capital. I was able to prepare clients for meetings with the USAID or Eurasia Foundation, since they had funding protocols, but most of my clients were too impatient and wanted to go to directly to Vladivostok's business centers to gain access to the money. I discussed the potential of expanding the business center's mission to include a TEFL (Teaching English as a Foreign Language) program for Russians students interested in studying abroad. With two of the new trainees destined to stay in Artyom as English teachers, it seemed like a good way to make better use of the space. Peter agreed and said that he would discuss it with Anna Gregorovna. Through poor communication the message became distorted and by the time it reached Anna she was told that I wanted to close the business center and turn it into an English-language center. She stormed into my office and began screaming at me, stating that I had no authority to make unilateral decisions affecting the business center. I had never seen her so angry, nor for that matter, had I seen anyone that angry at me in years. I finally had a chance to explain, telling her that I had only suggested incorporating the TEFL program into our office so that we could provide an additional benefit to the city. I mentioned that if we offered TEFL instruction, none of the local students would have to travel to Vladivostok to take the prep course. This was particularly of interest to her, since her own daughter had traveled twice a week to Vladivostok to take a course at the university. She calmed down and agreed that this was in fact a good idea and she apologized for not giving me a chance to explain. We spent the next twenty minutes excitedly talking about how we could make the change happen and she gave me a big hug before leaving.

Meanwhile, it looks like Helen, currently head of training, will become the new Peace Corps Country Director when Ken's term ends in January. Helen's authority and workload have steadily increased and I have seen more of a concerted effort on her part to get to know the volunteers in my group. I have gotten along well with her, primarily because of my help in dealing with the logistics of setting up the Artyom training program. During the prior week, she had taken me aside to tell me that she was working on assignments for the new group and wanted to know if I had any recommendations as to which trainees I wanted in Artyom. Out of the forty-five trainees, there were only two that I didn't particularly enjoy spending time with due to personality clashes. She smiled and reassured me that she would take this into consideration.

Two weeks later Helen called and greeted me with her usual cheerfulness before telling me that she had completed the assignments and that the two trainees assigned to Artyom were those exact two with whom I had trouble getting along. At the end of the day it didn't really matter because I had my own network of friends, but it was a nasty way to approach the situation. I asked her if she remembered our earlier discussion and she replied that she did indeed. I then asked if this was personal or whether they were simply the best fit. She laughed and then hung up on me. Was she just flexing her muscle to let me know that she was in charge and that I was a lowly volunteer, or had I done something to offend her? I felt betrayed and confused. I had been heavily involved in bringing the training to Artyom, had allowed the Peace Corps to use my relationship with the administration and mayor to push demands through and had been complimented often by Ken and the other staff. I guess I'd outlived my usefulness to the Peace Corps, or if not, then just to Helen.

That night I was still disgruntled and feeling a bit sorry for myself when one of the trainees called to ask if I would join her host family for dinner. I jumped at the chance considering that the host mother, Olga, was a gorgeous twenty four-year-old single woman who liked to have a good time. Olga was more of a host sister than a host mother, as the trainee staying with her was a twenty-two-year-old woman from Alabama, named Christina. Christina had also invited one of her fellow trainees. Olga was a small-business owner and told us that her interest in hosting an American woman was to understand better how American women had fought for equality, an answer that had won over the Peace Corps staff . . . although I think she primarily wanted to have an American party buddy.

I arrived with a bouquet of flowers and a bottle of sangria and found the three of them already well into a bottle of wine. Since Olga spoke only Russian, we fudged our way through dinner, finishing off two bottles of wine and my sangria in the process. I was in the midst of a story when I felt Olga's hand on my leg. I tried to keep a nonchalant appearance as she moved to a more sensitive area. Olga, acting innocent, pretended to listen to the conversation while making it very difficult for me to do the same. When the last of the wine was finished, the two trainees stood up to clear away the plates, which was not currently an option for me. As soon as they had entered the kitchen Olga stood up and in a single move straddled me, feverishly grinding away while aggressively kissing me. I offered limited resistance, but not wanting to make a scene, I whispered to her to walk me home. She agreed.

The next night I was sound asleep when the sound of running water jarred me awake. I squinted at the alarm clock and saw that it was only 4 a.m. I turned to go back to sleep when I again heard water splashing down onto my balcony. My upstairs neighbor had a Doberman pinscher that she was too lazy to walk. She would send it out to the balcony to shit and piss and then every few days, would hose it down so that the filth would drip down onto my balcony. What made the situation difficult was that she was the mistress of one of the mayor's buddies, which was not unusual; many of the mafia kept apartments in the building to house their mistresses. I would often pass them in the stairwell on their way to or from a booty call. They would wink at me and smile as if I was in on the game.

It was summer and I had no air conditioning, so I had left the windows open and now my entire apartment smelled like dog shit. Initially I had been intrigued by the sight of sexy lingerie hanging from my neighbor's clotheslines, but these late-night disturbances and the continual barking had overshadowed any fantasy-related benefits. I had to be careful in how I responded on account of her boyfriend, so in classic passive aggressive fashion, I used as much energy as I could to spit upwards onto the sexy undergarments hanging out to dry while I washed the filth down to the balcony below mine.

The next night my sleep was again interrupted, this time by a phone call from Olga. My first thought was that she wanted to take a ride on the "Richie," but she immediately blurted out in a panicked voice that her volunteer, Christina, was at the local hospital. They had been out to a picnic and after getting home, Christina experienced severe stomach pains, apparently from food poisoning. I took down the information and promised to forward it to Sarah, the Peace Corps nurse. Sarah told me that she would call the Russian doctor assigned to help us in these situations and that they would head straight to the hospital. The following morning I was sipping on a cup of coffee when Helen called. "Why didn't you call me first?" she screamed. I knew Helen was worried about Christina's safety, but I had reached out to the medial staff and had left everything in Sarah's hands. It wasn't my responsibility to notify the Peace Corps administration or Helen. Since I was still pissed about the Artyom work assignments, I politely let her finish yelling and then obnoxiously asked if she was done. "What?" was the only word that stammered from her mouth. "I need to go," I replied and hung up, knowing that our relationship was not headed in the right direction but feeling satisfaction that my actions had disturbed her, regardless of any intent on my part to do so.

AUGUST 20, 1995

Over the past few months I had been pushing Mama to start a catering company to supplement her meager pension, since Papa's company had gone into the Russian version of bankruptcy. The last time we had spoken, she mentioned that she had copied my pizza recipe and had made a dozen personal-size pizzas that she sold to workers in a nearby office building. Everyone had told her that they loved them. Mama loved to cook and since they had Papa's car to deliver the food, it seemed like a good fit. Mama ran with the idea and soon had several other companies ordering lunch from her each day. She was thrilled and at the end of each day she proudly counted out the money. I was proud of her and hoped that Papa wouldn't resent her new role as the family bread-winner.

AUGUST 22, 1995

Life at the business center continues to be frustratingly slow as the summer holidays have kept clients to a minimum. My role with the trainees has also been greatly reduced, partly due to my deteriorating relationship with Helen and partly because the trainees are spending eight hours a day in language lessons. Feeling a need to let off steam, I invited a few of the new trainees over for dinner and drinks hoping that the act of shopping and preparing a meal would put me into a better mood. I was thinking American comfort food and thus prepared three pizzas and a casserole of mac & cheese. As for beverages, you can't go wrong with vodka and Champagne. The average age in my own group had been twice that of this new group of volunteers, and it showed most in these gatherings where the alcohol flowed much more quickly with the younger folks. I was closer to them in age and had no trouble keeping up, particularly since I had sixteen months of living in Russia in which to build a tolerance.

One of my guests was Dawn, a trainee from New Jersey who had caught my eye early in the training. We had flirted innocently. It didn't take long before the vodka broke down our inhibitions and eye contact led to an unspoken tacit acknowledgement. During a break in conversation, I made an excuse to take her outside on my balcony where I pulled her toward me for a kiss. The sexual tension was running high, so once we kissed there was little chance of putting the horses back in the barn. I invited her to spend the night, and when she agreed, I pushed the rest of the guests toward the door. Sleeping with an American woman was different from sleeping with the local Russian women. The ease of communication and under-standing of customs led to a greater intimacy. I have never been adept at understanding women, but at least with Dawn we could refer to the same culture. Despite this much-needed respite and a yearning to embrace our new romance, we decided to keep things quiet since the Peace Corps had forbidden relationships between trainees. Even though I wasn't a trainee, my relationship with Helen was already quite strained and I didn't Dawn to suffer as a consequence. She shyly told me that she had requested a position in Artyom hoping that we would get together. It took all of my restraint not to tell her that I already knew which trainees were going to be assigned to Artyom; I am still hoping that Helen will surprise me and change her mind.

I called Mama as soon as Dawn had left, hoping to update her on my life, but instead I ended up consoling her. One of the Vladivostok mafia groups had put an end to her pizza business and the family's financial prospects were poor. Mama had managed to fly beneath the mafia radar by delivering the food quietly, but her success and financial gain meant that someone else was losing out. Unfortunately the person who had been providing meals to these offices had been paying protection money. They didn't want a payoff from Mama and calmly told her to shut it down with the implied threat of physical harm to her and the family if she didn't abide. Mama couldn't go to the police, since the mafia was more powerful than the police were. They had so many connections within the police that any effort to enlist police help would invariably lead to another visit by the mafia thugs. I felt guilty for having pushed Mama so hard to start her own business and I had committed the major mistake of thinking like an American without regard for the circumstances guiding business in Russia.

As soon as I hung up the phone, I packed a bag and grabbed a taxi to the train station. I thought back to all of my mafia contacts, wondering if any of them would have any clout in Vladivostok. Appeasing the mafia was an awful cycle that helped to perpetuate the damage to ordinary people and the inefficiency of the market place, but I was indulging in that line of thought. When I arrived at the apartment, Mama seemed on the verge of panic. She had unplugged the phone, kept the locks on the front door latched, and was ready to cry at the drop of a pin. I worried about their finances and wanted to help since Mama's pension barely kept food on the table, with little hope to support Timofey's university fees. If he dropped out of the university he would be conscripted into the army, which would take him to Chechnya. Papa offered to drive his car as a rogue taxi, but this too had strong negatives since many people ended up losing their cars to unscrupulous thugs posing as passengers. I had picked up several bags of groceries to stock their fridge and I promised that I would continue to do so until something changed. I knew that they wouldn't accept money from me, so my only option was to bring groceries whenever I visited, in the same way I had helped Vitaly. Ken had told my training group during our first week in Russia that at times we would feel helpless when hearing about the tribulations of our Russian friends and that we should always remember that these folks have lived a long time without our help and would continue to do so in the future. I realized again just how fortunate we are in America, or at least I was as a white middle-class citizen.

As for Vitaly, the plan to send him to Canada isn't proceeding very well either. Ken hasn't been able to garner any Peace Corps support and his *Newsweek* contact's enthusiasm has waned with respect to running a story. In the beginning, Ken's excitement was intoxicating, making both Vitaly and me highly optimistic of the plan actually happening. We completed the visa paperwork and hoped that the funding would come just as quickly. I recognize that Ken has a great deal on his plate and that, although this would make a nice story, it didn't rank as high on his priorities as it did mine. I haven't mentioned my frustration to Vitaly, but he is intuitive and I am sure that my recent silence on the progress is a strong indication that things aren't going well. My guilt at not being able to help more with Vitaly or my host family has been depressing, leading me to doubt myself and the value I provide to those I care about both in work and personally.

When I arrived at Vitaly's house, he was dressed in his work clothes, plastering the chimney. Despite having almost no money, he was meticulous in his dress when he was out in public. He took great pride in giving the impression that he was a person of character, despite the setbacks that had occurred in his life. When I saw him dressed in his old clothes, I knew he was serious about getting work done and that I too would soon be put to work. Not one to let a young man stand idle, he tossed me a pair of work gloves and a shovel. I spent the next four hours carrying buckets of sand and water to make cement. That was the easy part, because once we had enough to work with I climbed a homemade wooden ladder with the buckets strapped to my shoulders so that I could plaster the cracks in the chimney. Vitaly continually yelled at me to be careful and to point out any spot that I had somehow missed. Despite the physical discomfort, it felt great to push my body and free my mind from my recent shortcomings.

SEPTEMBER 4, 1995

Dawn and I have been spending every free moment together, which has inevitably led to our secret romance becoming not so secret. I was concerned about Helen's reaction once she found out, since she would have considerable sway over Dawn's future. Ever since our brief phone call regarding Christina, we'd barely acknowledged each other when passing at the Peace Corps offices or in Artyom. The day Helen had chanced upon Dawn and I walking hand in hand, she issued an announcement reminding all the trainees that anyone caught having a sexual relationship with another trainee or volunteer could be dismissed from the Peace Corps and sent home. No trainee or volunteer was younger than twenty-three and since we were adults, it seemed crazy to impose three months of celibacy on us. I could understand a warning that we would all have to rely on each other for support and that a relationship had the potential of going south and disrupting the peace, but to punish us for being attracted to each other was strange. I wondered whether it was a Peace Corps regulation or whether it was solely due to Helen's desire to punish me. We were far from home and living under stressful conditions and I couldn't see a problem with two consenting adults spending their private time together.

I couldn't stop thinking that I was harming Dawn's chances at a successful experience here in Russia. I stayed awake most of the night trying to come up with a solution. I decided to go to Ken's office and get his advice, since he knew what made Helen tick and might be able to relieve some of the animosity. Unfortunately, when I got to the Peace Corps office and knocked on Ken's door, I found him sitting in conversation with Helen. Unprovoked, Helen smiled and congratulated me on dating such a warm and intelligent woman. Ken agreed and after a little more small talk, he invited me to join him later for lunch. When I left his office to stop in to see Sarah, Helen followed me and asked whether I would be willing to help her plan an end-of-training barbeque for the trainees and their host families. I wondered whether this was a peace offering or whether she merely using me. I didn't have time to think it over so, in an effort to take a step in the direction of repairing our rift, I agreed, hoping to show that I was a team player.

Between the Peace Corps staff, the trainees, their host families, and select members of the city administration, there would be upwards of a hundred people in attendance. Cooking for such a large number would require a great deal of work, much more than I was willing to provide. The hotel that was hosting the event said that we could set up our own barbeque grill, but that everything else had to be arranged through their kitchen. I was excited to be in charge of the grilling and immediately called my buddy Toby, the chef at the Vlad Motor Inn, to place an order for Australian beef and pork. I had met Toby on a prior visit to the Vlad Motor Inn and we had become drinking buddies. We had a great deal in common including both having worked in kitchens, an enthusiasm for Scotch and the occasional bout of homesickness that often led to my visits. The mafia was a partner in the Vlad Motor Inn and thus he could get anything he wanted through customs without a hassle, including good-quality meat. On the morning of the picnic I drove to the hotel with Brian, our assistant country director. We packed the back seat of his jeep with forty pounds of ground sirloin and forty pounds of pork for the kebabs. Toby had thrown in a gallon of his own barbeque sauce as a gift and I was psyched to get the party started. On the way back to Artyom, we stopped at a local bakery and picked three dozen loaves of bread, which would have to substitute for buns. I was in my element managing the barbeque, calculating the portions and delegating tasks to Nicole and Tim, who were serving as my assistants.

This was easy for me and I could shut out all of the stressors in my life and focus solely on the task at hand.

Barbeque grills are still somewhat of a novelty here, so instead of trying to find one I stacked bricks in a 3-foot by 2-foot rectangle and placed oven grates over the top. It wasn't pretty, but it would do the job. I seasoned the beef and then let Tim and Nicole shape two hundred and fifty hamburger patties while I sliced onions and peppers to add to the marinated chunks of pork for the kabobs. I loved it! I was juggling bottles and flipping knives behind my back while yelling out instructions and feeling like I was back at work. When the first guests began to arrive, I was smiling from ear to ear and ready to relax with a cold beer. It was a beautiful day, perfect for a picnic. Ken and his wife Winnie showed up with a few cases of beer and soon we had a group playing Frisbee, screaming out in fun, and guzzling the occasional beer.

The night before, Helen had given out the assignments to the trainees. I recalled how anxious I had been when my group went through this process and hoped that Dawn and the rest of her group would get what was best for them, including my hope that Helen would change her mind and assign Dawn to Artyom. As expected, the news was bad, with Dawn assigned to a post six hours away. We have spent almost every free moment together for the past few weeks and I had high expectations for our relationship, but being so far apart with limited transportation, our prospects would be greatly diminished. A long-distance relationship is not easy even in America where there are good phone networks and a six-hour car or train ride would not be a huge impediment, but in Russia it will be a struggle. We held each other with tears pouring forth, each promising to do whatever it would take to stay in touch. Helen glanced over and caught my eye and gave me a look of satisfaction, making me feel that she was relishing in my anguish. Her smirk was a slap to my face and there was nothing I could do in response.

SEPTEMBER 7, 1995

The United States Deputy Ambassador to Russia, Dick Miles, had scheduled a stopover in Vladivostok and had arranged to spend an afternoon with a group of us at the Peace Corps office. This was my first meeting with someone from the American embassy in Moscow and it felt good to know that I might be able to be remembered for something other than getting medivacked the previous January. Being eight time zones away from the embassy, we often felt forgotten. The American consulate staff in Vladivostok treated us volunteers with indifference despite our being part of such a small expat community. Dick Miles was notably different, seeming genuinely interested about our work and in getting to know us. He had risen up through the ranks of the foreign service, serving in various State Department roles, including a stint as ambassador to Azerbaijan, before taking the job as Deputy Ambassador to Russia. His wife Sharon was every bit as warm, telling us all about their travel experiences. She was writing a cookbook about Russian and Eastern European cooking that sounded similar to the one I had just finished, so we spent quite a bit of time chatting and I ended up giving her a copy of my book and she promised to send me hers. Ken saw that we were getting along and asked if I would like to join them for lunch. Our lunch turned into a two-hour discussion of meals that we had eaten and those that we hoped would follow. After lunch we dropped Sharon at her hotel and Ken again told me how impressed he was with my ability to relate to everyone, including the big shots from Moscow. Anything that would strengthen the impression of our program could only boost our reputation in Moscow. It made me happy to feel appreciated after feeling utterly hopeless with Helen the night before. As Ken dropped me off at the train station, he asked if I would house-sit later in the month when he and Winnie left on vacation. There was no way I would turn down the opportunity for hot showers, a VCR with a library of American movies and a real bed to sleep in. "Hell yeah!" I replied.

SEPTEMBER 11, 1995

Dawn went on a two-day trip to her meet her future co-workers and to find a place to live, which gave me time to see my Russian friends. With the trainees off on their site visits, Artyom returned to its normal pre-American-invasion self. Several kiosk vendors expressed concern when I passed, particularly the beer kiosk, as the trainees were frequent customers and their leaving was sure to affect the local economy. Nicole and Tim also had time to relax for the first time in several weeks. The three of us had gotten close, but since the trainees arrived, their schedules had been non-stop with classes and field trips, limiting our time together to passing in the hallways. Tim stopped by my apartment occasionally on his way home and we would play backgammon, drink cognac, and bullshit about our lives. As for Nicole, I got the impression that she was hurt by my relationship with Dawn. She seemed more withdrawn and the bubbly interactions that had been our norm had ended.

I awoke Saturday morning with warming rays of sunshine bursting through the windows. I had planned on going to the market to buy a rooster for Vitaly's chickens and at the last moment decided to call Nicole in the hope she might want to join me. She had nothing planned and agreed to meet me at the market. According to Vitaly, chickens don't need a rooster to lay eggs, but they tend to lay more if the big guy is clucking around the hen house. I decided that with Nicole's help, we could pick up a rooster as well as another hen for the henhouse. Unfortunately, selecting a rooster requires a bit more skill than picking out a chicken. The market offered a wide variety, ranging from small and colorless to giant multicolored beasts that looked more like peacocks. Nicole pointed at the biggest rooster and I went along with her suggestion.

The second we stepped inside Vitaly's gate I dropped the bag containing the struggling rooster. My arms felt like they were going to fall off. The rooster had fought me the entire way from the market to getting on the bus, and then he entire uphill walk through the village. Even though I knew that I should hold him upside down by the talons to get him to relax, it turned out to be much harder to keep him that way than one would think. When the bag opened and the rooster hit the ground, he wasted exactly zero time establishing his dominance as he ran to a hen and promptly began humping away! Vitaly stared incredulously at me before asking. "What the hell is that?"

"It's a rooster!" I replied confidently. "That is no rooster!" he responded, as the rooster finished with one hen and began chasing another. I looked from the rooster to Vitaly, hoping that I hadn't somehow mistakenly selected some other type of Russian fowl.

"It's a monster!" he finally finished, flashing me a big grim. All three of us laughed at his joke.

Later that afternoon I took the train to the Vlad Motor Inn to see Toby. Spending time in a restaurant kitchen was like visiting an old friend and since Toby gave me free rein in the Vlad's kitchen, I had the opportunity to get my fix. I snooped through the refrigerator, selecting a piece of filet mignon and some asparagus to make a quick snack. I spent the next few hours working the grill and sauté stations, much to the amusement of the Russian cooks. At 10 p.m. the kitchen closed, so I went to the bar to wait for Toby to finish his ordering and other paperwork. The only other patron at the bar was a carefully dressed Russian "businessman" in a track suit, which was only partially zipped in the front to show off his gold necklaces. Apparently he was eager for conversation, since he bought my first drink before we had even nodded hello. I accepted a glass of Johnny Walker Black and offered my hand. We toasted to friendship and soon he had waved to the bartender for another round. Since this was one of nicer hotels, he must have assumed that I was a wealthy foreigner and he began laying the groundwork for what I assumed would be an investment opportunity. Sure enough, he told me about an idea to build a golf course catering to wealthy Japanese businessmen. He flashed a mischievous grin at the end of each sentence, reminding me of the character Jaws in the James Bond movies.

I was working on my third Johnny Walker when he told me to turn around and take a look at the table behind us. It was a strange request, but I turned and saw four beautiful women sipping Champagne. Their slinky silk outfits and finely tuned makeup were out of place here where the American and Canadian women came to relax after work in jeans and T-shirts. "They are my girls." His body wiggled as if he were dancing in his chair, reminding me of the Saturday Night Live skit with Steve Martin and Dan Akroyd being "Two Wild and Crazy Guys." "You are my friend, so pick one. Free, my gift." I smiled back stupidly as my brain and penis fought over how I should respond. "Thank you, my friend, but I have plans this evening with the chef." I stammered. This was not the first time I had been offered female companionship from a mafia figure. As tempting as the offer was, I no intention of cheating and living with the accompanying guilt.

Toby and I climbed into the back of a van, joining our two armed guards who had been stoically waiting without the hint of a smile. It had been so hard to find a Western chef willing to accept a contract to work in this Far East Russian outpost that the hotel had no choice but to protect their asset in this manner. Having already been on the wrong end of a night out in town, I had no issues accepting the protection. We were driven to a mafia disco called "Steals" that had all of the flash and glitz of a Vegas hotel. We had to pass through two sets of metal detectors before being shown to a table in the corner. Lockers were provided for those patrons who were carrying weapons, giving the place the feel of a poorly written gangster movie. Toby knew that I was on a Peace Corps budget, so before I could even pull out my wallet for the cover charge, he let me know that the night was on him. This was my first visit back to a mafia club, but the calming effect of having our own bodyguards allowed me to sit back and enjoy my Scotch.

We watched the scenes unfold around us, as the working girls strutted past patrons in their high heels, fishnet stockings and skimpy outfits. After a few passes, they ruled us out as customers and focused on those with bigger budgets. While sipping our drinks Toby mentioned that the US Meat Export Federation was in town and that they were looking for a chef to showcase their products at the high-end hotels in Vladivostok and Khabarovsk. They were hoping to stay ahead of the Japanese beef industry and form relationships with the Russians, and had asked Toby to represent them. Unfortunately the Vlad Motor Inn didn't want Toby moonlighting, so he thought I might be interested. Anticipating that I would, he had set up a meeting on Monday at the hotel. It sounded like a good opportunity and if it meant a few free steaks, I was all in.

SEPTEMBER 14, 1995

My meeting with the meat guys went well and I agreed to cook up a few hundred steaks in Vladivostok, followed two days later by a similar presentation in Khabarovsk. I was nervous, but not nearly as nervous as the two US Meat Export Federation representatives: they had smuggled in two hundred pounds of US Prime American beef in their suitcases. The guest list for the Vladivostok event included Russian chefs, local politicians, and businessmen; everyone was on the lookout for a free meal. The difficulty was that I was asked to cook the meat medium rare to show off the superior marbling of the meat, but having lived here I knew that the Russians wouldn't eat meat that wasn't served well-done. The only solution that I could come up with was to address the guests prior to the meal to explain the differences in tastes and why cooking the meat to well-done would diminish the taste and texture. I'd explain that as a compromise to local custom, I would cook half of the steaks medium rare and half at a medium temperature. If anyone wanted theirs cooked longer, they could ask the wait staff and I would be glad to accommodate them. I anticipated that none of the Russians would want to be seen as provincial and that nobody would send their steaks back to the kitchen.

The day after the demonstration in Vladivostok, a messenger showed up at my business center with a first-class airline ticket for me to fly to Khabarovsk on Friday morning. I made the decision to keep this a secret from the Peace Corps and the city administration for fear that one or the other would tell me not to go. Without anyone to fill in for me, I didn't want to break my word and leave the meat men without a chef. I should have asked for permission, but it was too late now and I hoped that nobody would notice my absence. As for my working outside of the Peace Corps environment, I had to explain that I wasn't permitted to get paid, but would be glad to pick a local charity for them to contribute to, or accept a few steaks and a bottle of Scotch if they insisted. I don't know whether they believed me or even cared as long as they had someone to do the cooking. They ended up giving me two hundred dollars for my expenses as well as a dozen rib-eyes and a bottle of Johnny Walker, which I split between my host family and Vitaly. I enjoyed the spotlight and cooking in a real kitchen again, not to mention an open tab at the bar following the presentation. The two representatives were very pleased and made sure that I had another drink in front of me well before my prior drink had been finished. They told me to look them up when I finished my tour with the Peace Corps if I was interested in a job.

Vitaly strolled into my office to tell me that the rooster is a "Sex Monster" and is causing havoc in his yard as he spends the entire day assaulting the chickens. I'd bought the rooster to encourage egg production, but instead he has had the opposite effect because he is so big that he crushes the chickens, leaving them too worn out to lay any eggs. I didn't know what Vitaly wanted me to do about the situation and sat quietly as he continued his dialogue. He finally told me that he wanted to trade the rooster to his neighbor for three chickens and a smaller rooster; he didn't want me to feel bad, so was asking for my permission. I gave him my blessing, trying not to laugh. My favorite part of the story was that his puppy had become protective of the chickens and every time the rooster mounted a chicken, the puppy would bite and pull the rooster's tail feathers. This led to the rooster chasing the puppy through the garden tearing up the plants and giving Vitaly additional grief.

Ken called me and he sounded subdued. "What's up?" I asked. He went on to say that he was concerned about me following a conversation he had with Peter. I had vented earlier in the week to Peter about a lack of clients and how I was spending most of my time working with the local schools to keep busy. I wanted more of a challenge to my everyday work and felt curtailed in my efforts by the administration pushing me toward teaching since many of the local English teachers had left to work as secretaries for the trading companies. I was also far from pleased with the way that Helen had been treating me, as if she wanted nothing more than to see me pack up and head home. I appreciated Ken's concern, particularly with the souring of my relationship with Helen, and I promised to talk to him to determine what we could do to provide a more challenging environment.

That night I took the train to Vladivostok to house-sit for him and Winnie. After months of having to heat water in a bucket in order to bathe, I couldn't wait to take a hot shower and to sleep in a bed in which my feet didn't dangle over the edge. In addition, it would seem like a vacation since Dawn had agreed to spend the weekend with me. We spent hours watching movies, eating microwave popcorn, taking walks through the city and going out for romantic dinners. Our time together was a reprieve from my feeling stagnant in my work. I tried to bring this up with Dawn, to express my frustration at work as well as how I dreaded the thought of having to rely on Helen when she replaced Ken at the end of his tenure.

Thoughts of leaving surfaced with each passing day that I sat in the office waiting for a new client to enter. The interference by the mayor and the realization that I had no capital contributed to the reduction in visitors, but beyond that, the population in Artyom was less than a hundred thousand, further reducing the potential for clients. I dreaded bringing up my thoughts of leaving to Dawn but it was weighing on my mind. I didn't want to spring it on her after I had already made a decision. I wanted a sounding board to discuss my feelings, but she must have sensed something was up and steered our discussion back to more mundane topics.

OCTOBER 3, 1995

We began our second in-service training session this week at a resort along the coast. Each of our three-day training sessions has been located somewhere between Artyom and Vladivostok, so I never had to travel more than an hour, while some of my colleagues had multiday travel itineraries. The primary focus of our sessions centered on the continued rumors that our business program was going to be shut down—the other business centers were experiencing similar issues to what I had experienced. Our discontent combined with a brutal political environment in Washington D.C. in which the Peace Corps funding was at risk if the Speaker of the House, Newt Gingrich, actually went forward with shutting down the government. The Peace Corps budget is wholly financed by Congress and a shutdown would lead to the canceling of all of our projects. This fear was realized when Ken opened our meeting by telling us that all projects had been suspended pending the outcome of the upcoming congressional budget meetings. This included funding that had already been approved, such as my efforts to build up the business centers resources. I had received a great amount of fanfare from the city administration when my grant had been approved, and now six weeks later I stood to lose my credibility when I had to tell them that there would be no new business course materials or equipment. I'd spent nine months preparing and presenting the grant and, once approved, had anxiously awaited the funds. Now that I only had a few months left in my service, the project would be unlikely to move forward while I was still in-country.

I was so frustrated at having so little control over my life that the idea of quitting the Peace Corps began to take shape. I am treading water with little to challenge me and living in an environment that will only get worse once Ken leaves. The prospective discomfort of having to tell Ken, Dawn, my host family, Vitaly, Tanya, and the rest of the city administration filled me with dread—it would seem that I wasn't just quitting the Peace Corps, but I was quitting them.

In between training sessions, I walked down to the water and took a seat facing the horizon with a beer in one hand and a paper and pencil in the other. I felt numb inside as I absorbed the realization of the impact of my decision would have on the people that I deeply cared about. I had joined the Peace Corps after earning my MBA and had given up the opportunity for a high-paying job to go out into the world to try to make a difference. Now I wondered whether I had been successful on any level. On the right side of the paper I wrote down why I should stay another six months to finish out my service and on the other side I listed the reasons why I should quit. Before making my final decision, I wanted to make sure I had weighed all of the factors so that I wouldn't later regret it. My head was reeling and I wanted an easy answer. I thought about my friends and family in America. I though about how happy my grandmother would be to see me. This line of thinking allowed me to focus more on my return home than on my leaving. I thought of the upcoming holidays and decided at that moment that I wanted to return home in time for Thanksgiving. Once you tell the Peace Corps of your intentions, they try to get you out of the country within a few days so as not to contaminate the minds of the other volunteers. My concern was that as soon as I put my plan in motion, I would have little time to say goodbye to all of the people that had been instrumental in my Russian experience. I see-sawed between feeling guilty and elated at the concept of returning home. I knew that I would be letting down my Russian friends, my fellow volunteers, and the Peace Corps staff, and I hated that I would be seen as a quitter. At the same time, I looked at the other volunteers in my group and saw that few were actually working in their assigned fields and instead had been moved into teaching positions. Our initial "can-do" attitudes had been tested along with our ability to be flexible.

The longer I dwelled on how I would say goodbye, the more difficult it became for me to pretend that everything was fine. I felt I owed it to Ken: he should hear the news from me. But I feared that my ability to leave on my own terms would be jeopardized. I spent the final night of the conference lost in thought. I wanted to get drunk, really drunk.

OCTOBER 4, 1995

I returned to Artyom just in time for the new trainees' swearing-in ceremony. They were excited and actually looked professional in their suits and dresses. The ceremony took place in a banquet hall that accommodated almost two hundred guests. I was proud of their transformation from nervous trainees to well-adapted, ready-to-save-the-world Peace Corps volunteers. They had come into Artyom, my city, and represented America well through their hard work and dedication to learning Russian and adapting to the local culture. They had lived with families that I helped pick, and for the most part, I would be sorry to see them go as they headed out to start their own experiences.

The ceremony got underway with first Ken and then the mayor giving short speeches saying how happy they were with how things turned out. Then Helen got up to speak. As head of the training program and the future Country Director, she thanked all of the people in the city administration for their support. For five minutes she named off the people who had helped, both the local Russians and the Peace Corps staff, smiling and making eye contact so that each felt appreciated. I listened attentively, waiting for my own name to be mentioned. When she had finished without addressing my contribution, I was heartbroken. Already emotional over my decision to leave, I felt humiliated in front of my colleagues and the other volunteers. I felt that I had been instrumental in bringing the trainees to Artyom and had continued supporting the staff, the trainees, and the city to make sure that things ran smoothly. I had no misconception that I was in charge or making the key decisions, but I did feel that if it weren't for my relationship with the administration, the city would never have agreed to host the group. If I'd had any doubt as to my leaving, it was now gone. I felt none of the joy that I saw around me when I looked around the room at all the laughing happy people.

Following the ceremony, I put on a smile and pretended to share in the excitement, offering hugs and congratulatory handshakes. Dawn, oblivious to my emotional state, was ready to party. Part of me wanted to blurt out in self-pity that I was pissed off and was quitting, but inside I knew that I needed to man up and not take away the pleasure from her big night. We had been invited to a few parties at the host family homes, followed by a much larger late-night party at the Miner's Hall. All through the night we went from house to house to celebrate and I drank to cover up the anger. When we finally got back to my apartment Dawn passed out on the couch before her head hit the pillow and I sat in a chair watching her while I sipped from a bottle of vodka. I stayed awake the entire night, processing and reprocessing my thoughts. I dreaded the conversation we would have in the morning, but couldn't put it off any longer. I had to tell her. I had been holding all of this inside for the past few days and it was eating me alive. When her eyes opened, I offered her two Advils and a cup of tea before explaining what had been going through my mind. She stared incredulously, trying to make sense of my words. I felt tears welling up inside and I wanted to hold her, to comfort her, and explain why I needed to leave. But before I could get a word out, she screamed that she hated me. She dressed with her back to me and then left without comment. I wanted her to say that she understood and that she forgave me, but she had her own emotions and crushed expectations to deal with, and I was the source of her pain. We had only known each other for two months, but we were both vulnerable and far from home and the connection was strong. I cared for her, but knew that if I remained in Russia solely for her, I would resent and blame her.

OCTOBER 7, 1995

Three days later Dawn moved to her site. It had been a rough few days for us as we finally sat down together to talk it through. Although she eventually acknowledged the difficulty and frustration of my situation, her hurt was real. She felt that I was quitting her as much as my position with the Peace Corps. I felt so guilty. I knew that we should make a clean break, allowing her to go on with her life and me with mine, but instead I promised that I would keep in touch and would return to Russia, which only seemed to muddy the waters. She told me that she loved me and I stood there like an idiot, not wanting to answer or even knowing how. My silence was all she needed to hear. Her tears caused such excruciating pain that I wanted to run and hide and pretend that this wasn't really happening. I hated myself as much as she probably hated me at that moment.

OCTOBER 8, 1995

I had subconsciously begun to shift my thoughts from painful goodbyes to the pleasure of surprising my family by showing up in New Jersey for Thanksgiving. These happy thoughts pushed the guilt and pain deeper inside, but whenever my mind turned to Vitaly and my host family, I would get severe heartburn. By telling Vitaly, I would undoubtedly lessen my own discomfort at the expense of adding to his. My method of dealing with emotional pain, depression, and anguish is to get into the kitchen and focus on making food. With Dawn now out of town, I knew it was time to tell Vitaly. So I went to the market and went crazy buying three shopping bags of food that I struggled to carry up to his house. He was kneeling in the garden when I came into view and he whistled hello, greeting me with a big smile. Before I could open my mouth, he told me to roll up my sleeves and grab a bucket. We spent two hours carrying pails of water and harvesting berries and vegetables, giving me a reprieve from the conversation I dreaded having with him. When we finished, I washed up and sipped on a cup of tea while watching him prepare our lunch. I fought the urge just to blurt it out, fearing a reaction that would make me even sadder. We had grown close and I knew the news would deeply hurt him as it had Dawn, but at least she was young and would soon be immersed in her own work and life, while Vitaly would be all alone until his son was released from jail. I had been his family for more than a year. I had trouble hiding my melancholy, which led to his asking why I looked so sad. I took a deep breath and then told him. He didn't say anything, just leaned his head forward and stared at the table. A few seconds passed in silence before he stood up and turned his back to me. I could see that he had begun to cry and I in turn did the same. Again I heard myself promising to return, trying to make myself feel better. He finally returned to the table with a bottle of vodka in hand. We drank to our friendship and then to seeing each other again. I felt like such a shit.

OCTOBER 9, 1995

The next day I went to see Ken to see if I could get a definitive answer on whether Vitaly's trip to Canada was still a realistic possibility. Due to the delays I sensed that we had lost traction, but felt I owed Vitaly one more attempt to pull this off. I felt dishonest asking for Ken's help without telling him about my plans to quit. While waiting at the Artyom train station, I ran into Thurston, one of the new volunteers who, in his sixties, was the oldest volunteer in the new group. He was also on his way to the Peace Corps office, so we waited and boarded together, talking about the adventures that awaited us both. The train was crowded with city travelers returning from their dachas and since many smoked, there was a curtain of cigarette smoke that filled the cars, which when combined with the smell of perspiration and the heat of so many bodies pressed together became claustrophobic. We stood chest to chest, the train swaying, forcing bodies against each other. With each successive stop, the train grew more crowded and we became one big pulsating mass. Suddenly Thurston's face turned gray and he lost consciousness, falling into me. I held him up by his shirt. His eyes were open, but there was no comprehension. I began shouting for the other passengers to move aside and when enough space had been cleared, I laid him on the floor. I'd unbuttoned his shirt and positioned myself to begin CPR when he coughed. His eyes gradually regained focus and I felt a huge relief wash over me. "It's alright, everything is going to be alright!" I stammered as much to myself as to him. The Russians, respectful of his age, helped me get him into a seat.

With his color slowly returning, he said that he was feeling well enough to continue on the train until we reached the Peace Corps' stop, which was only a few minutes further. When we arrived I carried his bags and we gingerly made our way directly to the medical office, where I turned him over to Sarah. I was emotionally spent and overwhelmed after the events of the past few days and needed to catch my breath before heading inside to meet Ken. I walked along the shoreline and stared at the sea until I felt strong enough to enter the building.

When I stepped into his office, my reception had less than the usual cheerfulness I had come to expect. I suspected that rumors of my leaving must have already reached him, but I didn't bring it up and instead asked right away whether he had heard anything new regarding Vitaly's visa. He told me that since neither the Peace Corps nor the international press seemed interested, he was giving up on the project. His time was limited before handing over the reins to Helen. If he had heard about my plans to quit, I couldn't blame him for being angry with me for not telling him first. I wished that I could explain everything without fear of the consequences, since he was the last person that I wanted to disappoint and one of the few people whose opinion I trusted.

As I walked down the hallway away from Ken's office, fingers dug into my shoulder with such force that I was completely turned around. I expected to see Gary or one of the other volunteers, but instead was greeted with Helen's screaming face. "Who the hell do you think you are?" she yelled, pushing her face within inches from mine. "Why didn't you tell me about Thurston?" She had picked the wrong moment to give me a hard time. I felt the rage gaining strength and it took all of my resolve to back up and take a deep breath. She was shaking with her own anger and I wanted nothing more than to go off on her and tell her exactly what I thought of her. Instead I calmly replied that my only responsibility was to get him to the medical office and that I didn't need to tell her shit, nor did

I owe her anything. Without waiting for her reply, I turned and walked off. My heart was pounding and I knew I needed to get out of the building and as far away from her as I could before I snapped and did something that I would regret.

The next morning I got to the office early and waited for Tanya to arrive. I loved Tanya and her family and as with the other people with whom I had become close, I dreaded telling her the news. I wanted her to hear the news first from me and I knew I could trust her to keep it a secret. I had prepared a pot of tea prior to her arrival, and per our Monday morning ritual, we sat down to discuss our weekends. I had trouble concentrating and without any notice, I blurted out that I was leaving. Her eyes filled with tears, but after a few moments, she let me know that she understood why I needed to go and was grateful for our friendship. "You have changed the lives of all of us in Artyom, most importantly mine." We hugged and I told her how much it meant for me that she included me in her family celebrations and that it made me feel like I was a part of the community.

OCTOBER 10, 1995

The past three days I have been a walking disaster, spreading sadness and pain wherever I go. Despite having told Dawn, Vitaly, Tanya, and a few of my fellow volunteers, I was still fearful of telling Mama. I sat her down and held her hand, telling her my prepared story of why I needed to quit. The news caught her so off guard that I thought she would faint. I am confident that I am making the right decision, but having these conversations is so awful. I feel like an ungrateful shit for letting down all those who care for me. I told Mama the same thing I told the others, that I hoped to return after securing a job with an American company. We spent hours drinking cup after cup of tea while I handed her tissues. The family's generosity and hospitality had changed my life and had helped shape my experience in Russia. I made Mama promise to keep my secret, since I wanted to put off my departure for another week and wouldn't be able to do so if the truth got out.

For the second time in three days I was going to the Peace Corps office. I found myself standing outside of Ken's door without even realizing that I had entered the building. I wiped my palms against my pants and after taking a deep breath, knocked. It appeared that he had been waiting for me; he didn't seem too surprised that I had come back to see him without having set up a meeting. He told me to take a seat. I looked at him and could feel the guilt exuding from my pores. I began my story with an apology and then proceeded to tell him everything. He admitted that he had heard the rumors, as I had assumed, but instead of being angry as I expected, he was genuinely sympathetic. As a gesture that there were no hard feelings, he offered to give me an extra week before making it official so that I could have more time to say goodbye. I promised to set aside a day for us to have lunch and then said goodbye, knowing that there was no turning back.

On Saturday night Karl hosted my going-away party. He invited our Russian friends, many of our Russian host families, and all of the local volunteers, which was basically everyone I knew in Vladivostok. I didn't want to go through a night of tears and sad goodbyes, so I got creative and prepared to auction off all of my possessions that wouldn't make the trip back home. These included spices, cooking utensils, and other accessories like my Frisbee and a dart board that were highly coveted by the volunteers. I didn't want money for any of my items, since I knew they were on limited budget, but I wanted to make sure that each item went to the person who wanted it the most. To determine who would get an item, I had the guests bid in vodka shots, with each item going to the person willing to drink the most shots for it. I brought my duffel bag packed with all of the items along with four bottles of Stolichnaya Vodka.

I kept the auction a secret until all of the guests had arrived and then explained the rules. Next I opened the first bottle of vodka and took out a shot glass. Nobody was sure of what I had planned as I pulled the first item from the duffel bag. It was a set of Indian spices that I had purchased from the Hari Krishna temple. I passed it around so that everyone could inspect it and then asked if anyone would be willing to drink one shot of vodka to own these spices. I increased the number of shots until only one hand remained. Gary drained the glass in one gulp, smiling from ear to ear, holding up the spices like a boxer holding up his championship belt. The Russians seemed a little puzzled, but once the first transaction had been completed, they became as eager as the volunteers. The challenge for the guests was that nobody knew what else remained in my duffel bag, so if they drank too much on the early items, they might not be in shape to compete later in the evening.

It took an hour to go through all of the items, with the noise escalating successively after each item. There was a great deal of laughter as wives and girlfriends had to pull down their partner's hands to keep them from getting too hammered. Everyone sat on the edge of their seats, gasping and groaning every time I poured more vodka into the glass. The highest bid went to Karl's girlfriend Vicka, who bid eight shots for a set of cocktail umbrellas. The most popular item among the volunteers was my dartboard, and that bidding ended with a head-to-head battle between Gary and Karl. The auction turned the goodbye party from a sad event to a fun one and allowed me time to say my individual goodbyes.

The next morning I returned to Artyom to pack up my bags and say goodbye to the mayor and my colleagues in the city administration. To save face for both Anna and the Peace Corps, I attributed my decision to leave to family issues in America so that it wouldn't negatively affect how the new volunteers in Artyom might be treated. As for the two women who were assigned to join me in Artyom, I wished them well and hoped that they would be treated as well as I had been and that they would enjoy their time with "my" community. I felt no ill will toward them and hoped that they found success and happiness while living there.

As for the people of Artyom, I submitted a letter that was published in the local paper thanking everyone for accepting me and making me a part of their lives. I told them that their love, generosity, and hospitality had made me comfortable and had allowed me to fall in love with Russia and that part of my soul would always be Russian. I had come to learn about Russia and its people, and in the process, I had learned far more about myself than I thought possible. I hoped that the letter would reach all of the people that had made my time so special. I wanted the kiosk venders, the butchers and clerks, the babushkas at the market, the chicken farmers, and everyone else with whom I had come in contact to know that I would miss them.

OCTOBER 26, 1995

The clock showed 8 p.m. when I returned to my apartment on my final night in Artyom. I felt hollow and incredibly sad. I had said all of my good-byes and now dreaded the silence that would last until the driver came to pick me up in the morning. Before I could feel too sorry for myself, there was a knock on the door, followed by Vitaly's voice telling me to open the door before he froze to death. He stood in the hallway, tottering as if at any second he would crash to the floor, a bottle of cheap Chinese vodka in his hand. I was so glad that he had come to say goodbye again that I hugged him for what seemed an eternity. We ended up sitting across from each other at my kitchen table trying to find the right words to say goodbye. We drank shot after shot, barely talking, until his eyes closed. I dragged him to the mattress and removed his shoes before covering him with a blanket.

The next morning the driver picked me up and brought me to the Peace Corps office to complete my exit papers. Several of the kids were playing outside my building and they ran up, yelling "Reech," to see if I wanted to play Frisbee with them. I told them that I was leaving for America, but that I hoped to come back and would bring each of them a Frisbee. They smiled and then ran back to their games. Once at the Peace Corps office, I said goodbye to all of the Russian and American staff before heading out to lunch with Ken and Winnie. Helen was conspicuously absent, which probably suited us both. At the end of the day, they dropped me off at my host family's apartment. I was tired, emotional, and still hung over from my night with Vitaly. I hoped for a quiet night alone with the family. Unfortunately, there was no way that Mama was not going to throw a party for me. Her friends and neighbors, many of whom had celebrated with us over the past two years, along with all of the Vladivostok volunteers and their host families showed up for a final farewell. Despite all of the preparations to ensure a good time, it became incredibly gloomy, with Mama clutching me with one hand and a box of tissues in the other. My biggest regret was that I hadn't been able to better connect with Timofey, but I understood his anger and frustration at all of the attention I had received. As for Papa, we shared a few private moments toasting each other with a bottle of cognac that I had given to him as a farewell gift.

The next morning, the entire family and Gary crammed into Papa's car to drive me to the airport. We were all hung over and nobody was talking much. Once at the airport, Papa and Gary grabbed my bags and I followed behind, clutching Mama's hand. It was a sobering moment as I stood at the gate. Suddenly I heard a chorus of people yelling my name. I turned to see Vitaly, Tanya, Oleg, Sveta, Yelena, and several other friends from Artyom. As hard as I tried to conceal my emotions, I began to cry. Seeing so many people going out of their way to see me off was so dear that I wanted to turn back the clock and delay my departure. Mama handed me a handkerchief, which I used to dry my eyes. When I offered it back, she insisted that I keep it since Russian tradition states that if you borrow something prior to leaving, it will guarantee your return. I hugged her and then turned to say one final goodbye before walking through the gate. These people had been my family. They were my support network, my friends, my confidants, and above all, the people who had enabled me to make it through the tough times. I would miss them.